D1249304

EUROCOMMUNISM

A Conference Sponsored Jointly by the American Enterprise Institute for Public Policy Research and the Hoover Institution on War, Revolution and Peace

EUROCOMMUNISM: THE ITALIAN CASE

Edited by Austin Ranney and Giovanni Sartori

American Enterprise Institute for Public Policy Research
Washington, D.C.

Library of Congress Cataloging in Publication Data

Main entry under title:
Eurocommunism.

(AEI symposia ; 78G)
Based on conference held in Washington, D.C.,
June 7–9, 1977.
Includes index.
1. Communism—Italy—Congresses. 2. Communism—. Europe—Congresses. I. Ranney, Austin. II. Sartori, Giovanni, 1924– III. Series: American Enterprise Institute for Public Policy Research.
HX289.E87 335.43′0945 78-17068
ISBN 0-8447-2135-2
ISBN 0-8447-2134-4 pbk.

AEI Symposia 78-G

Printed in the United States of America

CONTRIBUTORS

ENZO BETTIZA is a senator in the Italian upper house, elected in Milan as an independent. He is an authority on Communist and Eastern European affairs. For many years he was the Moscow correspondent for the *Corriere della Sera,* and he is now associate editor and columnist for *Il Giornale*. His most recent book is *Il Comunismo Europeo* (1978).

ANGELO M. CODEVILLA received his Ph.D. in political science from Claremont, and is a former national fellow of the Hoover Institution on War, Revolution and Peace. He is the author of *Modern France* (1974) and *Italy, the Partisan Democracy* (forthcoming). He is a member of the staff of the U. S. Senate Select Committee on Intelligence.

MASSIMO DE CAROLIS is a member of the Italian Chamber of Deputies for the Christian Democratic party. In the 1976 general election he received, in his Milan constituency, the largest preference vote in Italy.

MARINO DE MEDICI is currently the Washington correspondent for *Il Tempo* of Rome.

ROGER HILSMAN is professor of political science at Columbia University. From 1961 to 1963 he was director of the Bureau of Intelligence and Research, Department of State, and from 1963 to 1964 he was assistant secretary of state for Far Eastern affairs. His books include *The Politics of Policy Making in Defense and Foreign Affairs* (1971), and *The Crouching Future: International Politics and U.S. Foreign Policy—A Forecast, 1975* (1975).

HENRY A. KISSINGER is counselor to the Center for Strategic and International Studies of Georgetown University. From 1969 to 1974 he was director of the National Security Council and presidential adviser on national security affairs, and from 1973 to 1977 he was secretary of state. Prior to 1969 he was professor of government at Harvard University. His books include *Nuclear Weapons and Foreign Policy* (1957), *The Necessity for Choice: Propects of American Foreign Policy* (1961), and *The Troubled Partnership: A Reappraisal of the Atlantic Alliance* (1965).

WILLIAM E. KNIGHT is a retired U. S. Foreign Service officer. From 1948 to 1951 he served as third and then as second secretary of the American Embassy in Rome. He served in 1951–1955 as Italian desk officer in the Department of State, in 1961 as officer in charge of Italian-Austrian affairs, and in 1961–1962 as deputy director of the Office of Western European Affairs.

JOSEPH LAPALOMBARA is Arnold Wolfers Professor of Political Science at Yale University. His professional association with Italy dates from 1952, and in 1974 he was made a knight commander in the Order of Merit of the Italian Republic. He is the author of *Multinational Corporations and National Elites*.

LUCIO LIBERTINI is a senator for the Italian Communist party, and chairman of the Senate Committee on Public Works and Transportation. He is also a member of the Central Committee of the PCI. He was formerly a left-wing socialist.

AUSTIN RANNEY is a resident scholar at the American Enterprise Institute for Public Policy Research. A former president of the American Political Science Association and member of the Executive Committee of the International Political Science Association, he is the author of books and articles on American and British parties and politics.

GIACOMO SANI has taught at the Universities of Bologna and Florence and is now professor of political science at the Ohio State University. His articles on the government and politics of Italy have appeared in books and journals in Italy and the United States. In 1976–1977 he held a Guggenheim fellowship for work on Italy.

GIOVANNI SARTORI is professor of political science at Stanford University and a senior fellow of the Hoover Institution on War, Revolution and Peace. He was formerly professor of political science at the University of Florence and at the European University Institute. In 1972 he was awarded the Italian golden medal for cultural achievement. His books include *Democratic Theory* (1965) and *Parties and Party Systems: A Framework for Analysis* (1976).

CONTENTS

PART THREE
THE CURRENT STATE OF ITALIAN POLITICS

PART FOUR
The Future and Its Implications for American Policy

ABBREVIATIONS

CGIL	Confederazione Generale Italiana del Lavoro, General Confederation of Italian Labor
DC	Democrazia Christiana, Christian Democratic party
DP	Democrazia Proletaria, Proletarian Democracy
MPL	Movimento Politico Lavoratore, Workers' Political Movement
MSI	Movimento Sociale Italiano, Italian Social Movement
MSI-DN	Movimento Sociale Italiano–Destra Nazionale, Italian Social Movement–National Right
PCE	Partido Communista de España, Spanish Communist party
PCF	Parti Communiste Français, French Communist party
PCI	Partito Comunista Italiano, Italian Communist party
PDIUM	Partito Democratico Italiano di Unita Monarchica, Monarchist party (1968 only)
PLI	Partito Liberale Italiano, Italian Liberal party
PR	Partito Radicale, Radical party
PRI	Partito Repubblicano Italiano, Italian Republican party
PSDI	Partito Socialista Democratico Italiano, Italian Social Democratic party
PSI	Partito Socialista Italiano, Italian Socialist party
PSIUP	Partito Socialista Italiano di Unita Proletaria, Socialist Party of Proletarian Unity (1968 and 1972)
PSU	Partiti Socialisti Unificati, United Socialist party (1968 only)

INTRODUCTION

Austin Ranney

The Setting

On January 12, 1978, the U.S. Department of State issued a policy statement of a sort rarely made. The department declared its disapproval of the inclusion of a specified political party in the governing coalition of a friendly, allied, and democratic nation. The statement began by acknowledging reports that the Italian Communist party (PCI) was pressing hard for cabinet posts in the new government that would be formed after the resignation of the Christian Democratic party government of Prime Minister Giulio Andreotti.

> As the President and other members of the Administration have publicly stated on a number of occasions, our Western European allies are sovereign countries and rightly and properly, the decision on how they are governed rests with their citizens alone. At the same time, we believe we have an obligation to our friends and allies to express our views clearly. . . .
>
> Our position is clear: We do not favor [Communist participation in Western governments] and would like to see Communist influence in any Western European country reduced. . . . The United States and Italy share profound democratic values and interests, and we do not believe that the Communists share those values and interests. As the President said in Paris last week: "It is precisely when democracy is up against difficult challenges that its leaders must show firmness in resisting the temptation of finding solutions in non-democratic forces."[1]

Whatever one may think of the merits of the department's attitude toward increased power for the Italian and other Western European Communist

[1] The text of the statement is printed in the *New York Times,* January 13, 1978, p. A2.

parties, or of the propriety of expressing it so publicly, the January statement set forth, explicitly or tacitly, the position of the United States on most of the issues discussed in this book. Before we begin those discussions, let me briefly set forth the book's genesis and structure.

This volume stems from a conference on Italy and Eurocommunism held in Washington, D.C., on June 7–9, 1977. The conference, like the book, was sponsored jointly by the American Enterprise Institute for Public Policy Research and the Hoover Institution on War, Revolution and Peace. It drew together Italian and American scholars, journalists, and public officials to discuss the nature of Eurocommunism, the PCI's electoral fortunes and possible future participation in Italian government, and the consequences of such participation for Italy's political, social, and economic institutions, for democracy in Western Europe, and for the Western alliance. The conference focused on Italy not only because of Italy's historic importance to Western civilization and present role in the Western alliance, but also because it is the Western nation in which the Communists appear to be the strongest.

The Structure

The strategy of the conference has been followed in the organization of this book.

Part One focuses on Italian and American attitudes toward the *apertura a sinistra* (opening to the left) policy of the 1960s. In most respects that episode closely parallels the situation facing the two countries in the 1970s, and a look backward may well tell us something about the road ahead. As Angelo Codevilla's chapter details, in the late 1950s some elements of the dominant Christian Democratic party (DC) feared that the existing center coalition would not be able to cope with growing domestic problems and the coalition's weakening parliamentary and electoral support. They felt that the best solution would be to bring the Italian Socialist party (PSI) into the government, both for its support and for the purpose of isolating the Communists outside the "mainstream" left. Other DC leaders opposed such a move, on the ground that the PSI had been and remained unabashedly Marxist and therefore little more than a stalking-horse for the Communists. Giving the PSI a share of government power, they argued, would only smooth the way for the PCI's "long march" through Italian political and social institutions and lead to an eventual Communist takeover.

American councils were divided as well. As the chapters by Roger Hilsman and William Knight make clear, some of President John F. Kennedy's advisers, notably Arthur M. Schlesinger, Jr., and W. Averell Harriman, urged him to encourage the opening. Others, especially some leading members of the State Department's Italian and Western European sections, pressed Kennedy to use American influence to delay or block power for the PSI. No clear or forceful American policy emerged, but in 1963 the PSI accepted an invitation to join a government headed by the DC's Aldo Moro, and the opening was a *fait accompli.* Codevilla, Hilsman, and Knight all find some lessons in the opening to the PSI of the 1960s for evaluating a possible opening to the PCI in the 1970s.

Part Two reviews the current state of Communism in Italy. Giacomo Sani's chapter identifies the main demographic and attitudinal sources of the PCI's recent dramatic upsurge in voting strength as well as the modest decline of the DC and the greater decline of the PSI. He concludes that, while the PCI has benefited more than other parties from the recent lowering of the voting age, PCI has made gains in all segments of the population, and the main threat to those gains is likely to come, not from the DC or the PSI, but from the splinter parties to the PCI's left. Joseph LaPalombara's chapter describes some of the main developments in Italian society which have weakened the DC and PSI while strengthening the PCI. He calls attention to the fact that Italy is unique in that, whereas in other European countries the democratic socialist party is considerably stronger than the Communists, in Italy the PCI has much more support than the PSI. He reviews the PCI's professions of commitment to "democratic pluralism," and finds them hard to reconcile with the party's longstanding commitments to Marxism, Leninism, and "working class hegemony." Enzo Bettiza's chapter finds in the writings and speeches of Antonio Gramsci the basic philosphy and strategic plan of Italian-style Eurocommunism as it resembles and differs from Soviet-style Marxism-Leninism. Gramsci's basic strategy, says Bettiza, is for the PCI to abandon efforts to bring about the "preventive revolution" advocated by Lenin and Stalin and to concentrate on working for the "final revolution," which can be achieved only by PCI domination of Italian culture and mass communications. In this way there will be no need for violence or class war because eventually the society will demand Communism and achieve it through liberal institutions.

Part Three reviews the current political situation in Italy and presents the ideas of members of Parliament from the two main parties of the "imperfect two-party system" about their parties' problems and prospects. Marino de Medici outlines and updates the main developments leading to the present crisis. He stresses the decline of the PSI, the growing violence of Italian life and politics, the intransigence of the labor unions, and the weakness and irresolution of the DC. Massimo de Carolis argues that Italy's best hope lies in a reformed, revitalized, and modernized Christian Democratic party rooted not in an outmoded Catholic religiosity but in an up-to-date secular commitment to liberal political and economic institutions. Lucio Libertini argues that the Communists must take part in the government because no government can be effective without the active support of the PCI, and only the PCI can provide the organizational discipline and popular support for the economic austerity and modernization which alone can save the Italian economy. He also emphasizes the PCI's commitment to democratic pluralism, alternation in office, and Italy's foreign policy commitments, including NATO.

Part Four closes the book with two estimates of the shape of the future. Giovanni Sartori, cochairman of the conference and coeditor of this volume, develops a scenario for events after the PCI's accession to office. PCI participation in a governing coalition, he argues, must inevitably become PCI domination of that coalition. When the PCI assumes such power, its supporters will demand that it redeem the promises it made on the road to power. Since the economy will not permit the bill to be paid, the PCI will have little choice but to use "the iron fist," and at that point democracy will have left Italy, perhaps forever. Henry A. Kissinger presents his prospectus for NATO and the Western alliance in a situation in which Communist parties play major roles in the governments of Italy and other Western European nations. He is not impressed, he says, by the PCI's protestations of independence from Moscow and commitment to democratic procedures; those same protestations have been made by Western Communist party leaders outside the Soviet Union since the 1940s, and they have never been more than tactical rhetoric. If the Communists come to power in Italy, they can hardly be expected to favor Western interests over Soviet interests, and NATO is therefore likely to become little more than a German-American alliance. While the United States cannot and should not intervene in the politics of any other nation, including Italy, we can and must make our feelings known about the probable consequences of Communist takeovers.

The chapters of this book consist of revised versions of the papers presented at the conference. In addition to their authors, the other persons making formal presentations at the conference were: Professor Samuel H. Barnes, University of Michigan; Senator John H. Chafee, Republican of Rhode Island; Senator Frank Church, Democrat of Idaho; Professor Giuseppe di Palma, University of California, Berkeley; Mr. John Disciullo, American consul-general at Genoa; Professor Peter Lange, Harvard University; Professor Michael Ledeen, Georgetown University; and Dr. Alan Platt, Potomac, Maryland.

Honorable Mario Zagari, M.P., a leader of the Italian Socialist party, was scheduled to present a paper, but had to withdraw at the last moment because of an emergency meeting of the European Parliament, in which he plays a prominent role. We regretted his absence very much, for while we had papers by prominent members of the Christian Democratic party and the Communist party, we were left without a representative of the Socialist party.

The conference was attended by other prominent scholars of Western European and Italian affairs, including Graham Allison, Gabriel Almond, Hadley Arkes, James Billington, Karl Cerny, Furio Colombo, Mario Corradi, Milorad Drachkovitch, Stephen Hess, Samuel Huntington, Jeane Jordan Kirkpatrick, Norman Kogan, Leon Lindberg, Antonio Lombardo, A. F. K. Organski, Robert Osgood, Jan Triska, and Giuliano Urbani. The sessions were also attended by representatives from the Department of Defense, Department of State, National Security Council, Central Intelligence Agency, U.S. Information Agency, Foreign Intelligence Advisory Board, Congressional Research Service, and both houses of Congress. They were joined by representatives from the embassies of Belgium, Italy, and the Soviet Union, and from the Carnegie Endowment for International Peace and the European Economic Community.

Henry Kissinger's address to the final session, which appears as the concluding chapter of the present volume, was covered by all the American television networks and by many American newspapers and news magazines. All the sessions were reported in detail by correspondents from seventeen Italian newspapers. Their accounts created such a stir in Italy that Achille Albonetti, who attended the conference for the organization *Circolo Stato e Libertà,* assembled the principal reports in Italian, American, and Western European newspapers and published them in a much-discussed volume.[2]

---

[2] Achille Albonetti, ed., *Gli Stati Uniti, l'Italia e l'eurocomunismo* (Rome: Circolo Stato e Libertà, 1977).

PART ONE

AMERICAN POLICY TOWARD THE "OPENING TO THE LEFT" IN THE 1960s

1

U. S. Policy on the Opening to the Left: The Role of the President's Advisers

Roger Hilsman

Let me begin with two disclaimers. The first is that, though I was the director of intelligence and research at the Department of State in the early part of the Kennedy administration, I was not centrally involved in the development of U.S. policy toward the opening to the left in Italy. I would prefer that W. Averell Harriman had written this paper. Harriman was much more centrally involved in the development of that policy than I. I must also confess, however, that if Harriman were in my place *he* would probably want Arthur M. Schlesinger, Jr., to write the paper. For Schlesinger was even more deeply involved than Harriman.

The second disclaimer is, I am not an expert on Italian politics. Although I know something of the subject and follow Italian political events with fascination, other contributors to this volume and many readers are far more expert. Italian politics is said to be like blue cheese—it is an acquired taste.

Politicians often find themselves in a position—like mine here—of having to address experts on the subject of their expertise. Robert F. Kennedy, I remember, had a standard story for such occasions. It concerned a man who had lived through the Johnstown flood—a disaster that all Americans learn of in their childhood, in which a town in Pennsylvania was almost totally destroyed. This person would recount his experience in the flood to anyone who would listen—he dearly loved an audience of any kind. When he died and went to heaven, St. Peter greeted him and informed him that he would be granted one wish. Delighted, the old man asked that all the angels be assembled so he could tell them of his experiences in the Johnstown flood.

"All right," said St. Peter, "but I must warn you: Noah will be one of those in the audience." I think I know something of how the man from Johnstown must have felt.

This paper is not so much about Italian politics as about American politics. I have had some experience in the Department of State and on Capitol Hill in the policy-making process in the United States, and I have also engaged in scholarly writing and research on the subject. I had some role in making the Kennedy administration's policy toward the opening to the left in Italy—at least it can be said that I stood on the edge of the struggle. Accordingly, I will first try to lay out a theory of how U.S. policy is made—a conceptual model of the policy-making process. The second task is to see how the facts of this particular policy—toward the opening to the left—fit into this conceptual model of policy making. In dredging up memories of how this policy was developed, I am fortunate in having read published accounts, such as that by Arthur M. Schlesinger, Jr.,[1] and unpublished accounts, such as that by Alan Platt.[2]

A Conceptual Model of the Policy-Making Process

Some Puzzlements. Let me approach the first task of trying to lay out a conceptual model of the policy-making process in a somewhat unorthodox way—by taking note of some "puzzlements." Charles G. Dawes, the vice president under Calvin Coolidge, once said that the members of the cabinet are a president's natural enemies. Now this is a puzzlement. Members of the cabinet, after all, are appointed by the president with the advice and consent of the Senate and serve "at his pleasure." How can they be his natural enemies?

President Truman, as he contemplated turning over the presidency to Dwight D. Eisenhower following the election of 1952, found the prospect vastly amusing. "He'll sit here," Truman would say, tapping the presidential desk, "and he'll say, 'Do this! Do that!' and nothing will happen. Poor Ike—it won't be a bit like the Army."[3] This, too, is a puzzlement. The president, after all, is supposed to be the boss. Why would President Truman think that Eisenhower would find being president so different from being a general in the army?

Once at a press conference very early in his administration, President Kennedy surprised his aides by answering a question about allied trade with Cuba with a promise to put into effect certain measures still under discussion within the government. Afterward he said with some exasperation, that, on that day at least, he had "actually made a little

[1] Arthur M. Schlesinger, Jr., *A Thousand Days: John F. Kennedy in the White House* (Boston: Houghton Mifflin, 1965).

[2] Alan Platt, "U.S. Policy toward the 'Opening to the Left' in Italy" (Ph.D. diss., Columbia University, 1976); see also Alan A. Platt and Roberto Leonardi, "American Foreign Policy and the Postwar Italian Left," *Political Science Quarterly,* vol. 93 (Summer 1978), pp. 197–215.

[3] Quoted in Richard E. Neustadt, *Presidential Power* (New York: Wiley, 1960), p. 9.

policy." Here again is a puzzlement—if presidents don't make foreign policy, who does?

On numerous occasions, friends of President Kennedy would use their personal access to him to further one policy or another. They report he would often say that he agreed but he was not sure the government would. Here is still another puzzlement.

After President Kennedy had held a long series of meetings of the National Security Council on a policy toward the Buddhist crisis in Vietnam, several decisions were finally made at one morning meeting that seemed to mark a watershed. A cable was drafted by a group that included the national security adviser, the secretary of defense, the assistant secretary of state for Far Eastern affairs, the chairman of the Joint Chiefs of Staff, and others. Since the President was busy with a group of members of Congress, only McGeorge Bundy, Michael V. Forrestal, and I stayed to get the President's approval. When the three of us trooped into his oval office, the President looked up, grinned, and said that now we had "the inner club." Later, I asked Bundy if the President meant that we were the people who were really familiar with the problem. Bundy said the President meant not only that but also something more. It was a private joke of his. He meant that we were the ones who had known all along what we would do about the problem, and who had been pulling and hauling, debating and discussing, for no other purpose than to keep the government together, to get all the others to come around. This, too, is a puzzlement. Most people would have thought that a series of meetings of the National Security Council was supposed to look at alternative policies, not to put on a show for a reluctant group of members by those who had already made up their minds.

What do these anecdotes demonstrate? One thing is that, in spite of the great power they wield, presidents can very rarely command, even within what is supposedly their most nearly absolute domain—in the executive branch, and especially on matters of foreign policy. As Richard E. Neustadt once said, "Underneath our images of Presidents-in-boots, astride decisions, are the half-observed realities of Presidents-in-sneakers, stirrups in hand, trying to induce particular department heads, or congressmen, or senators to climb aboard."[4]

The Realities of Policy Making. Most Americans, with their flair for the mechanical and their love of efficiency combined with a moralistic Puritan heritage, would like to think not only that policy making is a conscious and deliberate act, one of analyzing problems and systematically examin-

[4] Richard E. Neustadt, "White House and Whitehall," *The Public Interest,* vol. 2 (Winter 1966).

ing grand alternatives in all their implications, but also that the alternative finally chosen is aimed at achieving overarching ends that serve a high moral purpose.[5] Evidence that there is confusion about goals or that the goals themselves may be competing or that they are mutually incompatible is disquieting. Most Americans think it only reasonable that the procedures for making national decisions should be orderly, with clear lines of responsibility and authority. We assume that what we call the "decisions" of government are in fact decisions—discrete acts with recognizable beginnings and sharp, decisive endings. We like to think of policy as rationalized, in the economist's sense of the word, with each step leading logically and economically to the next. We want to be able to find out who makes decisions, to feel that they are the proper, official, and authorized persons, and to know that the really big decisions will be made at the top, by the president and his principal advisers in the formal assemblage of the cabinet or the National Security Council and with the Congress exercising its full and formal powers. We feel that the entire decision-making process ought to be a dignified, even majestic progression, with each of the participants having roles and powers so well and precisely defined that they can be held accountable for their actions by their superiors and eventually by the electorate.

The reality, of course, is quite different. Put dramatically, it could be argued that few, if any, decisions of government are either decisive or final. Very often policy is the sum of a congeries of separate or only vaguely related actions. On other occasions, it is an uneasy, even internally inconsistent, compromise among competing goals or an incompatible mixture of alternative means for achieving a single goal. There is no systematic and comprehensive study of all the implications of the grand alternatives, nor can there be. A government does not decide to inaugurate the nuclear age, but only to try to build an atomic bomb before its enemy does. It does not make a formal decision to become a welfare state, but only to take each of a series of steps—to experiment with an income tax at some safely innocuous level like 3 percent, to alleviate the hardship of people who have lost their jobs in a depression with a few weeks of unemployment compensation, or to lighten the old age of industrial workers with a tentative program of social security benefits. Rather than through grand decisions on grand alternatives, policy changes seem to come through a series of slight modifications of existing policy, with the new policy emerging slowly and haltingly by small and usually tentative steps, a process of trial and error in which policy zigs and zags, re-

[5] In this passage and subsequent descriptions of the "political process" model of policy making, I am drawing on my previous work in the field, and particularly on my *The Politics of Policy Making in Defense and Foreign Affairs* (New York: Harper and Row, 1971).

verses itself, and then moves forward in a series of incremental steps.[6] Sometimes policies are formulated and duly ratified only to be diverted to an entirely different direction and purpose by those carrying them out—or they are never carried out at all. And sometimes issues are endlessly debated with nothing at all being resolved until both the problem and the debaters disappear under the relentless pyramiding of events.

This is the way it really is. On some occasions, presidents clearly are the ones to make the decision, even if they cannot make it exactly as they might wish. On other occasions, the decision is just as clearly made by Congress. But in action after action, responsibility for decision is as fluid and restless as quicksilver, and there seems to be neither a person nor an organization on whom it can be fixed. At times, the point of decision seems to have escaped into the labyrinth of governmental machinery, beyond layers and layers of bureaucracy. At other times, it seems never to have reached the government at all, but to have remained either in the wider domain of public opinion created by the press or in the narrower domain dominated by the maneuverings of special interests.

Just as our desire to know who makes a decision is often frustrated, so is our hope that the process of policy making will be dignified. A decision, in fact, may be little more than a signal that starts a public brawl by people who want to reverse it. Leaks of top-secret information are one of the first and most blatant signs of battle, and they are endemic in the policy process. When it became clear, for example, that the report of the Gaither Committee, set up by President Eisenhower in 1957 to study civil defense in terms of the whole of nuclear strategy, would be critical of the Eisenhower policy of "massive retaliation," the crucial battle took place, not on the substance of the report, but on the issue of whether there would be 200 copies of the top secret report or only 2. Everyone knew without its being said that if the President did not accept the Gaither Committee's recommendations, the report might be kept from leaking to the press if there were only 2 copies, but never if there were 200. The committee won the battle, and 200 top-secret copies were distributed within the executive branch. The President did not accept the recommendations, and, sure enough, within a few days the *Washington Post* published in two whole pages an accurate and comprehensive version of the top-secret report and its recommendations.

This example is not unusual. There flows out of Washington continual rumors, tales of bickering, speculations, stories of selfish interest, charges, and countercharges. Abusive rivalries arise between the govern-

[6] On this tendency toward "disjointed incrementalism," see Charles E. Lindblom, "The Science of 'Muddling Through,'" *Public Administration Review,* vol. 19 (1959); and also Lindblom, *The Policy-Making Process* (Englewood Cliffs, N.J.: Prentice-Hall, 1968).

ment agencies engaged in making policy, and even within a single agency different factions battle, each seeking allies in other agencies, members of Congress, interest groups, and the press. Officialdom, whether civilian or military, is hardly neutral. It speaks, and inevitably as an advocate. The army battles for ground forces, the air force for bombers, the "Europe" faction in the State Department for policies benefiting NATO, and the "Africa" faction for anticolonialist policies that are unsettling to our relations with Europe. All these many interests, organizations, and institutions—inside and outside the government—are joined in a struggle over the goals of governmental policy and over the means by which these goals shall be achieved. Instead of unity, there is conflict. Instead of a majestic progression, there are erratic zigs and zags. Instead of clarity and decisiveness, there are tangle and turmoil; instead of order, confusion.

Sources of the Turmoil. Even though we deplore the disorder and confusion, the seeming disloyalty of leaks, the noise and untidiness, and all the rest, the policy-making process should be examined more carefully before condemning it. What are the sources of all this turmoil?

Partly the turbulence comes from the nature of the Constitution itself. As scholars have pointed out, the Constitutional Convention of 1787 did not create a government of "separated powers," but a government of separate institutions sharing powers.[7] The executive is part of the legislative process, and so is the judiciary. Congress has a role to play in the carrying out of policies; and so do the courts.

Still another dimension of turmoil is the multiplicity of participants. The president, the White House staff, the members of the cabinet, and other political appointees make up what we think of as an administration, but below them are a host of civil servants. Then there is the Congress. And more are involved than just those who hold official positions. It is no accident that the press, for example, is so often called the "fourth branch of government." The press plays a role in making U.S. foreign policy. There are also lobbies, the spokesmen of special interests of every kind, from oil producers and farmers to the Navy League and Women Strike for Peace. The academic world plays a role, both formally and informally. There are also the quasi-governmental organizations, such as the RAND Corporation, which do research for various parts of the government. All these people and organizations influence policy. Although not accountable to the electorate, they have power and are as much a part of the governmental process as the traditional legislative, judicial, and executive branches. In making policy, many more people than those who hold official positions are involved, and many of them have more subtle ways

---

[7] Neustadt, *Presidential Power*, p. 33.

for shaping policy. In fact, there is turmoil in policy making because such a multiplicity of power centers are involved. Policy making is not hierarchical.

Policy Convictions. One cause of turmoil is the convictions about policy held by these many participants. Among the principal findings of a British government committee appointed to study the powers of ministers was that most people can go against their own pecuniary interests more easily than going against a deep conviction on policy. In the business of Washington, the stakes are high and the issues fundamental, both to our society and to the question of war and peace for the entire world. In such circumstances, it is not surprising when passions run so strong that the participants occasionally feel they must leak secret materials to the Congress or the press for the salvation of the nation. In the late 1950s, for example, intelligence officials leaked secret information foreshadowing a "missile gap" to sympathetic members of Congress and to the press, but not because they were disloyal. They had tried and failed to persuade the top levels of the Eisenhower administration to increase missile production, and they felt justified in going over the President's head to Congress, the press, and the public. It was undoubtedly the same kind of deep conviction that motivated Daniel Ellsberg to leak the Pentagon papers, the top-secret collection of documents showing how the United States became involved in the Vietnam War.

Inadequacy of Knowledge. The complexity of the problems and the inadequacy of our knowledge of how and why things work in the social and political affairs also cause confusion and turbulence. More and better understanding will not always lead to sure solutions of knotty problems, but it often does. If our understanding of a modern industrial economy had been better in the 1920s, for example, the depths of the Great Depression might have been avoided. When knowledge is inadequate, when problems are complex, and especially when such problems are new, presenting a challenge never before experienced, there is much room for disagreement, conflict, and turmoil.

Policy Making as Politics. These are some of the facets of policy making—the separate institutions sharing powers; the multiplicity of power centers inside and outside of government, including the press, the experts, the selfish and unselfish interest groups, and others who influence policy without holding formal power; and the difficulties and complexities of analysis, prediction, and judgment. These factors help to explain the turmoil, the hurly-burly of policy making that is disquieting or repugnant to so many.

This, of course, is the point of the presidential anecdotes. Truman had this in mind when he laughed about Ike being president and finding it not a bit like the army. Kennedy had this in mind when he talked about making "a little policy" or about "the inner club." It is what Neustadt had in mind when he talked about presidents-in-sneakers, stirrups in hand.

I would generalize these anecdotes by saying that the policy-making process is not a *rational* process. Neither is it an *irrational* process. The people involved in policy making use as much rationality as is available, and as much knowledge of how and why things happen as they can acquire. Even if more knowledge were available, however, policy would never be formulated by scientific equations fed into computers. Policy making is fundamentally neither a rational nor a scientific and logical process—it is a political process.

Policy making is a political process in that it involves multiple power centers that each have different goals for the society and different estimates of what alternative means will accomplish. When decisions are made on the larger questions that require sacrifices by the nation or the selection of one set of objectives at the cost of others, there is struggle and conflict. At the same time, there is a "strain toward agreement,"[8] an effort to build a consensus, a push for accommodation, for compromise, for some sort of agreement on the policy decision. Some participants in the process may block a policy, or sabotage it, or at least snipe away at it from the sidelines. Others may give the active and imaginative support and dedicated effort required to make the policy succeed if concessions aimed directly at them can enlist their cooperation. Finally, there is in all the participants an intuitive realization that prolonged intransigence, stalemate, and indecision on urgent and fundamental issues might threaten the very form and structure of the system of governance itself.

The Conceptual Model Summarized. Policy making, then, involves a number of different individuals and organizations. Each has power, and each may have either a different goal or a different idea of the best policy for achieving a commonly accepted goal. Each seeks allies by a variety of means—bargaining, persuading, leaking information, and a hundred others. There is conflict and struggle between these power centers, but there is also consensus building, an attempt to reach agreement.

Let me sum up this conceptual model with two quotations. In the first, Graham Allison describes the political process model of policy making. Allison says that government behavior can best be understood as

---

[8] The phrase is Warner R. Schilling's. See his "The Politics of National Defense: Fiscal 1950," in Warner Schilling, Paul Hammond, and Richard Snyder, eds., *Strategy, Politics, and Defense Budgets* (New York: Columbia University Press, 1962), p. 23.

the result of bargaining games. In contrast with a theory in which states are rational, unitary actors, he says,

> the governmental (or bureaucratic) politics model sees no unitary actor but rather many actors as players—players who focus not on a single strategic issue but on many diverse intranational problems as well; players who act in terms of no consistent set of strategic objectives but rather according to various conceptions of national, organizational, and personal goals; players who make government decisions not by a single rational choice but by the pulling and hauling that is politics.
>
> Men share power. Men differ about what must be done. The differences matter. This milieu necessitates that government decisions and actions result from a political process. In this process, some times one group committed to a course of action triumphs over other groups fighting for other alternatives. Equally often, however, different groups pulling in different directions produce a result, or better, a resultant—a mixture of conflicting preferences and unequal power of various individuals—distinct from what any person or group intended. In both cases, what moves the chess pieces is not simply the reasons that support a course of action, or the routines of organizations that enact an alternative, but the power and skill of proponents and opponents of the action in question.[9]

The second quotation comes from an earlier work of my own. I put it that Americans

> aspire to a rationalized system of government and policy making. This implies that a nation can pursue a single set of clearly perceived and generally agreed-to goals, just as a business organization is supposed to pursue profits. Yet is this realistic? Is the problem of making policy in a highly diversified mass society really one of relating the different steps in making a decision to a single set of goals or is it precisely one of choosing goals—of choosing goals not in the abstract, but in the convoluted context of ongoing events, with inadequate information, incomplete knowledge and understanding, and insufficient power—and doing so, in all probability, while pitted against opposition both at home and abroad? If so, the making of national decisions is not a problem for the efficiency expert of assembling different pieces of policy logically as if the product were an automobile. Policy faces inward as much as outward, seeking to reconcile conflicting goals, to adjust aspirations to available means, and to accommodate the different

---

[9] Graham Allison, *Essence of Decision: Explaining the Cuban Missile Crisis* (Boston: Little, Brown and Company, 1971), pp. 144–145.

advocates of these competing goals and aspirations to one another. It is here that the essence of policy making seems to lie, in a process that is in its deepest sense political.[10]

Policy on the Opening to the Left

The Schlesinger Account. Against the background of this analytical concept of policy making, let us look at the account by Arthur M. Schlesinger, Jr., of the development of U.S. policy towards the opening to the left. He begins with a very broad brush indeed, pointing out that the two great groups inhabiting the center-left in European politics had been the Christian Democrats and the Social Democrats, and arguing that if they could be persuaded to work together they might give Western Europe the "social leadership it needed to meet its new problems."[11] A center-left rapprochement seemed easier to obtain in Italy than elsewhere in Europe. If it succeeded there, Schlesinger says, it might offer a model for all the other Western European countries. This would be the best guarantee against the Communist effort to revive the old united front with the Socialists.

Turning to Italy, Schlesinger describes the formation of the Social Democratic party under the leadership of Giuseppe Saragat. He then describes how Pietro Nenni, who headed the Socialist majority, and his comrades became disenchanted with the Communist party after the Soviet intervention in Hungary in 1956, and began to move away from them. By 1960, Schlesinger says, Nenni's break with the Communists was complete, although some local Socialist-Communist coalitions lingered in many localities. This led a number of Italian Christian Democrats to begin to think of an opening to the left that would lead eventually to a coalition government between the Christian Democrats and the Nenni Socialists.

During the Eisenhower administration, U.S. policy had been one of "purposeful opposition" to such a move. That administration had not believed Nenni's break was genuine, but by 1961, no one could doubt that it was. Moreover, Schlesinger goes on to argue, "by ingenious reinterpretation, Nenni had defined his party's traditional neutralism as meaning the preservation of the existing European equilibrium; since Italian withdrawal from NATO would threaten that equilibrium, Nenni explicitly opposed such withdrawal as an unneutral act."[12]

Schlesinger says that for all these reasons, he and Robert Komer,

---

[10] *The Politics of Policy Making in Defense and Foreign Affairs,* pp. 14–15.

[11] Schlesinger, *A Thousand Days,* p. 876.

[12] Ibid., p. 877.

his colleague on the White House staff, concluded that the time had come for the United States to end its opposition and that the United States would welcome a government in Italy that would address itself to the social and economic needs of the people. Schlesinger and Komer suggested to President Kennedy that the visit of Prime Minister Amintore Fanfani to Washington in June 1961 would present an obvious opportunity. Schlesinger says that Kennedy "readily agreed that the United States from now on should indicate discreet sympathy for the opening to the left."[13] Schlesinger, it should be noted, says, not that he and Komer suggested discreet sympathy, but that Kennedy "readily agreed" to discreet sympathy. Also, Schlesinger notes, the opening to the left was not on the agenda for the meeting with Fanfani—Kennedy expressed this discreet sympathy "privately."

If anyone doubts the validity of the conceptual model offered in the pages above, Schlesinger's next few sentences should convince him: "The presidential decision was, of course, at once communicated to the State Department, and this should have ended the matter. In fact, it only marked the beginning of a long and exasperating fight. In the end, it took nearly two years to induce the Department of State to follow the President's policy."

Schlesinger then tells of his own visit to Rome in February 1962, which he describes as "passing through." He met with a number of Italian leaders, including Nenni. Schlesinger told Nenni that "Washington was pleased at the prospect of forward movement in Italian social policy but wondered about the implications of the *apertura* for foreign affairs." Nenni responded, Schlesinger says, by stressing his dislike of the Communists and his acceptance of NATO on a de facto basis. In any case, Fanfani's new government had the outside support of the Nenni Socialists, and, though the American embassy had maintained a "hands off" attitude, Schlesinger told the President that the opening was on its way—"not against the United States, but without it."

Schlesinger then pictures a continued fight in Washington. He says that the career officers in the State Department who dealt with Italy declared the Nenni Socialists were "not anti-Communist." Komer and Schlesinger, for their part, "enlisted" Robert Kennedy, Arthur Goldberg, and Walter Reuther "in the effort to cajole the department into abandoning the legacy of the past."

It was, Schlesinger goes on to say, an odd situation:

> We had, of course, the presidential decision and the patent backing of McGeorge Bundy. We had the sporadic sympathy of George Ball and William Tyler, when they were not out re-

[13] Ibid., p. 878.

> organizing Europe. As for the Secretary of State, he did not have, so far as I could find out, any views on Italian policy beyond a nervous response when President Segni, an old-time opponent of the *apertura,* told him that American interest in the Socialists would be interpreted as a rejection of our only "true" friends, the Italian conservatives.[14]

It was an endless struggle, Schlesinger says. He notes that those at the top of the U.S. government were preoccupied with major crises and that this is why the President's wishes were not honored. The major crises gave career officers on the working level the chance to pursue their own preferences. Schlesinger describes the battle in some detail, and says that it came to an end only when "Averell Harriman became Under Secretary for Political Affairs in the spring of 1963. With his expert knowledge of the Italian situation and his administrative vigor, he turned the bureaucracy around. By the time that Nenni and his party eventually entered the Italian government in December 1963, the Department of State was at last in accord."[15]

This, then, is the way U.S. policy was changed—as Schlesinger viewed it. A study by Alan Platt gives a fuller, more broadly based account, since he interviewed almost all of the U.S. participants, those who were against the opening as well as those in favor. The most curious discrepancy between Platt's account and Schlesinger's is that Schlesinger gives so much credit to Harriman for changing U.S. policy, but does not mention Harriman's visit to Rome in March 1961. Platt reports from an interview with Harriman that he had returned from that trip believing the following:

> (1) That the Nenni Socialists' entry into the government would be necessary to accomplish social and economic reforms.
>
> (2) That United States neutrality in the question of the *apertura* was in fact *support* for the idea of continuing the existing coalition.
>
> (3) That continued neutrality on the part of the United States would push the Socialists closer to the Communists.
>
> (4) That an opening to the left would have the result of weakening the Communists in Italy.[16]

Personal Recollections. Although only peripherally involved in these events as the director of intelligence and research, I can, perhaps, add a little to the story. Harriman's visit may have been omitted by Schlesinger

[14] Ibid., pp. 879–880.

[15] Ibid., p. 881.

[16] Platt, "U.S. Policy toward the 'Opening to the Left.' "

because he was writing from notes and documents soon after the events. Harriman's views were recalled several years after the fact, in an interview, without going over the record to refresh his memories. My own memories of what Harriman had to say following his return from the March 1961 visit to Rome are what Alan Platt reports. Harriman did, in fact, lobby rather heavily in Washington along these lines, but he put great stress on one additional point—*that an opening to the left was inevitable whether or not the United States approved of it.*

At first glance, Schlesinger's description of what happened seems to fit the analytical model with which I began—allowing, perhaps, for some slight exaggeration of Schlesinger's own role. But I think the fit is on the surface only, that it is a superficial fit. My own analysis would differ in a number of important respects. It starts with two assumptions. First, President Kennedy, Bundy, and Harriman—those who were particularly interested in Italy—did not believe that the United States could greatly influence what would happen in Italy. I think they believed that neither carrots nor sticks could impose the American preference on an opening to the left.

If the United States opposed an opening, and the Italians went ahead anyway, what could we do? We certainly could not cut off aid, or break relations, or sponsor a move to evict Italy from NATO. Our own public opinion, congressional opinion, press opinion, and expert opinion would have reacted with extreme wrath and prevented any such radical moves of punishment. I think those at the top levels of the Kennedy administration knew this, believed that the Italians also knew it, and realized that this knowledge would strengthen the Italians in their determination to do whatever they decided. The American government did not believe it could exercise any more than marginal influence on what happened.

If that was the case, the best thing to do would be to keep a very low profile. I think it was no accident that the opening was missing from the agenda of the meeting between Prime Minister Fanfani and President Kennedy. I think it may have been an accident that Kennedy indicated approval privately of an opening—if he in fact did so.

If the President publicly came out in favor of an opening *and nothing happened,* he would look rather silly and ineffectual. If the President came out *against* an opening, and it happened anyway, then he would look even sillier. If the President believed he could not influence what would happen, then the wise thing to do was not to take any sort of public stand either way.

My own impression is that he was willing to indicate discreetly that the United States would not do anything drastic either way but that he wanted to have no personal part in the matter. The reason it took Schlesinger and his allies so long to force the Department of State into line may have been that the President gave them nothing more than a hunting license to search for allies. The career officers were no innocents, and they had never seen a piece of paper signed by the President saying he wanted the policy changed—and immediately. They had only Schlesinger's word on what the President wanted, and career officials have had long experience with White House aides trying to inflate a hunting license into a presidential order. Under such circumstances, they would present arguments and engage in maneuvers designed to smoke out the President's personal views. Schlesinger accuses the State Department careerists of engaging in "strategems of obstruction and delay." I am sure they did. Anyone who has had any experience in Washington with presidents and top-level bureaucrats would expect both to behave just as they did—the one to stand aside, letting those on the lower levels fight it out, while keeping his own prestige intact; and the other to delay and obstruct, though never so blatantly as to invite retaliation.

My second assumption is, the top officials of the Kennedy administration disbelieved the predictions of both the anti-opening and the pro-opening American officials. The results might be good or bad, but they would not be earthshaking.

If the Socialists came in without either our opposition or our encouragement, these officials reasoned, there might be some improvement in social and economic policy, but it would scarcely change the social and economic situation overnight. At best, the Communists would be slightly weakened. There was, in a word, nothing to be gained for an American official or for the United States government from an all-out commitment either way.

Most top officials of the Kennedy administration thought that the Socialists would *not* try to withdraw Italy from NATO. I think they also believed that if the Socialists did try to do so, then the other parties and the Italian people would probably cast them out. As a result, the old coalition would be stronger than it had ever been.

If my memory serves me, this is what I was thinking at the time. The conceptual model with which we began suggests that Kennedy, Bundy, and others would let the Foreign Service bureaucrats in Washington and in the embassy in Rome, as well as White House aides and members of Congress and the press who felt passionately enough about the matter, fight it out among themselves. Then, no matter which way it went, the administration could either deny blame or take credit.

As John F. Kennedy once said in regard to another matter, "I hope this policy works. If it does, it will be another White House victory. If it doesn't, it will be another State Department failure."

2

U. S. Policy on the Opening to the Left: The View from the State Department

William E. Knight

It has been said by some concerning the opening to the left that the United States during 1961 and 1962 pursued two different policies at the same time, one favoring the opening and the other opposing. Was this true, or wasn't it?

By way of introduction, a few points should be made on President Kennedy's approach to the management of foreign relations during the early part of his administration, since it had a bearing on the situation that developed. President Eisenhower had built up under the National Security Council a highly structured system for the management of foreign affairs, the heart of which was the Operations Coordinating Board. The OCB constituted a forum in which all of the foreign affairs agencies met to catalog, and supposedly coordinate, almost everything done abroad in the implementation of policy. The fear was that, without such a centralized mechanism, the sprawling U.S. government was likely to go off in all directions, either acting at cross purposes with itself or coasting along, moving papers from the In Box to the Out Box, without doing much at all to achieve national objectives.

This was not a groundless fear. It had been known to happen before, and it would doubtless happen again. The question increasingly arose, however, whether the OCB was the best way of solving the problem. It was a tremendous paper factory. Kennedy arrived in Washington convinced that it was a great waste of time, and one of his first moves was to abolish it. His announcement said that responsibility for much of the board's work would be centered in the secretary of state, who would rely particularly on the assistant secretaries in charge of the regional bureaus, and they, in turn, would consult closely with other departments and agencies. Secretary of State Dean Rusk then told the State Department that the President expected the department to "take charge" of foreign policy. He told us to "use our elbows," if necessary. It later became apparent that Rusk himself had about the softest elbows in town, but he was happy to see us use ours.

All of this was music to the ears of most Foreign Service officers, who had always believed that this was the way the railroad ought to be run. Nowadays, of course, everyone loves and admires the State Department and considers it beyond fear and above reproach, but back in those days this was not so. We typically found ourselves subjected to a barrage of scornful clichés. We were told that we were marshmallows, and we were called the Foreign Affairs Fudge Factory. We were exhorted to call the shots as we saw them, without fear or favor, let the chips fall where they may. (Actually, it often developed that when the department took a firm stand on an issue, the groups that favored an opposite stand quickly developed a craving for marshmallows and fudge.)

In any case, the President's decision established the organizational context within which the debate on the "opening" developed, with the principal authority set at the level of the geographic bureaus in the Department of State.

Background of Policy toward Italy

There is no need for an extensive catalog of U.S. national interests in Italy in the early 1960s, but it is useful to remember the general range of those interests. On the military side, based on Italy's strategic position and membership in NATO, they included U.S. air bases, the headquarters in Naples of the U.S. naval command, the Leghorn logistical supply base, the line of communications, the Jupiter missile emplacements, and other odds and ends. They included, on the ideological plane, Italy's working democracy, which was as important to us then as it is today. They included U.S. trade with, and investment in, Italy, which was already high and rapidly growing. They included the millions of Americans with personal and religious ties in Italy, which added a special dimension of interest and concern. Finally, they included Italy's enthusiastic adherence to Western European integration, which the United States considered so important.

The policies that we had followed since the end of World War II had been grouped around these interests. As we consider the main points, we should bear in mind the possible implications for each one of them of the opening to the left as it was emerging at that time.

In brief, U.S. policy included the following objectives and tactical concepts:

- the establishment of a democratic form of government in Italy
- the consolidation of that government by the encouragement of economic growth and the strengthening of democratic institutions

through such measures as land and tax reform, the development of the south, and the establishment of grass roots popular organizations, such as free trade unions and cooperatives

- the participation of Italy in the Western community of nations through the Marshall Plan, NATO, and the European Economic Community
- the preservation of a close bilateral relationship with the United States
- particularly during the Eisenhower administration, the encouragement of steps by the Italians to reduce the Communist potential for revolution and subversion by a variety of measures aimed at removing Communists and fellow travelers from positions of authority in industry and government
- and finally working toward the ends listed above by supporting as the basis of government coalitions the forces of the political center, which ranged from the Social Democrat party on the left through the moderate leftist Republicans and the Christian Democrats to the conservative but democratic Liberals on the right (we had no theoretical quarrel with the inclusion of the Monarchists, but the practical political difficulties in Italy at most times ruled them out).

On both the far right and the far left, we saw parties opposed to many of the fundamental elements of our policies—the democratic method, NATO, Western European integration, close relations with the United States, and the liberal economic policies which we thought held the most promise for Italian advancement.

The Position of the Italian Socialist Party. The Italian Socialist party, led by Pietro Nenni, was the target of the opening to the left. In 1946, when the passions of World War II were still at fever pitch and a classical Marxist takeover in Italy seemed a real possibility, the PSI had renewed its prewar Unity of Action Pact with the Communists. Thereafter, during the late 1940s and early 1950s, it had fought valiantly beside the Communists against most of our objectives. However, as the 1950s rolled on and the situation in Europe at first stabilized and then gained strength, some in the party began to reappraise its tactics. A revolution was obviously not just around the corner, and political parties are, after all, machines whose reason for being is to win and exercise governmental power. They do not usually feel comfortable being forever out of power. Around the mid 1950s, the party began to show signs of separating itself a bit from the Communists, especially after the Soviet suppression of the Hungarian uprising in 1956. For many in the PSI that suppression was a shock that raised grave doubts about the whole Communist relationship.

In 1957, the party abstained from the vote on Italy's joining the European Economic Community and voted in favor of Italy's joining Euratom, despite the opposition to both measures by the Communists. Also in 1957, the PSI publicly endorsed the "democratic parliamentary method." In 1958, it canceled the Unity of Action Pact with the Communists and competed with the Communists in the national elections. It saw itself rewarded with an increase in its popular vote from 12 percent to 14 percent, while the Communists remained steady at 23 percent. It still remained within the General Confederation of Labor with the Communists, however, and it continued to be allied with them in the administration of many major and minor city governments.

The Growing Speculation of the Opening to the Left. From about the middle of 1958 on, the possibility of an opening to the left by the Christian Democrats toward the PSI became a matter of growing speculation. The reasons were partly the developments in the PSI, and partly the weakening of the old center party grouping in the Parliament. The Christian Democrats had never had the strength to govern alone, and the moderate left and the moderate right now found it increasingly difficult to work together. On the other hand, neither a center-leftist nor a center-rightist government could survive alone.

So what was to be done? There were mutterings of a possible right-wing authoritarian coup, but the principal speculation concerned a deal with the PSI. A growing body of opinion favored it among the Christian Democrat left wing, the Social Democrats, the Republicans, and the PSI right wing.

This proposal aroused strong feelings among its opponents—from devout Catholics who considered the Nenni Socialists to be Priest-Eaters as voracious as the Communists; from deeply committed democrats who viewed the PSI as inherently dictatorial; from "Atlanticists" and "Europeanists" who thought the PSI was at the very least neutralist, and possibly still secretly pro-Soviet; and from economic liberals who saw the PSI as an avowed enemy of free enterprise and a proponent of the nationalization of industry. Each group had chapter and verse from the PSI's quite recent past to nourish its fears.

The feelings were hardly less strong among the PSI hardliners, who labeled the suggestion a sellout to the bourgeoisie. This was, indeed, a potent political brew.

The Debate in the U.S. Government

Soon after the Kennedy administration took office, two fairly clear-cut groups had emerged in Washington and in the U.S. embassy at Rome, one tending to welcome and the other to be apprehensive about the opening from the U.S. point of view. The issue was *not* merely academic: it was whether we should encourage the opening to happen as quickly as possible, or whether we should use our influence, if not to oppose it, at least to affect the timing and the terms under which it would eventually take place. The viewers most concerned were centered in the embassy in Rome and in the Bureau of European Affairs at the State Department. I will make plain at the outset that—as the officer in charge of Italian and Austrian affairs in the Office of Western European Affairs at State—I was among those who were apprehensive. Our opinion was shared by the operational side of the CIA, by the defense attaché's office in Rome, and—among the influential private groups—by certain key people in the AFL/CIO, who could not forgive the PSI's continued alliance with the Communists in the Italian General Confederation of Labor. Of course, there was no complete unanimity of opinion in any of these units. There were those both on the desk and in the embassy who were in the favorable group or were without a firm opinion either way.

Those who favored the opening had as their most vigorous exponent Arthur M. Schlesinger, Jr., who was at that time a special assistant to President Kennedy, and who had an office in the White House. A substantial number of people came to share his view; indeed, more than a few had developed their opinions long before he came on the scene in January 1961. These included, in particular, most of the analysts in the research divisions of State and CIA. They also included certain members of the National Security Council staff, former Governor Averell Harriman, and various journalists and professional analysts outside the government.

Conspicuous by their absence from either group were the President himself and the people in the top echelons of State, such as the secretary and the under secretary.

The Arguments Pro and Con. Before going into the arguments that were marshalled for and against the opening within the U.S. government, I must emphasize that no two individuals saw the problem in exactly the same terms, or reached their opinions at precisely the same time. Rather than cataloging fine distinctions, however, I will try to present the essential points of the two sides.

To begin with, the two groups did not basically disagree on the nature of many of Italy's problems that so badly required solution; namely, the need for reform and modernization in taxation, education, public health, welfare, the judicial system, the bureaucracy, and other fields, and the need for more equitable sharing of the fruits of economic growth.

Nor was there much disagreement that, with the whittling away of the parliamentary majority of the center parties, their room for maneuver had just about disappeared. Those within the center on the left and on the right could each veto the measures of the other with the help of the more radical parties to their left and right, which exercised such votes not as a duty but as a pleasure.

In their purest form, the arguments between the Joyous Welcomers and the Worried Doubters of opening came down to differing assessments of three factors: the possible gains, the possible risks, and the timing. As a form of verbal shorthand, I will refer to the Joyous Welcomers as the pros and the Worried Doubters as the cons. Actually, some of the Welcomers were worried, and some of the Doubters were joyous.

The Possible Gains. To take the possible gains first, the pros as a group had high hopes and expectations that an opening government would bring major progress in the solution of Italy's social and structural problems. They tended to see Italy as increasingly divided into two broad groupings, which they labeled Conservatives and Progressives, the Progressives being all those who favored the opening to the left. They typically referred to the Progressives as "vigorous and reform-minded" and asserted that an opening would, as Schlesinger once put it, "begin the reclamation of the working class for democracy,"[1] thereby bringing new strength and stability to the government. They attached little weight to the accomplishments of the previous governments.

The cons were less sanguine about the problem solving that might flow from an opening. They suspected that Italian politics would still be Italian politics, with the usual difficulties in getting *anything* done. And some of the measures most likely to emerge, such as nationalization of additional sectors of private industry, were not equated with progressivism at all by the cons. In any case, the cons said, since strong opposition existed to the opening within the PSI, who knew how much of it Nenni could bring with him? The cons gave the Italian postwar governments considerable credit for what they had accomplished, particularly in pursuing the economic policies that had made possible the Italian "economic miracle," then well under way. Per capita income had increased 90 percent since 1948, and the rate of increase was rising. The cons thought that the biggest gains for the Italian man in the street were more likely to flow from this "miracle" than from governmental programs, essential as the latter were. Anything that interfered with the progress of the miracle might do more harm than good.

---

[1] Arthur M. Schlesinger, Jr., *A Thousand Days: John F. Kennedy in the White House* (Boston: Houghton Mifflin, 1965), p. 877.

And so, the pros and the cons disagreed first of all on the potential benefits to be reaped from the opening.

The Risks. As to the risks, the pros were confident that Nenni was not a Communist Trojan horse, that he could be trusted, and that the PSI would not upset the various foreign affairs and internal Italian democratic apple carts that meant so much to the United States. They averred that Nenni was now saying as many of the things that we wanted to hear as he could be expected to say without losing control of his party.

For many cons, Nenni's current statements were almost drowned out by the echoes of the hard-line revolutionary things he had said not very many years before. Even his current public pronouncements were not wholly reassuring. For example, he said in October 1961 that the PSI wished to free Italy's action from that of the blocs. Now, just what did that mean? Well and good that it was a formula that moved the PSI away from its solidly pro-Soviet posture; but it also suggested that Italy should move away from the Atlantic alignment as well. The PSI had always been neutralist. What would be the fate of the U.S. bases and the whole NATO relationship if it came into the government? The pros said that such statements by Nenni were merely rhetoric to placate the party's rebellious left wing.

In the matter of risks, just as important for the cons as the possible PSI influence in the direction of neutralism was the possible impact of the opening on the center parties themselves. The cons feared that an opening might lead to a split in the Christian Democrat party, on which the entire Italian situation, and Italy's foreign policy, depended. The cons did not identify the Italian working class as a whole with the PSI, since as a matter of simple statistics more workers usually voted Christian Democrat than Socialist. So the cons thought it unjustifiable to place such emphasis on the possibility of "reclaiming the working class for democracy" through an opening. As a matter of fact, the cons believed that the PSI was more likely to steal support from the Social Democrats and the Christian Democrat left wing, rather than from the Communists, as a result of the opening.

Finally, though the cold war had passed its peak, it had by no means disappeared entirely. Considerable effort had been devoted by the United States to urge Italian governments to root out potential subversives from the bureaucracy. There were many among the cons who were convinced that through the normal operation of the patronage system a new wave of pro-Soviet Marxists would almost inevitably worm its way back into the bureaucratic woodwork. The pros did not pooh-pooh this point. In his memo to Kennedy preparatory to the Fanfani visit in 1961, Arthur Schlesinger recommended that the President "reiterate the American position that we continue to favor strict and effective measures against Communist espionage and subversion."

To sum up, then, the cons saw much greater risks in the opening than did the pros.

The Timing. And this brings us finally to the question of timing. For all of the considerations I have mentioned, the cons thought that it would be better if the opening took considerable time to develop. This, they thought, would permit Nenni and the other supporters of the opening in the PSI both to bring their own new positions to maturity and to draw the party as a whole away from its longstanding neutralist positions on NATO, on relations with the United States, on European institutions, and on other matters. By the same token, it would give the Christian Democrat party time to adjust to the idea of an opening in such fashion that the party would not be torn apart over the issue.

Schlesinger and some other pros saw the opening as a fragile plant that would wither and die if it did not flower soon, and they thought that active U.S. encouragement was essential if the blooming was to occur. In contrast, by 1961 the cons thought that the opening was probably inevitable for a variety of reasons and that it ought to be permitted to develop at its own pace.

One other consideration on timing played a part in the equation, though it had nothing to do with Italy. Schlesinger hoped that a pattern of collaboration between Catholic and Socialist parties could be established generally in Western Europe, particularly in Germany after Adenauer and in France after De Gaulle, and he thought that a successful Italian opening would help make this possible. An unhurried scenario did not fit in well with this concept.

These, then, were the main elements of the debate. What was actually being done?

U.S. Actions

Since the immediate postwar period, the United States had pretty much written off the PSI, because of the PSI's Unity of Action Pact with the Communists, and treated its leaders essentially the same as it treated the Communists. Embassy contacts with PSI leaders at first were nonexistent and later carried out by a single middle-grade officer. PSI leaders had been offered no Leader Grants, and waivers had been required under the McCarran Act for PSI leaders wishing a visa for a visit to the United States. The United States did not want to give the impression to the Italian political community that it regarded the PSI as just another political party, like any other.

During 1961 and into 1962, U.S. officials in Rome and Washington took two basic positions.

- In public, they repeatedly asserted that the opening was a matter for the Italians themselves to decide, and that the United States had no wish to try to prevent it.
- In private conversations, at the same time, they expressed concern over the PSI's traditional neutralism and the possible effects of an opening on Italy's policies toward NATO, Europe, and the United States if not preceded by substantial changes in PSI policies and relations with the Communists.

Meanwhile, the pros, it need hardly be said, favored treating the PSI like any other party, with full embassy contacts, participation in Leader Grants, and the like.

In fact, as 1961 progressed a modest easing of U.S. relations with the PSI did take place. Travel grants were offered to a group of PSI people in the fall, though they did not avail themselves of them until the following year. Nevertheless, the U.S. official position remained essentially unchanged. And over many a practical question and many a study paper, the tug of war between the pros and cons went on. One of the highlights of this came in June 1961, when Fanfani visited Washington. Arthur Schlesinger maintained that, in speaking with Fanfani, President Kennedy had, in effect, made a clear-cut decision in favor of the opening. We on the Italian desk in State never saw evidence of such a decision. On the contrary, during all of this period I never saw any indication that the President had any personal views on the matter at all. We now know from McGeorge Bundy and others that the President was not very interested in the issue, which he considered of minor importance to the United States. This being the case, he was simply not willing to come out with a decision running flatly counter to the recommendations of State and others, particularly on a matter that could easily go sour.

The net effect of the President's attitude of noninvolvement, I am convinced, was to make those who favored the opening try to persuade State to change its own recommendations. Our position on the desk and in the Office of Western European Affairs was that as long as we were being asked for *our* judgments, we were going to give *our* judgments. The assistant secretary of state for European affairs, William R. Tyler, essentially relied on us, shared our concern, and accepted most of our recommendations.

It is hardly necessary to add that, had there ever been a clear-cut decision by the President, or by anyone above us in the operational chain of command leading to the White House, we would have saluted and carried it out, but none ever came. No one up the line felt inclined to inject himself into the matter. This was, as I have said, a relatively unimportant and esoteric issue from the U.S. point of view at the time, no development obliged those at the top to take a position, and there were other real crises to engage their attention. And so, a deadlock developed between the pros and the cons, during which the position of the cons, which reflected the established policy of the U.S. government, continued to be applied.

A Two-Policy Period? At this point, a situation arose which led some observers to conclude that the United States was following two contradictory policies at the same time. Arthur Schlesinger has recorded that, after failing to convince the State Department that the President desired a change in U.S. policy, he decided to go around, rather than through, State and the embassy. Late in 1961 and into 1962, he accordingly proceeded to do a variety of things intended to convey to Italian leaders a changed official policy toward the opening. He met with key Italian political figures in Rome, without the embassy's concurrence or participation (and, indeed, over the embassy's opposition), and wrote letters to them on White House stationery suggesting that the Kennedy administration, regardless of what the embassy in Rome or the State Department indicated, was sympathetic to the formation of a center-left government if the Italians themselves wanted such a government. He believed that in all this he had the tacit consent of the President.

These activities disturbed Ambassador Reinhardt in Rome sufficiently that he asked the President about them directly during a visit to Washington in the spring of 1962. He told the President that there were people close to the President who were pushing for the opening with the Italians actively and openly. The ambassador said that he thought this was a political error. While the United States was sympathetic to the opening, provided it did not affect Italy's foreign policy, he believed the United States should not become actively involved. Such a coalition government would involve hard bargaining by the two parties, and the U.S. interests could be damaged were we to become too intimately associated with its success or failure and the policies it followed.

The President replied that the ambassador's understanding of the policy was the correct one, and he was not to be misled by those who suggested otherwise.

By this time, I might add, the Fanfani government, which for the first time had the support, though not the participation, of the PSI, had been in power for about two months.

In short, it was not true that two different policies, each having official sanction, were being pursued at the same time, even though it undoubtedly appeared to the Italians that such was the case.

During 1962, there was a gradual cooling of the debate as the Fanfani government continued to work. In April 1963, in the regular elections, the Communists gained significantly in popular vote, the Christian Democrats lost significantly, and the PSI lost a trifle. This was viewed in the DC party as a rejection of the Fanfani formula, and Fanfani resigned to be replaced by a caretaker government. After intensive further debate and maneuvering within the DC and Socialist parties all through the fall, a full opening government with PSI participation was finally established in December 1963.

Conclusions

In retrospect, what should we say of this Great Debate—or perhaps we should say this Little Debate—in the light of what has come after? I would say that both the Welcomers and the Doubters were proven both right and wrong. The full opening government did come to pass, but only after years had passed, and considerable clarification and modification of attitudes and positions had taken place in both the Christian Democrat and the PSI parties. Perhaps the official U.S. position of reserve had played a useful part. The pro-opening group might feel that without their efforts the opening might never have come to pass. Who can say? Certainly, the opening proved neither the end of the world nor the coming of heaven on earth. Italy remained a firm member of NATO and the European community and an equally firm friend of the United States. The domino theory did not work, as it so often doesn't. That is, the French and Germans did not follow the Italian example. The Christian Democrat party did not split, although it was rudely shaken and there was one moment when it seemed that it might be about to divide. One faction did split away from the PSI. The Italian political process did continue. Some useful things were accomplished, particularly during the first year of the opening, but no great era of reform or modernization was initiated. The hardest battles were fought over matters of more interest to politicians than to the public—such as the establishment of additional regional governments and the nationalization of electric power generation. The parliamentary problem was eased for a few years, but neither the PSI, nor the center parties, nor Italian democracy in general was lastingly strengthened. Neither the pros nor the cons can claim a monopoly of prescience.

In closing, I wish to offer one final point. The opening to the left, as it stood in 1961 and as it appears today, is fascinating, and worth contemplating, surely, but, from the standpoint of the essential health of Italian democracy, it may be the *wrong* topic for a volume of this kind. An even more vital question for Italy is, Why does the Italian political system perform so poorly over the long run in solving the nation's practical problems?

I have a theory as to at least a part of the answer, born of ten years' work on Italian affairs. In my opinion, the energies of the Italian political establishment are so taken up with the play of factions that very little time and attention is left over for solving the nation's hard substantive problems. The Italians call this the *giuoco delle correnti* ("interplay among factions"). I call it Italian checkers. We were playing Italian checkers in 1961 and we are playing it again today. In Italy, they play it all day every day.

The Italian political world is a living museum of the movements of the past. Once a party has played a significant role at any stage of Italian history, it may shrink in size as times change, but it almost never dies. The Republicans, the Monarchists, the Liberals, the neo-Fascists, the Christian Democrats, the various Marxist parties, they all remain, playing the great game of maneuver.

The election laws not only make this longevity possible, they almost impose it. Practically any party, no matter how small, can sweep up enough votes across the nation to ensure the election of at least its top leaders.

That is only the beginning. Each party has its left wing, its center, and its right wing, and several have additional identifiable factions within their wings. A count made some years ago showed nine recognizable organized factions in the Christian Democrat party. There may be more by now. Both in the DC and the PSI, the factions are organized like miniature political parties. Each has its own periodical. As one writer pointed out, whenever a faction does not control the official party organization in a given province, it will often create its own machine, paralleling, and to some extent competing with, the provincial party organs.

It is no mystery why this is so. The way to get ahead in Italian politics is to set oneself up as the head of a faction, or to join someone else in doing so. To do this, some identity must be established on programs, tactics, or constituency, which is distinguishable from the positions of all other factions. And that identity must be kept alive, by whatever means necessary.

Now the faction head is in business. His opinions are sought by political journalists who must scan the range of opinion from one horizon to the other. He will appear on television; his opinions will be sought on each issue that arises in Parliament. The votes of his faction will be duly entered in the running box scores. At election time, the leaders of the party will usually take steps to ensure the reelection of the faction head through the workings of the preferential voting system, since they fear to alienate the bloc of voters presumably represented by that faction.

Finally, when governments are being formed, the faction head will be able to bargain for positions or patronage.

For the outsider, this arrangement is marvelous. Every component of the scene may be identified, categorized, and quantified. In this system, political change is registered between elections by gradual shifts in the positions of factions, often more apparent than real, or by the migration of individuals from one faction to another, which is unceasing.

This is the true business of politics in Italy, and I suggest that it is a major part of what is wrong. The political world is so deeply engaged in this never-ending maneuver that it has scant energy for, or interest in, national problem solving. And if well-meaning leaders have the best will in the world to try to solve problems, the system places almost insuperable obstacles in their paths.

How might the disease be cured? That is for the Italians to say. The essential first step is recognition of the nature of the problem. A new electoral law getting away from the particular ills of the proportional representation system would be a step in the right direction, but obviously that will not happen. Why should the politicians do away with a system that serves them so delightfully?

Meanwhile, returning to the opening to the left 1977-style, admitting the Communists to the government could conceivably lead to a catastrophe of one kind or another, though I suppose that this could be prevented in the short term by careful handling of the nature of the Communist participation in the governmental ranks. But, even if the Communists prove to be little democratic pussycats, we should not delude ourselves that their participation would answer any question except where the next day's parliamentary majority is coming from. Because, in that case, the Communists would be playing Italian checkers, too, and the game would go on as before.

3

The Opening to the Left: Expectations and Results

Angelo M. Codevilla

The Relevance of the Opening

The focus of Italian politics in the 1970s has been the drive of the Communist party (PCI) to enter Italy's government. The prospect of the Communists' presence in the government of a major Western country has occasioned scholarly as well as political controversy. The purpose of this paper is to shed light on this controversy by examining one in the past that bears some kinship to it.

In summary terms, the current controversy is as follows. Some believe that Italy may be heading for tragedy. They point out that the PCI plays a far greater role in Italian life than it did even in 1944–1947. They cite the burly men who march down Italy's streets in military formation, the party's growing patronage throughout Italian society, and its growing hegemony over the media of mass communication. Moreover, they charge that the PCI's promises of liberalism are transparently self-serving and that the party has already used its influence to restrict liberty. It is reasonable to expect that with greater power the PCI will impose greater restrictions. Finally, they note that history contains no example of a country which has escaped tyranny once Communists have played as large a role in it as the PCI now does in Italy.

Others believe the PCI may be the only solution to Italy's problems. They attribute these problems—a bloated public sector, the treasury's cash debt ($25 billion in 1975, 15 percent of Italy's GNP), the rate of inflation (over 20 percent for three years in a row), Italy's $19.5 billion foreign debt,[1] as well as the wave of violence which has submerged the country—to the government's having been run for thirty years by the

---

[1] See Mauro Lucentini, *Commentary* (November 1976), p. 49.

Christian Democrats (DC). The DC, so goes the argument, does not have the confidence of the nation's workers. A consensus can be built behind the measures needed to restore peace and prosperity only with the help of a party the workers can call their own—the PCI. The argument sometimes takes note of the PCI's practice of democratic centralism, and of its praise for the "superiority" of the Soviet Union's moral climate over that of the West, and concludes that, though the PCI's promises of adherence to liberal democracy may be questioned, the best way to wean the PCI from any sentimental attachment to the Marxist understanding of democracy is to involve it in the running of a modern Western society. These arguments have about them a sense of *déjà vu.*

The opening to the left[2] is the antecedent of the present situation in terms both of chronology and of political logic. That is to say, the most significant aspects of the political situation in Italy today have developed since 1960 in connection with the center-left. We need recall but one of these aspects to grasp their importance. Since 1960, it has not been enough for a government to obtain a majority of the votes in Parliament in order to govern. To be spared the wrath of labor unions and other mass organizations, the cabinet must be acceptable to the Italian Socialist Party (PSI), and since January 1976 (or sporadically since 1968) the PSI has insisted it would approve of governments only in tandem with the PCI.

As we examine the opening to the left, however, we should keep in mind that the Italian political predicament of the early 1960s differed from that of the late 1970s. Above all, the PSI, unlike the PCI, has never ruled itself by democratic centralism, and it has always contained elements with impeccable credentials as civil libertarians. Moreover, the Italy of the early 1960s differed from Italy today: neither the DC nor the minor parties was as dispirited as it is today. There was a much more tolerable level of violence, and the word "moderate" had not yet become commonly accepted as an adjective of opprobrium in political parlance. Finally, in the early 1960s the military preponderance of the United States

[2] The opening to the left (*apertura a sinistra*) is the process by which the Italian Socialist Party (PSI) became part of the governing majority in the Italian Parliament, and which practically foreclosed the DC's option of alliances with forces on its right. The resulting majority came to be known as the center-left (*centro-sinistra*). The process went through three main stages: (1) In July 1960, Fanfani's cabinet (DC, PLI, PSDI, PRI)—the post-Tambroni "cabinet of national unity" or "parallel convergences"—received the "benevolent abstention" of the PSI. From February 1962 to May 1963, Fanfani's cabinet (DC, PSDI, PRI) received the PSI's official "outside support." From May to November 1963, Leone's caretaker cabinet (DC) received the PSI's outside support. (2) From November 1963 to June 1968, there were three Moro cabinets (DC, PSI, PSDI, PRI). (3) Between 1968 and 1976, with the exception of the Andreotti cabinets of 1972–1973, the DC continued to depend on the PSI's support, tacit or open, within or outside the cabinet.

over the Soviet Union was so well known that very few in Italy or elsewhere felt that communism was the wave of the future, which one must learn to ride at all costs. That is no longer the case in the 1970s. In sum, in today's Italian political struggle, the stakes are higher, and the capacity of the Communists is greater, while that of their opponents has diminished.

The politics of the opening to the left offers no precise indications concerning the present situation. Nevertheless, the process by which the PCI draws close to government power today resembles the PSI's approach, especially in that it is accompanied by contrasting expectations. From our vantage point, we can try to understand why some of the expectations of the early 1960s were realized, while others were not. Although the expectations of the early 1960s cannot be identified with those of our day, we can hope to acquire insights concerning the opening to the PCI now in progress.

The Opening: Why and How?

The DC: Factions and the Necessity for Choice. In 1947, Alcide de Gasperi decided to form a government without the Communists and their Socialist allies and to ask the non-Communist labor movement to cut its ties with the PCI and PSI. While the voters approved de Gasperi's judgment in the 1948 election, some elements of the DC did not. Gronchi, Ravaioli, Dossetti, La Pira, and their followers believed that a coalition with the mass parties of the Marxist left helped to give the DC access to "the masses," especially in the labor unions, and to give it credentials as a "popular" party. Indeed, some elements in the DC never fully broke with the left. They maintained personal contacts with the PSI-PCI, and worked for the day when the DC would again "open" to the left. These factions worked with some success to move the party—and therefore the government—in a recognizably leftist direction. As a result, in the local elections of 1951–1952, the DC began to lose heavily to self-proclaimed rightist parties. In the 1953 parliamentary elections, the vote for the right rose in comparison with the previous election from 8.6 percent to 18.5 percent, while that of the DC dropped from 48.5 to 40.6 percent. The PCI-PSI increased their total by 3.7 percent.

Having lost its parliamentary majority,[3] the DC now needed to bargain for the support of other parties in order to form a government. But, while the logic of the election returns argued for a move to the right, partisan political factors prevailed and brought about the first moves to-

[3] The following are the results of the 1948 and 1953 elections for the Chamber of Deputies. Note that the Liberals' percentage of the vote is higher than the percentage

ward the opening to the left. The Social Democrats (PSDI) and Republicans (PRI), like the DC, had lost more voters on their right than on their left. Nevertheless, as a condition for joining the government, they demanded some extensive and presumably popular spending. In order to bargain with the Social Democrats and Republicans, de Gasperi opened negotiations with the Monarchists, whose forty votes would have easily given a combination of the DC and the moderate Liberal Party (PLI) a majority.[4] But the ire of the DC's leftist factions—which within a year would destroy de Gasperi politically—forced him to desist, and, eventually, to echo their charge that alliances toward the right were illegitimate.[5] Thus de Gasperi was compelled to explore the possibility of gaining Socialist support. But the center-right factions of the DC dug in their heels and stipulated that any deal with the PSI would have to be accompanied by a break of the ties between the PSI and the PCI in local government, in the labor movement, and in the cooperatives. Since the PSI was unwilling to make even token concessions, and the DC's position was firm, this first attempt at the opening failed.[6]

Over the next decade, the DC changed. De Gasperi's description of the DC as a party of the center which was moving to the left is well known. At least as significant was the DC's increasing emphasis on the economic relations between clients and patrons, stressed after 1954 by the left-of-center *Iniziativa Democratica* faction led by Amintore Fanfani. By basing the party on the patronage created by "progressive" legislation, the DC left tried to diminish the influence of the Church and the civic committees, and of those who voted for the DC for conservative reasons. The *Iniziativa*'s success multiplied the bases for factions. Christian Demo-

---

of seats they received. This is because the Liberal vote is scattered.. With the partial exception of Torino, the PLI never had a concentrated base.

	1948			*1953*	
Party	Percent of vote	Number of seats	Party	Percent of vote	Number of seats
Christian Democrat	48.5	305	Christian Democrat	40.6	261
Uomo Qualunque	2.0	6	Social Movement	4.9	29
Liberal	3.8	19	Liberal	8.3	14
Monarchist	2.8	14	Monarchist	5.3	40
Social Democrat	7.1	33	Social Democrat	4.5	19
Republican	2.5	9	Republican	1.6	5
Socialist and			Socialist	12.0	75
Communist	31.0	183	Communist	22.7	143
Other	2.3	5	Other	0.1	4
Total	100.0	569	Total	100.0	590

[4] *Il Tempo,* June 11, 1953.

[5] *New York Times,* March 19, 1954.

[6] See *Corriere Della Sera,* June 16, 1953, and *Avanti,* June 14, 1953, for contrasting news on these negotiations.

crats, never insensitive to factional interests, became absorbed by them, and in factional struggles, the left had a trump card: the support—actual or promised, open or tacit—of leftist forces outside the party. This card was played spectacularly for the first time in 1954, when a joint session of Parliament elected the president of the Republic. The DC had designated its own official candidate, but the leftist DC factions, supported by the PCI and PSI, elected another, Giovanni Gronchi. Albeit in a limited instance, the opening to the left had occurred, and Gronchi's years of work for the opening had benefited, first of all, himself.[7]

Christian Democrats were quick to draw practical lessons from the case of Gronchi as compared with that of Mario Scelba, whose mere nomination to a ministry would prompt at least a small strike. Progressive politics paid off not just in patronage, but also in support by the left. Moreover, only the progressives could persuade the left to cooperate in passing profitable *leggine* ("special-interest laws"). With few exceptions, the literature on the subject has not sufficiently stressed that the Christian Democrats learned about the advantages of the opening on the lowest level of political life, and that the opening coincided with a quantum leap in the corruption of Italian politics.[8] Principles remained at issue, but now "progressive policies" enlarged political access to the resources necessary to support factions. As individual Christian Democratic leaders competed with one another for material and factional advantages, the support of the left became more precious.

The Moderates' Arguments in Favor of the Opening. There were three basic reasons why some moderates in Italy and abroad supported the opening.[9]

(1) Many moderates believed that the policies advocated by the Socialists (for example, egalitarianism in education, a higher ratio of

[7] Gronchi described his years of effort on behalf of the opening in *La Nazione,* Firenze, December 24, 1963.

[8] Nicola Matteucci, in *Il Mulino,* January 1971, p. 17, suggests that his fellow progressives have no reason to be surprised at the growth of the PCI since they long since accepted it as a partner in the old game of logrolling.

[9] The following are but a few of the places where arguments in favor of the opening appeared: Arthur Schlesinger, Jr., *A Thousand Days* (Boston: Houghton Mifflin, 1965); Ugo la Malfa, "The Socialist Alternative in Italy," *Foreign Affairs,* January 1957; Giuseppe Saragat, *Quaranta anni di lotto per il socialismo* (Milan, 1966); Victor Sullam, "Kennedy and the New Frontier," *Il Mulino,* January 1961; Leo Wollemborg, "A Progressive Coalition at Last?" *The New Republic,* February 19, 1962; Claire Sterling, "Italy's Opening to the Left," *The Reporter,* March 15, 1962; Raphael Zariski, *Italy: The Politics of Uneven Development* (Hinsdale, Ill.: Dryden Press, 1972); and Alan Platt, "U.S. Policy toward the 'Opening to the Left'" (unpublished Ph.D. dissertation, Columbia University, 1973). Platt gives the fullest account yet available of the grounds on which pro-opening American politicians and officials intervened in Italy on the opening's behalf.

public to private expenditure, social and economic planning) were necessary for social peace and prosperity. They held that communism is born of a reaction to poverty and unequal opportunity. Increases in egalitarianism in the schools, in public programs to aid the disadvantaged, and in public planning and public consumption were to eliminate the causes of social extremism.

(2) These moderates argued that the government ought to embrace not only Socialist policies, but also the Socialists themselves. They believed that the assumption of responsible and lucrative government positions would help to bolster the Socialists against any lingering temptations of totalitarianism and lead them to spurn their alliances with the Communists. In turn, the Communists, deprived of their most valued allies, would be forced either to shed their own totalitarianism or to wither in isolation. In sum, many moderates believed that the best way to fight Communists—and ultimately to integrate them, too, into liberal democratic societies—was to give power to the Socialists.

(3) Some believed the opposition between liberal-democratic societies and Communist societies could not last. Over time, it was thought, the latter would lose their harshness and allow more individual liberty, while the former would have to achieve greater equality and more planning in economic, cultural, and other matters. In short, it was felt to be futile to fight for something destined to pass away and to fight against something even then in the process of change. Conflict is expensive. Moreover, it retards salutary and inevitable changes on both sides.

Among the many in the United States who advocated the Italian opening to the left on one or more of these grounds were Averell Harriman, Arthur Schlesinger, Jr., Senator Hubert Humphrey, Dana Durand of the CIA, John Di Sciullo of the Department of State, James E. King of the Institute for Defense Analysis, and Leo Wollemborg of the *Washington Post*. According to Schlesinger, professional foreign service officers in charge of Italian affairs had grossly exaggerated the risks involved in the opening. He deprecated their attitude as "typical" of the Foreign Service, and resolved to disregard their views.[10] He agreed with James King, who said that future collaboration between the PSI and the Communists would be an impossibility, and that "the DC would never enter into a left-center coalition until the vast majority of the party were satisfied regarding the anti-Communism of the PSI."[11] Senator Hubert Humphrey believe that Pietro Nenni was so anti-Communist that he and who-

[10] *A Thousand Days,* pp. 414–415.

[11] Quoted in Platt, "U.S. Policy toward the 'Opening to the Left,' " p. 114.

ever would follow him would leave the PSI if it insisted on closer ties with the PCI.[12] These views were reflected in the National Intelligence Estimate on Italy in 1961. Schlesinger and Humphrey led an effort to persuade Italians that the United States would be pleased by the opening to the left.

With few exceptions American academics judged the opening favorably.[13] Perhaps the most widely used U.S. textbook on Italy at the time said that Nenni's party had crossed the Rubicon and supported a bourgeois government.[14] The authors of another textbook saw it as a shrewd trade—a new alignment on economic issues by the DC in return for a greater political acceptance of institutions by the PSI.[15] They rejoiced that the opening made possible two majorities instead of one, which did not question the legitimacy of the system. Raphael Zariski wrote of a "giant step forward to safeguard democratic stability."[16]

Among the many in Italy who spoke and wrote on behalf of such views were Amintore Fanfani, Aldo Moro, Emilio Colombo, Carlo Donat-Cattin, Giulio Pastore, Giovanni Gronchi, Giuseppe Saragat, Giuseppe Romita, Ugo la Malfa, and Oronzo Reale, as well as some in the autonomist faction of the PSI. Their arguments in favor of the opening were articulated by scholars and publicists such as Giorgio Galli and Luigi Pedrazzi in *Il Mulino,* the foremost Italian journal of public affairs, between 1958 and 1972. According to *Il Mulino*'s vision, the opening would transform Italian politics into a contest between two moderate groups. Entry into the government would permit the Socialists to free their party of the PCI's heavy economic and ideological mortgage. Once free, the PSI could join with the Social Democrats to form a great moderate Socialist party. These United Socialists would be so attractive to both voters and politicians of other parties that moderate reformists—from the left wing of the DC to the more practical bourgeois Communists of Emilia—would rally to the new group. The DC would have to shape up and serve the country better in order to compete, because, for the first time since World War I, Italians could vote against the party in power without throwing themselves into the arms of totalitarians. The extremists of the left and right either would have to choose oblivion or would integrate themselves into the moderate Socialist or the moderate

---

12 Ibid.

13 Angelo M. Codevilla, "The Opening for Communism in Italy," *Politeia,* Spring, 1965.

14 J. Clarke Adams and Paolo Barile, *The Government of Republican Italy* (Boston: Houghton Mifflin, 1972), p. 161.

15 Dante Germino and Stefano Passigli, *The Government and Politics of Contemporary Italy* (New York: Harper & Row, 1968), p. 106.

16 Zariski, *Italy: The Politics of Uneven Development,* p. 170.

DC group.[17] Indeed, in the February 1966 issue of *Il Mulino,* Giorgio Galli published an article entitled "The PCI in a Blind Alley." During the early years of the center-left, the PCI was widely pictured on both sides of the Atlantic as giving proof of its stupidity by failing to recognize that it had been maneuvered into dire straits.[18]

The Italian public was presented with less theoretical arguments. In our time it has become common for political changes to be accompanied by the raising of wild hopes and by assurances that the fulfillment of those hopes will cost next to nothing. Thus Italian newspapers of the early 1960s offered promises that the center-left would mean greater prosperity, universal access to the university (and therefore to the professional class), and so on. For example, Ugo La Malfa, usually known for his fiscal responsibility, declared that the institution of regional governments (a promise of the center-left) would cost the taxpayers, not $2 billion as had been estimated, but rather nothing additional at all.[19] Carlo Donat-Cattin pledged the prospective regional government would bring government closer to the people and would require fewer public officials.[20] The socioeconomic problems of migrant workers could be solved only by the regions. People in Cuneo, asked if they wanted the establishment of the regions, said they had been told it would bring a much-needed tunnel. In Emilia, it was a port on the Po River. Indeed, Professor Achille Argigo went so far as to say that, as a result of the opening and its reforms, the PSI in the city of Bologna would switch sides and throw the Communists out of city hall.[21]

The Opening as Seen by the Left. From the left, the opening looked quite different. Socialists, indeed, thought of the opening as a Rubicon of sorts, but only a small minority thought the PSI rather than the DC was doing the crossing. Everyone thought of the opening as a deal, but most leftists, including the Social Democrats, thought that they had become exclusive purveyors of political support to the DC, and looked forward to raising the price of their support. Of course, Socialists differed almost as much among themselves as they did with the DC on precisely what the opening should mean.

---

17 See especially the articles by Giorgio Galli in *Il Mulino,* September 1966 and January 1967.

18 *Il Mondo,* January 1, 1963, echoing the *Washington Post.*

19 *L'Europeo,* January 13, 1963.

20 Ibid. One should have asked why politicians are interested in these reforms if indeed they will not increase the number of posts available to their supporters? Italians have since learned that, whatever else they achieve, reforms surely provide more patronage for their authors.

21 Ibid., January 20, 1963.

No prominent figure in the PSI, however, conceived of the opening as a means of fighting Communists. Even when the push for the opening was most intense, Nenni declared that his party was "not prepared to make any concessions to those on its right on the grounds of anticommunism, which is repugnant to its democratic nature."[22] Indeed, scholars have not paid enough attention to the Socialists' penchant for using the term "democracy" now in its Communist, now in its liberal, meaning.[23] Be that as it may, the PSI was thoroughly united in considering the opening a weapon to be wielded against forces to its right, and not against the PCI. When Nenni originally outlined the opening to his party in late 1952, he did so backed by the authority of Joseph Stalin, who had personally pinned the Stalin Peace Prize on his chest in October.[24] When he officially presented it to the PSI's Thirty-first Congress, he did so in unimpeachably Marxist terms:

> One of the characteristics of confessional parties is that they reproduce within themselves . . . the contradictions that exist within each society and each state: between poor and rich, exploited and exploiters, protected and protectors. That is to say they carry within themselves a latent class struggle. . . . This conflict inside Christian Democracy interests all parties and it interests in the highest degree the Socialist Party, which is neither indifferent nor extraneous to the prevalence of one or the other force.[25]

The opening was to deepen the contradictions within the DC, and to help "progressive" forces within it to prevail. Occasionally, Nenni or other spokesmen, including Rodolfo Morandi, who was always close to the PCI, would disclaim any intent to "subvert" Catholic organization.[26] Nonetheless, until the very end of the opening in the 1970s, when Socialists explained it to party audiences they rarely omitted references to "deepening the contradictions within the DC."

Some elements in the PSI were highly interested in the patronage they would receive as a result of joining the government. There is evi-

---

22 PSI *Bulletin No. 6* (Rome, November 1959), p. 6.

23 The Twenty-fourth Congress of the PSI (1946) is one of many places where one can find Socialist assurances that the Communists have changed, that they are now defenders of democracy, and that the distinction between "Socialism with liberty and Socialism without liberty is nothing but a polemical artifice."

24 See Nenni's speech upon his return, *Atti Parlamentari,* October 16, 1952. Compare with Stalin's statements in his interview with James Reston, *New York Times,* December 25, 1952, and with Nenni's speech to the Thirtieth Congress of the PSI, 1953.

25 *XXXI esimo Congresso del PSI* (Milan, 1955).

26 Ibid.

dence that state funds and favors designed to mollify willing Socialists found recipients beginning in the mid-1950s.[27] On the other hand, some Socialists, led by Tullio Vecchietti and Lelio Basso, unabashedly argued that the PSI should regard the opening as a means to insert the PCI into the government. In sum, the question Why did the Socialists want the opening? cannot be answered simply, for different Socialists seem to have been moved by different purposes. Even individual Socialists have explained their own intentions in different terms at different times. One can only look at what results the PSI has achieved.

The PCI, for its part, did what it could to foster the opening. Speaking at the Fourth Party Congress in June 1955, Palmiro Togliatti encouraged the most pro-Communist Socialists to back Nenni's policy. From 1956 until the opening was consummated, Togliatti tried to keep the left wings of the PSI behind Nenni.[28] Togliatti hoped that the PSI would open the DC so wide that it could no longer help but deal with the Communists. He also hoped that the PSI would not become so interested in its new sources of power, and would not so identify itself with the government, as to despise its "proletarian" identity and the useful organizations it shared with the PCI.

The PCI knew, of course, that the DC and some in the PSI had different expectations, and that the operation involved some risk. But it judged the odds to be in its favor. On the DC's side was a congeries of individuals and factions, many eager to strike a deal before the others could. By picking and choosing carefully with whom it dealt, the PSI could progressively control the terms of the relationship. The PCI believed it possessed the same advantages over the PSI that the PSI enjoyed over the DC, only to a higher degree.

Above all, the PCI helped to apply the pressure without which the DC would not have consented to the opening. The strikes and riots of 1960, mounted by the CGIL and the National Association of Partisans, could not have taken place without the PCI's commitment. The party valued the 1960 campaign for the opening as a means of exercising and replenishing its corps of young street activitists, and it did not expect the DC to collapse as it did in July 1960. When it did, the PCI claimed the victory as its own.[29] Indeed the party claimed the opening to the left itself was the fruit of its labors.[30] "Bourgeois" proponents of the opening barely noticed the PCI's cooperation with a process which they said would

---

[27] *Il Borghese,* October 1, 1968.

[28] See, for example, Togliatti in *L'Unità,* January 11, 1962, and Amendola in *Rinascita,* January 11, 1962. Also see Domenico Settembrini, *La Chiesa nella Politica* (Pisa, 1964), pp. 332–342.

[29] Giorgio Galli, "Il PCI rivisitato," *Il Mulino,* January 1971, p. 31.

[30] Ibid., p. 32.

destroy it. When they did, they postulated that the PCI was either stupid or hiding fear with rejoicing.

Arguments against the Opening. The moderate opponents of the opening argued that since most of the PSI had not broken with the Communists either materially or psychologically, the PCI would become the opening's major beneficiary. At the Eighth Congress of the DC in January 1962, Mario Scelba predicted that, as a result of the opening, the state would lose the ability to restrain the organizations jointly run by the PSI and the PCI—especially the labor unions. By virtue of their connection with both the government and the opposition, these groups would be beyond the reach of the law. Moreover, Scelba reasoned that, while Nenni's avowed divergences from the Moscow line and his occasional criticism of the PCI impressed progressive elites, the Italian people could not fail to notice the thousands of ties still binding the PSI and PCI at the grass roots. The Italian people could only conclude, said Scelba, that if the DC accepted the PSI into the government despite its ties with the PCI, the PCI itself must not be entirely unacceptable to the DC. Stopping the growth of the PCI's organization and of its electorate would become harder, not easier. Therefore, Scelba predicted, the PCI's vote would rise, and the PCI would be anything but isolated. He also judged it probable that the DC would lose votes both on the right and on the left. Scelba was not alone. There is no doubt that independent businessmen and investors, both large and small, had no faith in the opening. The Italian economic miracle, as well as great growth in the overall real value of stocks, ended in 1963. The pro-opening press, however, attacked Scelba's judgment as ridiculous, and the attitude of businessmen and investors as simply criminal.[31]

The misgivings of the American Foreign Service were based on two considerations: (1) the continuing ties between the PSI and PCI, and (2) the difficulties the DC would experience in trying to control the opening. Outerbridge Horsey, deputy chief of mission at the U.S. embassy in Rome from 1959 to 1962, spoke for most American diplomats who had served in Italy when he contrasted the purposefulness of the grass roots organizations shared by the PSI-PCI with the ephemeral and self-serving nature of the Socialists' moves away from the PCI. He also noted that the opening would change the relative weight of the forces within the DC. By the very fact that it was entering into the deal, the DC would tend to lose the ability to enforce the terms of that deal. Since the evidence pointed to the PSI remaining its old self (that is, equivocal but, in a pinch, on the Communist side) and to the weakening of the DC, the center-left coalition "eventually

[31] See, for example, *Il Mondo,* February 13, 1962, and April 9, 1962, respectively.

would come to be dependent on the Communists."[32] Moreover, Ambassador Reinhardt believed that since the DC was agreeing to the opening under duress, and at the urging of the Kennedy administration, it could not easily threaten to withdraw from the arrangement, and its bargaining power would diminish. In countering any demands from the left, the DC could henceforth do little more than drag its feet.

The Opening, Shaped by How It Took Place. In the very process of achieving the opening, expectations for it clashed. The crucial episode of that process was the rise and fall of the Tambroni cabinet in 1960. The episode is worth examining because of its relevance to the current Italian situation, and because no period of Italian history has been more the subject of mythmaking.[33]

The crisis of 1960 had its immediate origins in late 1958 when Amintore Fanfani, the prime minister and secretary of the DC, arranged with Nenni for the DC to bargain for the parliamentary abstention of the PSI and a greater measure of social peace. Fanfani agreed to sponsor certain reforms, to banish the conservative Liberals from future coalitions, and to make certain concessions on personnel to the Socialists. In January 1959, when the DC rejected this bargain, Fanfani resigned his posts and, in effect, dared his party to proceed without him and the support he could mobilize. The next prime minister, Antonio Segni, later president of the Republic, governed for a year during which the leftist factions of the DC openly joined the Social Democrats, the Republicans, and the PSI in calling for the opening. These forces, with the parliamentary help of the PCI, could have brought down the government at any time. But in February 1960, the Liberals preempted them and caused a government crisis in order to bring about a test of strength. The PSDI and PRI declared they would support no cabinet that did not merit at least the abstention of the PSI.

These advocates of the opening were in a difficult position. Their refusal to join could not keep the DC from forming a government which would enjoy a relative majority over the PCI-PSI. The PSDI and PRI could cause any such government to fall by joining their votes to those of the PCI-PSI, but they were unwilling to join the Marxist bloc in a popular

---

[32] Quoted in Platt, "U.S. Policy toward the 'Opening to the Left,' " p. 222.

[33] The myth of Tambroni's fascism appears made of the same stuff as that of Tonypandy, a village in Wales where, in 1910, according to newspapers and even to historians, troops sent by Home Secretary Winston Churchill massacred striking mineworkers. In fact, there was a minor disturbance, no one was killed, and Churchill was not involved. But the Tonypandy "massacre" haunted Churchill until his death. Together with its kind, it haunts history still. It is rooted in partisan interest and propagated by inertia, and no amount of fact seems capable of eradicating it. See Josephine Tey, *Daughter of Time* (New York, 1953), p. 99.

front government. If they had joined a negative majority to cause the government to fall, and then refused to form a government with that majority, they would obviously have been acting irresponsibly. If the DC then asked President Gronchi for new elections, not only would their irresponsibility be punished, but also the DC would be forced to ask its electorate to approve its resistance to the opening, which no one doubted would be forthcoming. Fortunately for the advocates of the opening, President Gronchi was on their side and did not want elections. Therefore those in favor of the opening could choose the course which maximized their leverage and minimized their responsibility. The PSDI, the PRI, and some DC leftists would abstain. If the new government could manage a relative majority over the PCI-PSI bloc, they would join the PSI-PCI to make its life unpleasant. Hence, strikers and demonstrators became a common sight on the streets and factories of Italy, while the organs of the parties of the left—and of the leftist factions of the DC—promised worse for the future. Thus would the rest of the DC's resistance be worn down.

In April 1960, President Gronchi asked his old disciple Fernando Tambroni, a member of the laborist faction of the DC, to form a government during which the political situation could clarify itself. Tambroni appointed an all-DC cabinet, which was approved by a relative majority of the Chamber of Deputies. The Christian Democrats who did not vote for it were outnumbered by the votes of the MSI. Supporters of the opening charged that this made the cabinet "Fascist," and therefore illegitimate. In deference to them, Tambroni resigned his mandate. Gronchi then handed it to Fanfani, who worked out a deal with Nenni similar to that of eighteen months prior. But the DC would ratify it only on condition that Nenni pledge publicly to break with the Communists in local government, labor, and mass organizations. Nenni refused angrily, and Fanfani resigned his mandate. The country now needed either a caretaker government or new elections. To avoid the latter, Gronchi decided to ask his friend Tambroni to submit his cabinet to the Senate. He did, and it passed.

The powerful groups that fought the Tambroni cabinet could have defeated it in Parliament any time, and thus forced its resignation, as indeed they could have prevented its birth. The secretary of the DC, Aldo Moro, had announced his support for the deal Fanfani had struck with Nenni. Moro and the DC left could have deserted the cabinet on any bill and forced its resignation. But this might have brought about elections, and it would have done nothing to persuade recalcitrant Christian Democrats to accept the opening.

Instead, the pro-opening forces preferred an extraparliamentary strategy and gathered under the banner of "anti-Fascism." The cabinet they refused to defeat in Parliament was to resign under pressure from "the people" because it was "Fascist." The charge had two particulars: Tambroni was in office thanks in part to votes of a party accused by its enemies of being Fascist, and Tambroni ordered the police to disperse demonstrators who had shut down cities. Tambroni, so the story goes, showed his true colors by authorizing the police to defend the right of the MSI to hold its regular national congress in Genoa. On the day of the congress, July 1, 1960, Genoa was a battlefield. The PCI-PSI labor unions and mass organizations and the organizations controlled by the DC left trucked in 80,000 activists from all over northern Italy, organized into squads, each under its own flag. They bypassed the usual "Fascist" targets and attacked the police, wounding forty and destroying six police vans. During the following days the pattern was repeated in Rome, Catania, Reggio Emilia, and most other major cities. Tambroni resigned. Fanfani then formed a government approved by the PSI.

The popular myth would have it that "the people" saw the Fascist danger, that housewives dropped their pasta and turned back the police just as they were about to slip the noose around the country's neck, and that in so doing "the people" taught the reactionaries a lesson and ushered in an age of liberty. Raphael Zariski writes that "under Tambroni, Italy had appeared to be tottering on the brink of a new right-wing dictatorship."[34] Germino and Passigli say that the Tambroni cabinet was "an attempt to put into practice" a coalition with the MSI, which failed "under the pressure of popular riots."[35] Another work on the subject is entitled "Opening to the Right: The Tambroni Experiment."[36]

But the myth of Tambroni's Fascism was fabricated only because it served as a weapon. If Tambroni's association with the MSI (which denies it is Fascist) makes him a Fascist, doesn't the PSI's immeasurably greater connections with the PCI make it Communist? And what should be made of the PCI's unbroken organizational connections with the Soviet Union? For that matter, according to the standards of the Tambroni case, how should one have judged the PCI's outright coalition with the MSI in the *Milazzo Giunta* in Sicily? But, of course, the Tambroni test has been used only against the opponents of the left.

Unquestionably, the physical and intellectual violence of the summer of 1960 shaped subsequent events. Whenever the DC seemed to be delaying the consummation of the opening, the left brandished the experience of July 1960. Milan's newspaper *Il Corriere Della Sera* ended 1960 by advising the DC to tell the public precisely what it had asked the

[34] Zariski, *The Politics of Uneven Development,* p. 229.

[35] Germino and Passigli, *The Government and Politics of Contemporary Italy,* p. 94.

[36] Robert K. Nilsson, "Opening to the Right: The Tambroni Experiment" (unpublished Ph.D. dissertation, Columbia University, 1964).

Socialists to do to demonstrate their independence of the Communists; then, if the PSI refused, the DC should ask for new elections and let the people decide. The pro-opening *Il Mondo* replied that this suggestion was a direct threat against the policy of the left—from the left wing of the DC to the PSI—and that if the DC followed the advice of the *Corriere,* it must be prepared for a repetition of July 1960.[37] Any attempt to govern without leave of the left—including the calling of elections—would be considered "rightist subversion" and dealt with accordingly.[38] When Aldo Moro pressed the Eighth DC Congress to give official approval of the opening to the left, the theme of his five-hour speech was that the DC's only option was the opening to the left or the kind of violence it suffered in 1960.[39] In sum, the DC had placed itself in the position of being threatened with violence by even the most mild-mannered progressives if it should refuse to follow the paths of progress.[40]

The intellectual violence done in 1960 has had an even greater effect. The anti-Tambroni campaign introduced to Italy the following syllogism: All that is not certified by the left to be on the side of the left is on the right. All that is on the right is Fascist. Therefore, all that the left does not recognize as its own is Fascist. After 1960 Italians heard repeatedly that by opposing the opening to the left, centrists placed themselves on the same ground as the right, and therefore exposed themselves and the country to a "counterreactionary shove" that would make the events in Genoa in July 1960 "appear a midsummer picnic!"[41] A similar argument appeared even in the pages of *Il Mulino*: The very same centrism which was once a good thing is now to be considered neo-Fascist. Why? Because from 1947 to 1957 centrism helped to forestall powerful conservative forces. Now it had served its purpose and only sat in the way of progressive forces.[42]

Disagreement with the opening to the left (except from a standpoint further left) was enough to get Luigi Einaudi himself accused of "talking like Mussolini or Goering."[43] Einaudi had written that a political change as momentous as the opening should be submitted to the voters for approval or disapproval, rather than coming about as a deal between parties. This argument reflects a criticism of the party monopoly on politics in Italy. Those who regret that Italian voters cannot influence decisions on

---

[37] *Il Mondo,* January 3, 1961.

[38] Ibid., February 6, 1962.

[39] *VIII Congresso Nazionale della DC* (Rome, 1963).

[40] See, for example, Giorgio Galli in *Il Mulino,* January 1972.

[41] *Il Mondo,* February 5, 1963. Also: "After the nationalization (of the electric industry) . . . psychologically the Milanese Right is today Fascist or parafascist." *Il Mondo,* February 19, 1963.

[42] Pietro Scoppola, *Il Mulino,* January 1972.

[43] *Il Mondo,* January 31, 1961.

men or measures as do British, French, or American voters have called the present Italian arrangement "*partitocrazia.*" To the left, however, this critique is tantamount to Fascism. Without explaining its substance, Adams and Barile tell American students that this term "often comes from the pen of former Fascists or Fascist sympathizers with little insight into or sympathy for the democratic process."[44]

Clearly such physical and intellectual violence had to affect the struggle between the several interpretations of the opening.

The Results of the Opening

With the beginning of the opening to the left, the struggle intensified to determine its eventual meaning. As the first center-left cabinet took office, *Il Mondo* announced that in this round of the class struggle "the right must be made to pay."[45] According to this argument, the DC would be less able to resist pressures for the development of the opening than it had been to resist the opening itself.[46] People who were not wholly pro-opening had to be eliminated from state-run credit agencies, industrial development boards, chambers of commerce, newspapers, and elsewhere.[47] The notion of granting jobs on the basis of qualifications rather than politics was openly ridiculed. *Il Mondo* reflected the attitude of the new regime when it said that the proper political attitude is the primary qualification for important jobs.[48] Here was an ideological justification for doing what politicians in power enjoy doing anyway: building their patronage. In order for the center-left to be successful in democratizing Italy, its supporters must hold positions not only in government but also in banks and the great state holding companies. Indeed all enterprises influenced by the state must be staffed by people with the correct intentions. One of the first acts of the center-left was the nationalization of the electric power industry. Riccardo Lombardi, who, together with Nenni, received the lion's share of the posts in the new state electrical agency (ENEL), once described it as a stick thrown between the legs of Italian capitalism.

Il Mondo, speaking for a substantial part of the leftist opinion, declared on January 9, 1962, that, having forced the DC to open to the PSI, "Those democrats most committed to and most concerned with the future naturally turn their attention to integrating the masses and the leadership of the PCI into the life of the state." The concrete task of

---

44 Adams and Barile, *The Government of Republican Italy,* p. 168.

45 *Il Mondo,* March 6, 1962.

46 Ibid., March 19, 1963.

47 Ibid., February 20, 1962.

48 Ibid., January 8, 1963.

these "democrats," according to *Il Mondo,* would be "to impose [upon the DC] a relationship, albeit mediated and indirect, with the Communists."

The First Trials. Moderates did not have to wait long for indications that the opening was bearing fruits other than the ones they desired. They should have expected the elections of 1963 to show an increase in the strength of the center-left parties and a drop in the vote of the Communist party, now presumably isolated. The opposite happened.[49] The PCI, which had done little more than hold its own in the 1950s, began a climb in popularity which has still not stopped. The Socialists lost a little at the polls, but they lost almost a third of their membership. Once the opening had taken place, the PCI stopped discouraging leftists in the PSI who wanted to split. Now it could afford to press the PSI from the left, to spur it, and to threaten it, so as to keep it headed in the desired direction.

In January 1964, Tullio Vecchietti formed the Italian Socialist Party of Proletarian Unity (PSIUP) in protest against the low price Nenni had received for participation in the cabinet and the slow pace at which the center-left was paying its bill to the left. In short, the Socialists lost members on their left. They felt vulnerable to Communist reproaches that they were not energetic enough in promoting the interests of the proletariat. The PSI thought that, if the PCI itself took some governmental responsibility, it would no longer grow at the PSI's expense. At the same time, the PSI decided not to leave itself so open to Communist attacks. Therefore, as soon as the PSI entered the cabinet in 1963, it called for "broadening the base of the majority"—that is, including the Communists—and for building a Socialist society.

In keeping with these convictions, the PSI provoked a government crisis in June 1964 by voting against a routine bill for aid to Catholic

[49] The following are the results for the 1958 and 1963 elections for the Chamber of Deputies.

	1958		*1963*	
Party	Percent of vote	Number of seats	Percent of vote	Number of seats
Christian Democrat	42.4	273	38.3	260
Communist	22.7	140	25.3	166
Socialist	14.2	84	13.8	87
Social Democrat	4.5	22	6.1	33
Social Movement	4.8	24	5.1	27
Republican	1.4	6	1.4	6
Liberal	3.5	17	7.0	39
Monarchist	4.8	24	1.7	8
Other	1.7	5	1.3	4
Total	100.0	596	100.0	630

schools. The DC denounced this "attempt to consider the center-left as an instrument for the creation of a Socialist society, an objective which obviously could never be and is not that of the coalition. There has been a deformation of the concept of the limits of the majority."[50] On the same occasion Flaminio Piccoli urged the PSI to stop thinking about the center-left in "romantic" terms, and the editorialist of the *Corriere* suggested it was incongruous for the PSI to have its officials serve simultaneously in the government and in the CGIL, which opposed that government.[51]

But what were the true objectives of the coalition, and what could truly be called a deformation or romantic or incongruous? The answers were to be found, not by wishes or by declarations, but by trials of strength, unity, and determination in the real world.

The three such trials in the first year of Socialists' participation in government all suggested that the PSI did not intend to fight the Communists.

(1) In January 1964 with the birth of the PSIUP—which immediately allied itself with the PCI—the PSI might have been expected to leave Communist-dominated local governments. Instead, the three parties declared "the leftist majorities represent the most advanced points of the workers' democratic power."[52] The DC hardly seemed to notice the contradiction between what it had assumed the PSI would do and what it actually did.

(2) During the June 1964 crisis, as part of its demand for an "advanced" center-left, the PSI stipulated that no one but Aldo Moro should form the new government. Once again it urged the PCI and CGIL to press its case, and the PCI agreed. Togliatti declared that any cabinet except Moro's would be "an authoritarian involution" and therefore unacceptable. The two parties evoked the specter of 1960, and the CGIL, together with the National Association of Partisans, called a mass rally in Rome.[53] The DC shrank at that prospect, and complied with the joint demands of the PSI-PCI.

(3) In December 1964, a joint session of Parliament elected the president of the Republic. The DC nominated Giovanni Leone, and expected the parties of the center-left coalition to back him. The elections, which were televised, extended over three weeks and twenty-one ballots, during which the PSI demonstrated that it would never vote for the DC's official candidate and that, after all the bargaining was done, the PSI

[50] Mariano Rumor, secretary of the DC, *Corriere Della Sera,* June 30, 1964, speaking before the party directorate.

[51] Ibid.

[52] *L'Unità,* February 25, 1964.

[53] *L'Unità,* June 29, July 3 and 4, 1964.

would vote alongside the PCI. Indeed, though the PSI started out voting for Saragat, it stopped when the DC resigned itself to voting for him. The PSI declared it would again vote for Saragat only if the DC persuaded the PCI to do so.[54] Meanwhile the PSI-PCI voted for Nenni. The DC called for the election of Saragat by "a wide spectrum of democratic forces . . . excluding all requests and negotiations for Communist votes,"[55] while the PCI called for a "democratic consensus, without any discrimination or preclusion."[56] But the TV screens were soon filled with reports of meetings between Moro, Longo, and Saragat, while leftist spokesmen ridiculed the DC's impotence. Saragat was finally elected by the center-left-plus-PCI. The election had shown a national TV audience that the DC could be led piecemeal to deny its own words about "delimitation of the majority," and that it could be forced to overlook cooperation between the PSI and PCI.

A Major Trial: Socialist Unification and Local Giunte. The sine qua non of the moderates' conception of the center-left had been the PSI's abandonment of its grass roots ties with the PCI, among the most important of which were the local *Giunte*. Although the PSI had given general assurances about breaking with the Communists, it maintained those ties. At the end of 1966, the PSI and the Social Democrats united, at least on paper, to form the United Socialist Party (PSU). Now some reshuffling of the *Giunte* could no longer be postponed.

By this time, the more perceptive moderate advocates of the center-left were beginning to doubt the Socialists' ability to make the break. In September 1966, Giorgio Galli wrote:

> Locally, one looks at persons [Socialist officeholders] and one sees much evidence of their prudence, and precious little of their dynamism; they count the posts which heads of city departments would have to leave, they assess the weight of the counter-blows which would be dealt them [by the PCI] in the municipalized companies, in the cooperatives, in the clienteles, in friendships: and everything leads one to think that almost nothing will happen, that in every case they will go slow and try to break and lose as little as possible.[57]

Galli urged the Socialists to refrain from making a mockery of the center-left, to withdraw from Communist-dominated governments, and either to form governments with the other parties of the center-left or at least

---

[54] *Corriere Della Sera,* December 27, 1964.

[55] Ibid., December 28, 1964.

[56] Ibid.

[57] *Il Mulino,* September 1966.

to join them in opposition to the PCI-PSIUP, so that in the next elections voters would have a more attractive alternative to Communist government. Galli picked out 102 cities, mostly in Emilia and Tuscany, as test cases.[58] Five months later the results were in. *In no important city had the Socialists acted to topple a Communist government.* In Parma, for example, eight city councilmen from the PSI and three from the PSDI formed the new PSU group in the council. The group then voted, eight to three, to stay in the coalition with the PCI.[59] The PSDI had not pulled the PSI *out* of the coalition. Rather, the PSI had pulled the PSDI *in.*

Many leading Socialists who considered leaving Communist *Giunte* found they would have to give up positions of influence and refused to do so. Labeling themselves *Movimento Autonomo Socialista* (MAS), they stayed in office and allied with the PCI. This made the Socialists' break with the Communists—in the few places where it did occur, such as Reggio, Modena, Ferrara—a purely formal act. In Bologna those Socialists who did not adhere to the MAS formally left the *Giunte.* But instead of opposing the PCI, they abstained in its favor, allowing it to continue in power, and continuing to receive favors. In sum, according to Galli, "The Socialists' readiness to detach from the Communists has manifested itself where it was easiest for the latter to maintain power uninterruptedly. Where they could have caused a problem for that continuity, the Socialists revealed themselves much more timid."[60]

The Reformists Defeated. By early 1967 Galli recognized that the moderates had erred in their conception of the center-left. In his view, the Socialists could have dealt serious blows to the power and prestige of the PCI in its stronghold, but refused to do so. For the center-left to work as it should, the Socialists, reinforced by the Social Democrats, should have attacked the PCI's ways and argued with and embarrassed the PCI's corps of activists, prying some loose and sowing doubts in others. Only in this way could the PCI have been defeated electorally and the 80,000 activists at its core have been won over to democracy. Instead, for very practical reasons, some Social Democrats and even Christian Democrats had been drawn closer to the PCI's orbit.

Galli urged the Socialists to change their ways before it was too late.[61] Four years later he had to acknowledge that they had not done so.

[58] In Bologna and 113 other cities the center-left could not oust the PCI-PSIUP without accepting help from the right. Galli did not propose they do this. Nonetheless, he thought the Socialists could not remain in power alongside the PCI without making a mockery of both the center-left and Socialist unification.

[59] Giorgio Galli, *Il Mulino,* January 1967.

[60] Ibid., p. 65.

[61] Ibid., p. 67.

The Socialists and leftist Christian Democrats did not challenge the PCI activists, but rather

> they approve them and they support them, both by cooperation in the labor movement and by accepting at face value the vague contrasts with the U.S.S.R. produced for the benefit of elites. And therefore the leadership of the PCI need fight only on its left . . . only against the ultraleft groups, even using Socialist and Catholic militants as auxiliary troops, above all during labor demonstrations.[62]

In fact, Galli noted, the leaders of the center-left, each for his own reasons, had hastened to congratulate the PCI on its carefully worded dissent from the Soviet invasion of Czechoslovakia. As a result, the PCI actually gained prestige from this barbarous invasion. How could the PSU gain at the PCI's expense if it did not fight the PCI?

It would be inaccurate, however, to think that in refusing to fight the Communists, the PCI withstood pressure to do so from the Christian Democrats. In fact, the moderate strategy for the center-left failed in large part because of the DC's failure to press that strategy on the PSI. Space does not permit me to document the DC's own loss of strength and determination vis-à-vis the Communist party. Surely the Catholic party suffered when Bruno Storti and his colleagues of the CISL accepted unity of action with the CGIL, despite being habitually greeted at "unitary" meetings by choruses of "United, yes, but against the DC." The succession of DC slogans about the PCI from 1948 to 1968 indicates how the relationship between the two parties changed: Anti-Communist Crusade, Anti-Communist Dike, Struggle, Challenge, Anathema, Reprobation, Vigilance, Irreducible Contrast, Very Clear Distinction, Enlightened Anti-Communism, Democratic Recuperation, Democratic Competition, and Constructive Dialogue.

In one important respect, Italian Communists seem no different from other living things: when their natural enemies abandon the field, they prosper.

The election of 1968 resulted in yet another gain for the PCI at the expense of the Socialists—that is, the precise opposite of what the moderates expected from the center-left plan. The PSU's loss was not great. In 1963 the PSI received 13.8 percent and the PSDI 6.1 percent of the vote for the Chamber of Deputies, for a total of 19.9 percent. The PSIUP should have been expected to draw off about 4 points. In fact, it polled 4.5 percent in 1968, while the PSU received 14.5 percent. The two added up to 19 percent—remarkably close to the figures for 1963. In fact, the PSU lost only three of its ninety-four seats in the Chamber, and none of

[62] Giorgio Galli, *Il Mulino,* January 1971, p. 47.

its forty-six in the Senate. Giorgio Galli was quite right in saying the center-left had not suffered a numerical defeat but a political one.[63] At some cost, the Socialists had been in the forefront of the forces which had split and dispirited the DC, but the Communists were reaping all the rewards. Many Socialists, especially in the north and center, where the PCI had made some gains at their expense, wanted at all costs to become indistinguishable from the party which seemed to hold the key to success: the PCI.

After the elections, PSU Vice Secretary Brodolini declared, "The center-left must be regarded ever less center, ever more left, otherwise one should ask himself if it be worth the trouble to let it survive."[64] The first (and last) congress of the PSU was dominated by one question: How can the party participate in governments opposed by the PCI without "losing contact with the masses," that is, with the "mass organizations" influenced by the PCI? A majority of what had been the PSI were so concerned about the security of their posts in the Communist-dominated localities, unions, and elsewhere that they wanted to refuse to cooperate with the government until the DC made its policies more acceptable to the PCI. The ex-Social Democrats tipped the balance in favor of joining the government first and pressing these demands later.

By the end of 1968, however, it was clear that with few exceptions the ex-Socialists would unite against the ex-Social Democrats and insist that governments be ever more acceptable to the PCI. The Social Democrats found themselves in the position they had escaped in 1947. Once more they fled "Socialist unity," but this time they had to leave behind most of their assets in the labor movement.

The Reformists Trapped. All the moderates in the center-left shared the Social Democrats' predicament in some way. In their rush to strengthen "the forces committed to reform," they backed the PSI's refusal to meet the conservatives' demands that it break with the Communists. In so doing, they contributed to the defeat of center-right forces in the DC, but then they found that no power in the land could make the PSI more friendly to them than to the PCI. In December 1968 and January 1969 *Il Mulino* published articles by Enrico Finzi and Giorgio Galli exploring the reasons why, from their own moderate Socialist perspective, the center-left had failed. Finzi's article, titled "The Reformists' Anger,"[65] admitted that people like himself had been mistaken about the center-left, both intellectually and politically. The Socialists, on whom they had

[63] *Il Mulino,* January 1969.

[64] *La Stampa,* May 22, 1968.

[65] *Il Mulino,* December 1968.

staked so many hopes, had not used their newly-found political and economic influence to make their party independent of the Communists. Instead of substituting new kinds of patronage for old, the Socialists had simply tried to add the new to the old. In this and in the shabby way they had managed the so-called unification of the PSI and PSDI, the Socialists had proved themselves greedy and shortsighted. Both they and the Christian Democrats, Finzi charged, approached reforms, especially the reform of the school system, with one paramount consideration: to make them yield the maximum number of posts. They helped to raise wild hopes, and they hid from the public the cost of the reforms. Above all, they refused to challenge the PCI. They would denounce the PCI publicly on Sunday, and the rest of the week make profitable deals with it under the table.[66]

Giorgio Galli, speaking officially for *Il Mulino,* said the journal's editors felt isolated because, as it turned out, neither the Socialists nor the Christian Democrats responsible for the opening had appreciated the importance of making "frontal attacks" on the PCI's power positions, such as those in local government and parliamentary committees. Those who had made the center-left, said Galli, only paid lip service to the proposition that "a new left either will be built on the rubble of the present PCI, or will not be built at all."[67] He realized both that the leftist elements in the center-left had refused to stop "understandings and deals" with the PCI, and that his appeal for the government to "stop channeling public funds to the PCI" was not likely to be heeded.

Contradiction and Resolution. In 1960, when the DC gave up its demand that the PSI cut its ties with the Communists as a condition for participation in the government, it accepted a contradiction: Socialist politicians thereafter took part simultaneously in both the government and the grass roots of the opposition. This ambivalence was reflected in the PSI's statements on important matters (for example, on NATO: "We Socialists cannot accept the *raison d'être* of the Atlantic Pact, but that does not create a need for denouncing that pact").[68] The center-left gave rise to some interesting verbal attempts to cover contradictions—for example, "parallel convergences."

Not surprisingly, the most often asked question about the center-left concerned the "soul" of the PSI. Did it lie in the Maximalism of Lombardi, or in men like Santi of the CGIL, whose lives were built around cooperation with the Communists? Or did it lie with men like Giolitti,

---

[66] Ibid., p. 1010.

[67] *Il Mulino,* January 1969.

[68] Pietro Nenni, speech to the Thirty-fifth Congress of the PSI, October 1963, *35 Congresso del PSI* (Milan, 1964).

who had become wholly involved with government power and patronage? Was one to believe in the party's attacks on Communist totalitarianism or in its steadfast refusal to break with the Communists? Whose partner was it really? Was it a Trojan horse in the Communist camp, or was it a Trojan horse in the camp of liberal democracy? The answer, of course, is that the PSI has always contained contrasting elements. The contradictions between these elements—when they do not lead to scissions—are resolved in different ways at different times.

In the years after the 1968 election these contradictions were progressively resolved in favor of the PCI. But even as the PSI moved closer to the Communists, Nenni gave excellent reasons why it should not be doing so: the PSI's vision of politics, said he, was like that of the Czech Alexandr Dubček, while the PCI stood with those who crushed Dubček.[69] After the formal scission of the Social Democrats in 1969, even as the "new majority" favorable to the PCI was consolidating its hold, the party newspaper *Avanti!* published an anti-Communist editorial. The PCI was about to decide the fate of Luigi Pintor and others in the Manifesto group. *Avanti!* warned that if the PCI took "bureaucratic measures" against its dissidents, it would demonstrate that it was still as much a part of Soviet Communism as in the days of Stalin and Zhdanov, that it was really on the side of those who had invaded Czechoslovakia, and that its touted dissent from the invasion had been but a tactical artifice.[70] In due course the PCI "bureaucratically" expelled the Manifesto group. To be sure, especially since the local elections of 1970 were approaching, the PSI cried foul. Nenni even charged once again that the PCI's attitude on Czechoslovakia was fundamentally pro-Soviet with a few sprinkles of eyewash for willing dupes.[71] Why, then, did the PSI continue to draw closer to the PCI?

One reason the PSI acted as it did was the way the PCI and the DC each acted. After the 1970 elections the party secretary, Mancini, sent the following guidelines for Socialists to follow in negotiations for local *Giunte*: the programs of the PSI and PCI were drawing closer; the PSI must ally with the forces whose programs were closest to its own; where this was not possible, center-left coalitions must be formed, but only on condition that these not include the Social Democrats.[72] Thus, while a partner in the center-left government of Emilio Colombo, the PSI abandoned any pretense of intending to break with the PCI, declaring that while the DC would be held to the terms of the center-left, the PSI would

---

[69] See Ugo Finetti, *Libro bianco sulla crisi socialista* (Milan 1972), p. 103.

[70] *Avanti!*, October 14, 1969.

[71] Ibid., May 18, 1970.

[72] See Finetti, *Libro bianco sulla crisi socialista*, pp. 91–93.

not. The DC—by failing to make the PSI at least pay lip service to the moderate conception of the center-left in return for PSI participation in the cabinet—utterly abandoned the moderate conception. The Communists, however, used their position as the most influential members of the "workers' movement" to threaten the PSI both materially and psychologically. The PSI's "new majority" officially explained its actions thus: the "true pressures coming from the nation" required "more advanced equilibria."[73] "More advanced equilibria" was a euphemism for greater participation by the Communists in the life of the nation. The "true pressures," according to Nenni, were "a new situation in the world of work."[74] That is, the PCI had become the only party capable of controlling its own activists in the labor movement. Thus, the PSI knew intimately how illiberal were the ways of the PCI but had to follow it or give up thinking of itself as part of the "movement." One kind of reason overruled the other.

The PSI's "new majority" took as its model the Communist-Socialist coalition in Chile. In March 1971, Francesco de Martino was elected president of the Central Committee to pursue it. His opening remarks confirmed the worst charges the opening's opponents had made a decade before: though he rejected "ideological confusion with Communism," de Martino said the PSI would seek "the unity of the real social forces interested in reforms, and therefore the *political opening* [emphasis added] toward the parties which express and represent those forces."[75] The center-left, he continued, had served its purpose by strengthening "democratic forces" and weakening their opponents. Now the concerted action of the PSI-PCI would bring the nation to new thresholds and "overcome the moderate version of the reforms."[76] Moderation had become the PSI's official enemy.

The contradictions were resolved—at least for a while. Despite recurring, heartfelt declarations of mistrust, cooperation between the PSI and the PCI increased. In the 1971 presidential election the PSI voted with the PCI on all twenty-six ballots. After the 1972 elections, when Andreotti attempted to govern with a centrist coalition, even the PSI's arch-autonomist, Pietro Nenni, vowed to fight with all his energy alongside the PCI to make this attempt fail. Said he: "The critique to be made of the center-left is one of the left, not of the right." Therefore, he continued, while the PSI would remain distinct from the Communists, it would work with them against "rightist involutions," such as the current

[73] Document of Nuova Maggioranza, *Avanti!,* September 4, 1970. Of course an "advanced equilibrium" belongs to the same genus as a "parallel convergence."

[74] See Finetti, *Libro bianco sulla crisi socialista,* p. 103.

[75] *Avanti!,* March 16, 1975.

[76] Ibid.

one.[77] In practice, Nenni, the most autonomist of the Socialists, countenanced any sort of cooperation with the PCI in forcing the DC to submit to the majority within the Socialist party that moved only in tandem with the PCI.

Since January 1976, the PSI's position has been unequivocal: it will not cooperate with any government opposed by the PCI, and it will make impossible any government not approved by the PCI.

The Opening to the PCI. *Il Mulino, Il Mondo,* and of course *L'Unità* had all expressed hopes that the opening to the left would lead to the integration of the PCI into the life of the nation.[78] But, clearly, each of these journals harbored very different hopes. *Il Mulino,* and to some extent *Il Mondo,* hoped the PCI would be weakened and would be drawn, probably piecemeal, into the orbit of the other parties, after proving it had changed its international preferences as well as its habits regarding civil liberties. Neither journal foresaw that a larger, stronger, richer, and more self-confident PCI, backed by a Socialist party unwilling to break with it, would increasingly exercise veto power over the internal affairs of a splintered and dispirited DC, and over the minor parties. When the outlines of this situation first became obvious in 1969, some Italian politicians and publicists began to discover signs of democratic probity in the PCI and to speak of some sort of deal with it. According to Galli, it was then that Aldo Moro began to think of repeating with the PCI what had been tried with the PSI a decade before.[79] The "reformers" of *Il Mulino* judged this a bad caricature of what they had originally proposed—a caricature born of frustration, fear, and unwillingness to admit one's own mistakes.[80]

As the PCI progressively entered into the calculations of the center-left politicians, their perspective on Italian politics changed. Before, and to a lesser extent during, the 1960s, center-leftists had attributed much of Italy's trouble to the existence of a strong antisystem party, the PCI. But the center-leftists' own acts to propitiate the PCI made them less comfortable in applying the label "antisystem" to it. In 1969, however, the very year when they stopped using the label, the labor movement initiated serious action against the system, and the PCI exercised the strongest in-

[77] See Finetti, *Libro bianco sulla crisi socialista,* p. 103.

[78] See *Il Mondo,* January 9, 1962, *Il Mulino,* February 1966, and *L'Unità,* January 11, 1962.

[79] Giorgio Galli, *Il Mulino,* September 1969, pp. 835–836. Galli believed that Moro and many other Christian Democrats intended to tame the PCI by *transformismo,* that is by verbally adopting some of its platform while actually working out a system for sharing the spoils of office with it.

[80] Ibid., p. 837.

fluence within the movement. The PCI attributed the troubles to the ubiquitous Fascists. By and by the center-leftists came to agree that the system's only enemies were the right, and the groups to the left of the PCI. *Il Mulino* did not concur. Galli doubted that the nation's troubles could honestly be ascribed to the small part of the electorate that voted for the MSI, and he deemed the new "anti-Fascist" fad an escape from reality.[81] Nicola Matteucci's critique of this attitude was even more pointed. He noted that those being intimidated and eliminated by the violent groups were primarily anti-Communists, and that the PCI was pressing the state to fight only "Fascism," and not "the two extremisms." This attitude, he wrote, "is *perhaps* anti-Fascist, but certainly not democratic."[82] In sum, it was clear from 1968 on that the opening to the PCI involved both a political and an intellectual change.

As in the case of the opening to the PSI, the moderates who favor the opening to the PCI have widely varied motives, but, as in the early 1960s, the mechanics of the process are rather simple. Matteucci described the leftist elements within the center-left as constantly leapfrogging each other in a race for firmer contacts with the PCI. Thus, he wrote, "The great coalition presents itself as the hegemony of the strongest anti-system political force, and therefore of the PCI, over a splintered center."[83]

Reasonable Expectations

The expectations of the *Mulino* group, of the DC left, of Arthur Schlesinger, Jr., and of many other American academics concerning the opening to the left and the role of the PSI in Italian politics were not a priori unreasonable. Neither were those of, say, the Communist party. Why were the hopes of one group disappointed and those of the other substantially fulfilled? Both sets of expectations were based in part on evaluations of the PSI, and both could have been correct. Marxism-Leninism and liberal democracy do coexist not just within the party's doctrines but also in the convictions of its individual members. The difference between the two sets of expectations lies in the realm not of theory but of practice.

At the beginning of the 1960s, the choice whether to "open" the government to the PSI and under what conditions belonged to moderates and centrists. They, more than the PSI itself, made Italy's public life hinge upon the PSI's internal contradictions, and made the nation's welfare hang upon the resolution of those contradictions. Of course, as the condition of the opening, the PSI could have been compelled to resolve its contradictions in favor of the centrists. But they could not withstand the

---

[81] *Il Mulino*, December 1969, p. 1173.
[82] *Il Mulino*, January 1971, p. 7.
[83] Ibid., p. 12.

combination of their own desires and fears—factional as well as ideological—and of the pressure of the PCI-PSI. The centrists began negotiations with the PSI already committed to an ultimate agreement. As usually happens in such cases, their ability to influence the other party to the bargain decreased drastically. They gave up a lever that might have helped the PSI's own moderate tendencies to prevail. Unable to get an agreement favorable to themselves, the moderates would also prove unable to enforce the terms they did get.

On the other hand, the moderates may have expected more from the PSI than any political party can give, even under pressure. A definitive break with the Communists would have meant unemployment (at least temporarily) for thousands of PSI members in and around municipal governments. In the cooperatives, it would have meant the rupture of profitable relations and perhaps the loss of jobs for tens of thousands of party members. In the labor movement, Socialist activists would also have been faced with a choice between defection and loss of their places. In 1966 we saw how few Socialists were willing to make concrete sacrifices for the sake of the center-left.

Nothing explains the outcome of the opening to the left better than the methods the moderates used to influence the Socialists. Above all, the moderates did not challenge the Socialists' ideology. This indulgence for the PSI's class-analysis of society should be surprising because Marxism is the basis of the cooperation between the PSI and PCI. If their moderate partners were not scandalized by Marxist classism, why should the Socialists have felt ashamed of the heritage they share with the Communists, and why should the Socialists have been expected to wage ideological war on the Communists? Instead of providing the Socialists with firm guidance in the realm of ideas, the moderates offered to the Socialists—and to themselves—profitable "reforms." By means of these reforms, the parties of the center-left used the Italian economy and culture to create colonies of dependents of a "New Class." Then the parties argued over the division of the spoils.

The Communists, too, could offer the PSI access to posts, but they were able to offer more. The PCI could lend its united strength to help the Socialists increase their share of the center-left's spoils, but more importantly it could offer the Socialists justification for what they were doing. On the Communists' side is the confidence that partisan activity is at the service of noble goals, which have been pursued by generations of secular "saints." On the Communist side, partisan activity takes place within an intellectual framework that appears to justify it.

The moderates who entered the center-left alliance failed because they did not base their work on a critique of that framework, those goals, and those "saints."

PART TWO

THE PRESENT STATUS AND ROLE OF THE ITALIAN COMMUNIST PARTY

4

Mass Support for Italian Communism: Trends and Prospects

Giacomo Sani

In the late 1970s the Italian political system is in a phase of transition characterized by an impasse. Since the general election of June 1976, there has been no viable majority in Parliament. The coalitions of the past are no longer acceptable to some of the parties; the new alignments that have been proposed are rejected by other political forces. Uncertainty is reflected in the solution adopted: a minority cabinet led by Christian Democrat Giulio Andreotti, which relies on the indirect support of five other parties.[1] Although inaugurated as a temporary and transitional solution, the cabinet survived far longer than expected, largely because no other alternative was acceptable to all concerned.

As they struggle to find a way out of this impasse, Italian political elites are constrained by a variety of domestic and international factors.

The author wishes to thank his colleagues, Samuel Barnes, Alberto Marradi, and Giovanni Sartori, for sharing with him data from their studies of the Italian electorate. Giuseppe Di Palma provided useful advice for the preparation of the manuscript. The assistance of the Polimetrics Laboratory of the Ohio State University is gratefully acknowledged. Research for this chapter was carried out in 1976–1977 when the author held a Guggenheim Fellowship.

[1] Indirect support for the Andreotti government came from the Communists, Socialists, Social Democrats, Republicans, and Liberals when, in August of 1976, these parties abstained from the vote of confidence and thus allowed the cabinet to be inaugurated. A more formal agreement on a limited program was reached among these parties and the Christian Democrats in July 1977. The cabinet remained formally a minority cabinet, however, and the views of the protagonists as to the meaning of the agreement differed considerably. While the Communists tended to stress its importance and argued that it represented a marked departure from the past, the Christian Democrats stated that the agreement was an essentially transitory measure required by circumstances. For examples of divergent views, see the interview with PCI official, Gianni Cervetti, in *Espresso* (September 11, 1977), p. 7; Guglielmo Zucconi, "Ira a Torino, baci a Perugia," *La Discussione* (August 8, 1977), p. 1; Mario Ferrari Aggradi, editorial, *La Discussione* (September 5, 1977); Gerardo Chiaromonte, "Il subito e il dopo," *Rinascita* (September 9, 1977); Luca Pavolini, "Il confronto e la lotta," *Rinascita* (September 2, 1977), p. 1.

One constraint is the relative strength of the contending forces which, in turn, depends on the distribution of partisan preferences within the electorate. In this chapter, I shall focus on political orientations at the mass level and raise two questions: What accounts for the electoral trends of the past? What reasonable conjectures can be made about the behavior of Italian voters in the near future?

Since the essence of the "Italian problem" is the present and future role of the Communist party (PCI), much of the analysis concerns the bases of its popular support; but the discussion touches also on some of the other parties. The first two sections of the chapter deal with the growth of the Communist party in the postwar period and with the rapid increase of the party's strength in the mid 1970s. The third section contains a review of the factors that, in my opinion, have been associated with this growth. In the last part of the chapter, I present some conjectures on the likely dynamics of the Italian electorate in the near future.[2]

The Long March of the PCI: The Electoral Dimension

The Communist party emerged from the first general election held in Italy in the postwar period (1946) as the third largest party. Its share of the popular vote was considerably smaller than that of the Christian Democrats (DC) and slightly lower than that of the Socialists (PSI). Thirty years later, the returns of the parliamentary elections of June 20, 1976, gave the Communist party 34.4 percent of the popular vote; the Socialists had been overtaken and outdistanced, and the gap with the DC had been reduced to merely four percentage points (Table 1). More significant than the size of this overall advance—it took the PCI thirty years to gain fifteen percentage points—is the nature of that growth. Several characteristics stand out.

For most of the postwar period, the growth of the Communist party has been *gradual*. Between 1946 and 1972 the party's share of the vote grew by 8.3 percent, with a mean increase from one election to the next of approximately 1.4 percentage points. In the mid 1970s the rate of growth has been considerably higher. But this acceleration was in part

[2] A number of propositions advanced in this paper are based on data I have presented in previous works. For the details, see Giacomo Sani, "Mass Level Constraints on Coalition Re-Alignment: Anti-System Parties in Italy," *British Journal of Political Science,* vol. 6 (January 1, 1976); "Le elezioni degli anni settanta: Terremoto o evoluzione?" *Rivista italiana di scienza politica,* vol. 6, no. 2 (1976); "The PCI on the Threshold," in *Problems of Communism,* vol. 25 (November 1976), pp. 27–51; "Generations and Politics in Italy," unpublished paper presented at the Seminar on the Italian Crisis, Turin, Fondazione Luigi Einaudi, March 24–27, 1977; "La nuova immagine del PCI e l'elettorato italiano," in Donald L. M. Blackmer and Sidney Tarrow, eds., *Communism in Italy and France* (Princeton: Princeton University Press, 1975).

TABLE 1
PERCENTAGE OF THE VOTE FOR THE THREE MAJOR ITALIAN PARTIES, 1946–1976

Year	*Communist Party*		*Socialist Party*	*Christian Democrats*
1946	18.9		20.7	35.2
1948[a]		31.0		48.5
1953	22.6		12.7	40.0
1958	22.7		14.3	42.4
1963	25.3		13.9	38.3
1968	27.0		14.5[b]	39.1
1972	27.2		9.6	38.7
1976	34.4		9.6	38.7

[a] Communists and Socialists contested the election of 1948 together.
[b] The Socialists ran with the Social Democrats in 1968.
SOURCE: Computed by the author from official election returns.

a consequence of the expansion of the electorate after the voting age limit was lowered.

The second point worth noting is the *general* nature of the phenomenon. The strength of the PCI has increased in the industrial regions of the North as well as in the underdeveloped areas of the South; in the heavily Catholic areas of the Northeast as well as in the so-called red belt of the center (Figure 1). To be sure, the rate of growth has not been uniform. Higher gains have occurred in areas where the party was initially weak, especially in the southern provinces. But the party has also made significant advances in regions such as Emilia-Romagna, Tuscany, Umbria, and Marches, which were its strongholds at the beginning of the postwar period. As a consequence, regional differences have been somewhat reduced, but the geographical distribution of the vote continues to display a great deal of continuity with the past. Although the party has done particularly well in the large urban centers, its strength is by no means confined to the cities. The PCI enjoys a considerable level of support in many rural areas and smaller towns as well.[3]

[3] In fact, the percentage of the vote for the PCI is only slightly higher in the urban than in the rural areas. In the ninety-four provincial capitals, the party received 34.9 percent of the vote, and in the rest of the territory, 34.2 percent. Of the 1,362 Communist mayors, 21 were in provincial capitals, 510 in communes with over 5,000 inhabitants, and the remainder incumbents in small communities. Cleso Ghini, *L'italia che cambia: Il voto degli italiani, 1946–1976* (Rome: Editori Riuniti, 1976), p. 609. Data on mayors are from the *Almanacco PCI 1977* (Rome: PCI, 1977), p. 30.

FIGURE 1

PERCENT OF THE VOTE FOR THE PCI, 1946, 1953, 1963, AND 1976

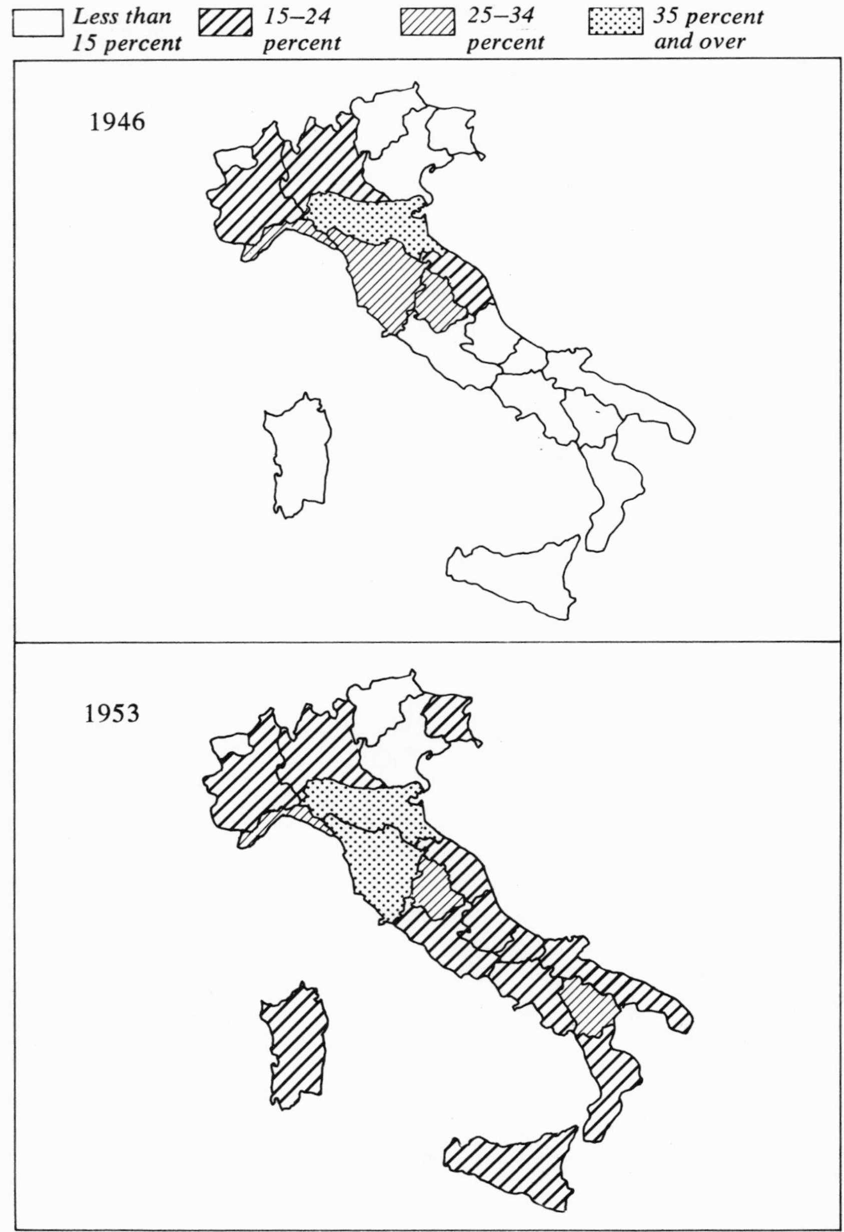

FIGURE 1 (continued)

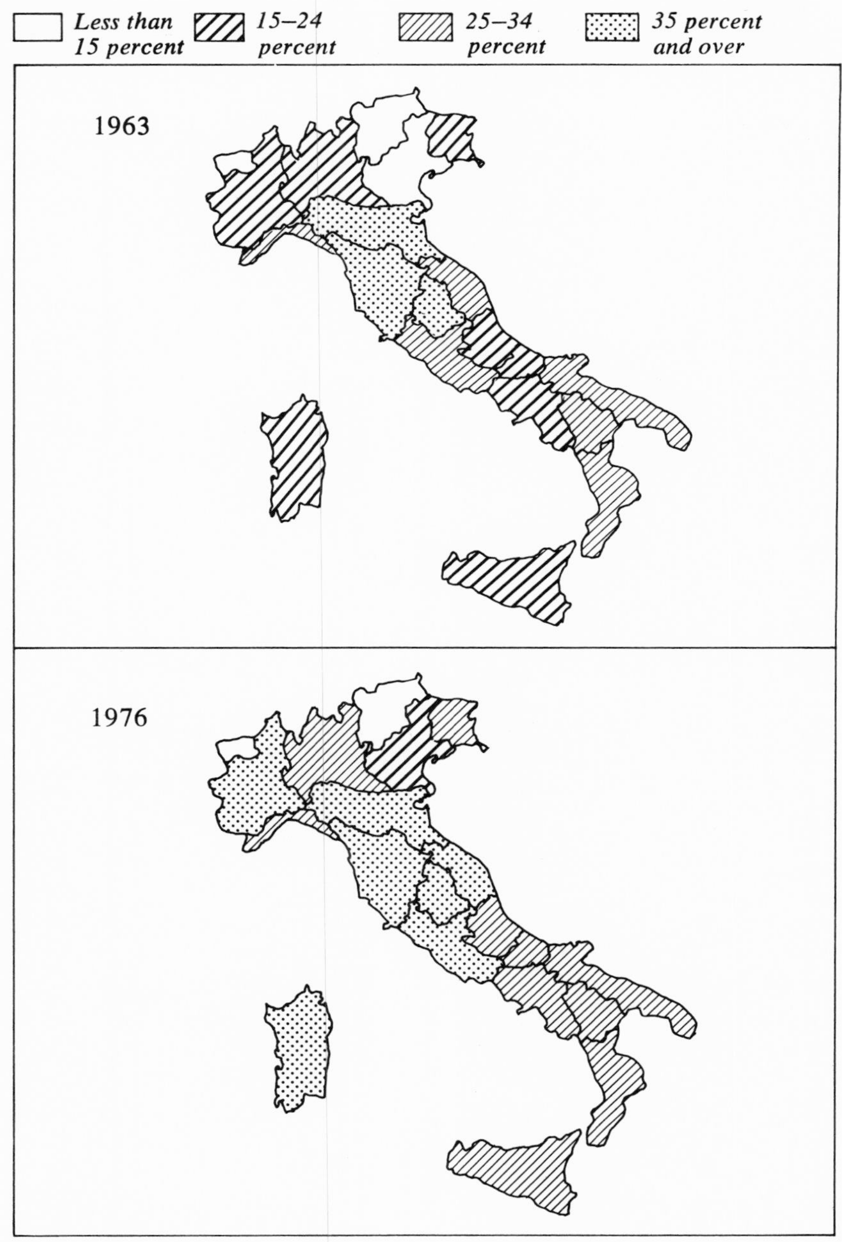

TABLE 2

VARIATIONS OF THE ELECTORAL STRENGTH OF THE PCI IN EIGHTEEN REGIONS, 1946–1976

(percent)

Region	*1946–53*	*1953–58*	*1958–63*	*1963–68*	*1968–72*	*1972–76*
Piedmont	+0.6	−2.4	+4.2	+2.9	+0.2	+9.2
Lombardy	−2.3	+0.9	+1.4	+2.8	+0.9	+7.8
Liguria	−2.7	−1.1	+3.8	+2.5	+0.7	+7.5
Trentino–Alto Adige	+0.7	−3.7	+0.6	+0.9	+0.9	+5.6
Veneto	+0.5	−0.8	+1.4	+1.9	+0.6	+6.4
Friuli	+2.0	+1.1	+2.0	+1.4	+0.5	+6.4
Emilia-Romagna	−0.8	—	+4.0	+2.5	+0.7	+4.6
Tuscany	+1.4	−0.6	+4.1	+2.5	+1.2	+5.4
Marches	+1.3	+2.6	+4.3	+2.2	+0.6	+7.1
Umbria	+0.2	+2.6	+8.0	+3.0	−0.1	+5.6
Lazio	+8.9	−0.2	+2.7	+2.1	−0.5	+8.8
Abruzzi-Molise	+10.0	—	+2.6	+0.9	+1.3	+8.2
Campania	+11.9	+2.5	+0.3	+1.0	−0.6	+9.6
Puglia	+9.0	+0.3	+2.2	+1.0	−1.5	+6.0
Basilicata	+12.9	—	+3.0	−2.8	−1.2	+8.4
Calabria	+7.6	+2.2	+3.3	−2.4	+2.0	+7.1
Sicily	+13.9	+0.1	+1.6	−1.2	−1.2	+6.3
Sardinia	+8.7	−1.4	+2.7	+1.2	+1.6	+10.3

— No change in electoral strength.

NOTE: Figures are the difference in the percentage of the vote polled by the PCI in two adjacent elections.

SOURCE: Computed by the author from official election returns.

The third point is that the growth of the Communist party has been mostly *continuous*. At the national level, the PCI has never suffered a setback. Even in the difficult circumstances of 1958 when the party was on the defensive, the PCI managed to hold onto its share of the vote and to improve its position marginally. At the regional or provincial level a certain amount of fluctuation has occurred, but in general the steps backward have been few and relatively small, and they have been quickly compensated by gains in following elections. This pattern is immediately evident from an inspection of Table 2, which contains data on the fluctuations of the Communist vote in eighteen Italian regions in all parliamentary elections during the postwar period. Of the 108 values of the table, only approximately 18 percent represent a loss, and several of these are marginal. Moreover, in only three regions are there two consecutive losses. The data also show that the PCI has been steadily gaining ground in the North, while in the continental South and Sicily during the same period the vote has fluctuated more markedly. This pattern of growth suggests that the success of the PCI has been founded on a steady core of support from a rather large mass of voters who have confirmed their choice of the party in successive elections. Findings from survey research corroborate this proposition: Communist voters tend to have a high degree of partisan identification and loyalty to their party.[4]

The fourth point is that the growth of the PCI has been *diffused* among social classes rather than specific to any one. Even in the earlier part of the postwar period, the Communist electorate was considerably heterogeneous. Although working-class electors did represent an important component of the party's following, sizable segments were drawn from the middle and lower-middle classes. Over the years, the social composition of the Communist electorate has become even more heterogeneous.[5] Recent survey evidence confirms that in the mid 1970s the Communist party draws its electoral support from a variety of social strata. As a consequence, the PCI electorate has a "catch-all" configuration that resembles the social profile of the electoral body (Table 3). The picture is still somewhat skewed toward the bottom of the social ladder, but, on the whole, the social composition of the party appears to be rather well balanced.[6] The statistical representativeness of the party has increased in other respects as well. Traditionally, the following of the PCI has been characterized by an unbalanced ratio of more males than females, but in recent years this phenomenon has become less pronounced. In the past, partly as a consequence of the class composition, the mean level of education of Communist electors was lower than the mean for the adult population; but in recent years the level has risen, in part because of the success of the party's appeal to younger and better-educated voters.[7]

The fifth characteristic of the PCI's growth is that it has taken place concurrently with the gradual decline of the Socialist party. At the be-

---

[4] Giacomo Sani, "L'immagine dei partiti nell' elettorato," in Mario Caciagli and Alberto Spreafico, eds., *Un sistema politico alla prova* (Bologna: Il Mulino, 1975), especially p. 113.

[5] Mattei Dogan, "La stratificazione sociale dei suffragi," in Alberto Spreafico and Joseph LaPalombara, eds., *Elezioni e comportamento politico in Italia* (Milan: Comunità, 1963), pp. 407–474; Gianfranco Poggi, *Le preferenze politiche degli italiani* (Bologna: Il Mulino, 1968), especially table I.1, p. 19; Samuel H. Barnes, "Italy: Religion and Class in Electoral Behavior," in Richard Rose, ed., *Electoral Behavior: A Comparative Handbook* (New York: Free Press, 1974), pp. 171–226; Paolo Sylos Labini, *Saggio sulle classi sociali* (Bari: Laterza, 1974).

[6] Additional evidence in the same direction comes from a 1976 survey commissioned by the PCI and carried out by the Demoskopea Institute. The results of the study were reported in summary form by Chiara Sebastiani, "Un paese indisfatto e politicamente maturo," *Rinascita,* May 13, 1977, pp. 6–7.

[7] Sani, "La nuova immagine del PCI," especially p. 332.

TABLE 3
SOCIAL STRATA IN A SAMPLE OF ITALIAN VOTERS AND PCI SYMPATHIZERS
(percent)

Strata[a]	*Full Sample*	*PCI Voters*	*Difference*
Businessmen, professionals, executives	14.5	10.3	−4.2
White-collar workers	26.9	22.5	−4.4
Skilled workers	17.7	21.1	+3.4
Farmers, sharecroppers	7.3	4.4	−2.9
Unskilled workers	19.3	23.6	+4.3
Peasants, farmhands, laborers	14.3	18.1	+3.8
Number of cases	2,413	641	

[a] Respondents were classified on the basis of their profession or the profession of the head of household.

SOURCE: The data were furnished to the author from an unpublished study conducted in 1975 by Giovanni Sartori and Alberto Marradi.

ginning of the postwar period, there existed in Italy a socialist political tradition with strong roots, particularly in the regions of the Northwest and of the center, that is, in the areas where the socialist movement had developed and prospered in the late nineteenth century and the earlier part of the twentieth. After the fall of fascism, this tradition resurfaced and provided much of the initial support for the parties of the left.[8] By 1953 the PCI had already taken a sizable lead; in 1963 the Socialists received half as many votes as the PCI; by 1972 there were three Communist voters for every Socialist elector, and in 1976 the balance was even more tilted in favor of the PCI (34.4 percent as against 9.6 percent). In part, the decline of the PSI can be traced to deep divisions within the Socialist ranks which led to the formation of splinter parties in 1947 (the Social Democrats, PSDI) and in 1974 (the PSIUP). The gradual erosion of the strength of the PSI is also explained by the number of Socialist voters who have shifted to the PCI over the years. Perhaps more important than this direct benefit to the Communists has been the indirect

[8] The significance of political traditions in Italy has been emphasized by a number of scholars. Giorgio Galli and others, *Il comportamento elettorale in Italia* (Bologna: Il Mulino, 1968); Barbara Bartolini, "Insediamento culturale e distribuzione dei suffragi in Italia," *Rivista italiana di scienza politica,* vol. 6, no. 3 (December 1976), pp. 481–514; Giacomo Sani, "Political Traditions as Contextual Variables: Partisanship in Italy," *American Journal of Political Science,* vol. 20, no. 3 (August 1976), pp. 375–406.

TABLE 4
PARTISAN PREFERENCE OF FATHERS AND OFFSPRING IN A SAMPLE OF ITALIAN LEFTIST VOTERS

Partisan Preference of Father	*Partisan Preference of Offspring* (percent of sample)			*Number in Sample*
	Communist	Socialist	other	
Communist	82.4	8.2	9.4	267
Socialist	38.0	34.2	27.8	216

SOURCE: The Sartori-Marradi survey (1975).

contribution. Survey findings show that voters from families with a Socialist background have been attracted to the PCI as much as, or more than, to the party of their elders. As the figures on political mobility across generations of voters clearly indicate, this exchange of voters between the two major parties of the left is a net gain for the PCI at the expense of the Socialists (Table 4). In sum the PCI has gradually become the main beneficiary of the socialist tradition.

The sixth and last point is that dissent within the Communist party has been sporadic and marginal and has not significantly hurt the electoral strength of PCI. To be sure, the secession of the Manifesto group in 1970 and the formation of several small challenges to the Communist party from its left have had considerable symbolic significance. But their impact at the mass level has been, so far, negligible. I will argue later that the potential for Communist losses to the forces of the radical left is greater now than at any previous time. Nevertheless, it remains true that until today the PCI has shown a remarkable capacity to isolate the dissidents and to limit the consequences of their attacks. In many cases, the party has been able to reabsorb them into its ranks.

To sum up, in the postwar period the Communist party has gradually but consistently extended its support at the mass level. It has attracted voters in all parts of the country and from different social strata. It has inherited and expanded its share of the socialist tradition. It has forged strong bonds with its electors and maintained their loyal support. This record suggests that the growth of the PCI has been relatively insensitive to the political vicissitudes of the day and to short-term factors. For an interpretation of the party's gains it would therefore seem profitable to look at the long-term changes in the political culture of the country that over the years have contributed to making the PCI's appeals more persuasive.

The Growth of the PCI in the Mid 1970s

A brief examination of the electoral developments of the last few years is useful for several reasons. In the regional elections of 1975 and parliamentary elections of 1976, the popular support for the PCI grew at an unprecedented rate. This growth occurred in conjunction with the addition to the electorate of a sizable contingent of voters from the young generations. Some observers have interpreted the voting behavior of the mid 1970s as a shift from the pattern of the past, arguing that votes were cast in response to current issues rather than as a result of strong identification with a specific party.[9] A study of recent electoral dynamics might provide some clues as to future developments.

In the parliamentary elections of June 20, 1976, 12.6 million Italian electors voted for the Communist party. This represented an increase of approximately 3.5 million over the returns of the preceding election in 1972. The party gained in all provinces, and the gains were distributed fairly evenly throughout the nation. In order to understand better the nature of this advance, it is useful to look at the various components of the Communist vote: stable supporters, new electors, voters who switched to the PCI from center-right parties, and voters who switched to the PCI from the Socialist party and other groups of the left.

Stable Supporters. The stable supporters are voters who had already chosen the PCI in 1972 and who confirmed their choice in 1976. To estimate the size of this component, losses suffered through demographic attrition and defections are subtracted from the 9.1 million votes the party received in 1972. On the basis of statistics on mortality, demographic attrition can be set at approximately 0.4 million. Survey data collected in the fall of 1975 suggest that very few voters defected from the party—at the most, 0.2 million people. In all likelihood, the stable component of the Communist vote therefore amounted to approximately 8.5 million votes.

New Voters. People who had not been eligible to vote in parliamentary elections before 1976 make up the new voters. Because of the lowering of the age limit from twenty-five to eighteen years, this body of freshmen electors was unusually large: it included seven one-year cohorts of voters, or a total of 5.5 million people.[10] On the distribution of the approxi-

[9] Arturo Parisi and Gianfranco Pasquino, "Relazioni partiti-elettori e tipi di voto," in Parisi and Pasquino, eds., *Continuità e mutamento elettorale in Italia* (Bologna: Il Mulino, 1977).

[10] The new law lowering the age limit for voting was passed in the spring of 1975, thus making a number of young voters eligible to vote for the first time in the regional elections of 1975.

mately 5.2 million votes cast by these freshmen voters, there is no full agreement among observers, but the estimates that have been suggested differ by only a few percentage points. Thus, we are on relatively safe ground if we assign to the PCI a segment of the new electorate consisting of between 2.0 and 2.2 million votes, corresponding to 38 to 42 percent of all the ballots cast by the new electors. There is little doubt that this was an important component of the PCI's advance. It can, in fact, be estimated that if the percentage of Communist voters among the youth in 1976 had been the same as that in the overall electorate in 1972, the Communists would have gained some 0.7 million votes less than they did.

Moderate Voters Shifting to the PCI. In the aftermath of the election, there has been a tendency to overestimate the number of people who shifted to the PCI and to attribute the success of the Communists almost exclusively to the defections of electors who in the past had voted for the moderate parties—the Social Democrats (PSDI), the Republicans (PRI), the Christian Democrats (DC), the Liberals (PLI), and the neo-Fascists (MSI). Survey data and ecological analysis conducted at the provincial level indicate that the phenomenon *did* occur but that the flow of moderate voters was probably smaller than had been assumed. On the basis of estimates from survey research and analysis of alternative flows of voters among the parties, I have suggested that approximately 1.5 million moderate voters moved to the left in 1976.[11] Approximately two-thirds of these defectors accrued to the PCI while the remainder can be plausibly assigned to the Socialists, the Radicals, and other groups of the left. Translated into number of votes, this would mean that approximately 1.0 million electors who had previously voted for the center-right parties, in 1976 gave their preference to the Communists.

Leftist Voters Shifting to the PCI. In 1972 support for the non-PCI left amounted to 4.2 million votes or 12.9 percent of the total vote. It included people who voted for the Socialists (PSI), the left-wing Socialist Party of Proletarian Unity (PSIUP), or for other small groups of the left, such as the Manifesto, MPL, and Marxist-Leninists. In the period between the two elections, some of these groups disappeared (PSIUP, MPL) and other forces emerged, namely the Democrazia Proletaria (DP) and the Radicals (PR). In 1976 PSI, Radicals, and Democrazia Proletaria polled 12.3 percent of the vote, which already constituted a marginal loss. But this net balance tells very little about the flow of voters to and from these parties. It also ignores the fact that the Radicals and the Democrazia Proletaria group attracted a disproportionately large number of young

[11] Sani, "Le elezioni degli anni settanta."

TABLE 5
ESTIMATES OF THE DIFFERENT COMPONENTS OF THE VOTE FOR THE PCI IN 1976

Component	*Millions of Votes*
Votes received in 1972	9.1
Losses due to demographic attrition	−0.4
Losses due to defections	−0.2
Stable voters	8.5
Vote of new electors	+2.1
Votes of electors who switched to the PCI from the center right	+1.0
Votes of electors who switched to the PCI from other parties of the left	+1.0
Total number of votes received in 1976	12.6

SOURCE: Author's estimates.

electors and that in all likelihood there was also a flow of moderate voters to the PSI.[12] When these two inflows are taken into account, one is forced to conclude that there must have also been an outflow of voters away from these groups which for the most part benefited the PCI. Analysis of the alternative patterns of circulation of leftist voters suggests that this flow of voters toward the PCI ranged from a minimum of 0.6 million to a maximum of 1.4 million.[13] The more plausible estimate, in my view, is a figure of about 1.0 million votes, of whom some 0.4 million came from the ranks of the Socialists and 0.6 million from the other leftist groups. There is ground for believing that the Communist party did benefit considerably from the circulation of votes within the left.

A summary of the composition of the 1976 Communist vote is displayed in Table 5. Needless to say, the values, and especially those pertaining to the shifts of voters, are not firm figures but tentative estimates that could be reasonably set at slightly higher or lower values. It is my belief, however, that on the whole the values are a fairly accurate description of the vote for the PCI in 1976. A number of conclusions can be drawn from this analysis. First of all, it is apparent that the Communist party has gained voters from a variety of quarters: young electors, moderate voters, leftist voters. Second, the contribution of new voters has

[12] A comparison of the votes obtained by the parties in the election for the House and the election for the Senate indicates that DP and PR received approximately 10 percent of all votes cast by new electors. The figures are reported in Parisi and Pasquino, "Relazioni partiti-elettori e tipi di voto," table 7, p. 26.

[13] Sani, "Le elezioni degli anni settanta," pp. 282–283.

been a significant factor. Without the expansion of the suffrage, the PCI would still have advanced but not as rapidly. Third, one should not overlook the contribution to the party's gains made by the core of stable PCI voters; without their continuing support the jump of the mid 1970s could not have occurred. Fourth, 4.1 million, or approximately one-third of the 1976 Communist voters, are newcomers, people whose attachment to the party has not yet been tested through time, and whose behavior is likely to be of great significance in future elections.

An Interpretation of the PCI's Gains

Not unexpectedly, the increase in the level of mass support for the Communist party has received considerable attention from observers and politicians. With few exceptions, however, the comments made in the aftermath of the election are not very helpful in identifying the factors connected with the party's growth, in part because the observations on the components of the vote are often mixed with comments on its political significance and its consequences for governmental coalitions. Perhaps the thesis that best exemplifies this confusion between causes and consequences is the notion that the vote of 1976 was a vote for change. According to this view, widely shared among observers of the left, after thirty years of corrupt and incompetent rule by the Christian Democrats, Italian electors finally decided that it was time to replace them, or at least to bring new forces into the government. This would make it possible to halt and eventually to overcome the crisis that has gripped the country for several years. Even if the obvious bias is disregarded, this view is clearly more political diagnosis, with a suggestion of therapy, than an interpretation.

In my view, a number of propositions are more useful for understanding the Communist advance. These will be reviewed briefly in an order that does not necessarily reflect their importance.

The Opposition Role of the PCI. In democratic political systems the function of opposition parties is to identify problems, solicit reforms, press for change in policies, amplify popular dissatisfaction with measures that the incumbents have taken (or failed to take), and articulate and voice demands. In so doing, the opposition attempts to achieve two goals: to focus the blame for the shortcomings of the situation on the party or parties in government and to present itself to public opinion as a more effective alternative to the incumbents. When, because of objective reasons, or because of the ineptness or corruption of the incumbents, a society finds itself in a difficult situation, the role of the opposition parties is facilitated and their prospects at election time, other things being equal, are more favorable. It seems to me that the recent gains by the PCI can be understood in part in this context.

Italian life has been characterized since the beginning of the 1970s by a difficult economic situation, widespread social malaise, and mounting political violence, to mention only the most commonly cited ills. Popular expectations have increased while only half-hearted attempts have been made at solving problems that have been piling up for a long time. Measures that were taken to relieve the pressure of demands have made things worse (as the current crisis of overpopulated universities indicates). Given these conditions, it was not difficult for the major opposition party to focus the blame on the incumbents and particularly on the Christian Democrats. The more so, since the charges of patronage, corruption, mismanagement of the economy, and abuses of power directed toward the DC were often well grounded in fact. Furthermore, by presenting its own elaborate proposal for legislation and reform in a variety of different areas, PCI leaders and militants could easily refute the argument that they were playing their role in an irresponsible manner. This stance could enhance the credibility and persuasiveness of their appeals with those segments of the electorate who no longer believe that the center-left coalitions can carry out the needed reforms. There is little doubt that the poor performance of the incumbents coupled with the good reputation of the PCI created widely contrasting images of the major parties in the eyes of the Italian public. Comparison of data collected by the DOXA Institute over the last decade shows that the public's evaluation of the DC has become more negative, while a progressively larger segment of the electorate has tended to express a more favorable view of the Communist party. Regardless of the trait considered—for example, honesty, competence, having good ideas, being against violence—the trend runs in one and the same direction. The curve for the PCI goes up and that for the DC goes down (Table 6). The evaluation of the Socialist party follows a zig-zag course. Although the PSI image has not been tarnished as much as that of the DC, it is clear that in public opinion there is a considerable gap between the two parties of the left. It would not have been too difficult to foresee, on the basis of these figures, that the Communists would do much better than the Socialists at the polls.

The Growing Democratic Legitimacy of the PCI. The PCI could not have reaped the rewards of being the opposition if some of the longstanding predispositions against it had not diminished in recent years. One of these objections against the party had to do with widespread doubts about the democratic nature of the PCI. Throughout the postwar period, anti-Communist appeals stressed the fact that the Communist party was antithetical to the pluralistic tradition of the West, that it subscribed to a rather different view of democracy, and that if it succeeded in getting power it

TABLE 6
CHANGES IN THE POPULAR EVALUATION OF COMMUNISTS, SOCIALISTS, AND CHRISTIAN DEMOCRATS, 1967–1976
(percent)

Evaluation	Parties Rated	Period			
		1967	1974	1975	1976
Have good ideas	PCI	21	34	45	60
	PSI	32	32	40	41
	DC	43	27	26	34
Are honest	PCI	22	28	29	45
	PSI	32	23	30	26
	DC	36	22	21	23
Are against violence	PCI	16	26	31	46
	PSI	42	48	53	67
	DC	72	60	64	58
Are united	PCI	60	56	59	—
	PSI	31	29	33	—
	DC	33	21	16	—
Are competent	PCI	—	43	44	65
	PSI	—	33	38	41
	DC	—	38	33	40
Are modern	PCI	23	41	46	—
	PSI	35	29	35	—
	DC	45	23	17	—
Defend people like me	PCI	29	39	45	—
	PSI	33	35	46	—
	DC	39	27	25	—

— Question not asked in this year.

NOTE: Figures are percentage of respondents in a national sample agreeing with a given statement about each of the parties.

SOURCE: DOXA Institute, *Bollettino DOXA*, vol. 30 (September 17–18, 1976), pp. 140–149.

would eventually attempt to transform the system and alter drastically the rules of the game. The revolutionary tradition of the party and the ties with the international Communist movement were (and are) often brought into the picture to reinforce doubts about the nature of the PCI. For most of the postwar period this kind of anti-Communist argument was very effective with large segments of the electorate, but in recent years its persuasiveness appears to have decreased. Survey data from the mid 1970s show that considerable segments of the non-Communist electorate view the PCI as a democratic and nonrevolutionary force (Table 7). Not

TABLE 7
OPINIONS ON THE PCI IN A SAMPLE OF NON-COMMUNIST VOTERS
(percent)

Questions and Answers	*Partisan Preference*				
	PSI	PSDI-PRI	DC	PLI	MSI
Is the PCI a revolutionary party?					
Yes	44.4	40.7	52.8	54.1	63.2
No	38.7	36.4	17.5	29.7	21.8
Uncertain, do not know, no answer	16.9	22.9	29.7	16.2	14.9
Is the PCI a democratic party?					
Yes	47.2	31.3	19.8	27.0	20.7
No	29.6	49.2	50.5	56.8	70.1
Uncertain, do not know, no answer	23.2	19.5	29.7	16.2	9.2
Number of cases	284	118	610	37	87

NOTE: Percentages may not add up to 100 because of rounding.
SOURCE: The Sartori-Marradi survey (1975).

surprisingly, views more favorable to the Communist party are more frequently found among Socialist sympathizers, but they are by no means limited to this part of the political spectrum.

Although the doubts have not altogether disappeared, they no longer carry the day with segments of the moderate electorate, and the democratic legitimacy of the party has increased in the eyes of the public. In part, this new perception is a consequence of the statements and behavior of party leaders who in recent years have pledged to uphold pluralism, civil rights, and political and religious freedom, and who have stressed the original character of the "Italian road to Socialism." The changing image of the PCI may also reflect the longstanding integration of the party in the political structures of the country and the fact that in the postwar period the party has abided by rules of the democratic game.[14]

[14] For an overview of the evolution of the PCI see Giuseppe Mammarella, *Il partito comunista italiano, 1945–1975* (Firenze: Vallecchi, 1976). For recent assessments of the structural integration of the PCI in different political arenas, see: Samuel H. Barnes, *Representation in Italy* (Chicago: University of Chicago Press, 1977); Giuseppe Di Palma, *Surviving without Governing: The Italian Parties in Parliament* (Berkeley and Los Angeles: University of California Press, 1977); Sidney Tarrow, *Between Center and Periphery* (New Haven: Yale University Press, 1977).

TABLE 8
OPINIONS ON THE NATURE OF THE PCI AND ITS PARTICIPATION IN GOVERNMENTAL COALITION
(percent)

Questions and Answers	*Partisan Preference of Respondent*					
	PCI	PSI	PRI-PSDI-PLI	DC	MSI	Not given
Is the PCI similar to the communist parties of Eastern Europe?						
Yes, similar	15.0	24.5	50.0	53.0	70.7	21.8
No, different	73.1	54.2	31.9	19.8	20.7	23.7
Uncertain, do not know	11.9	21.3	18.1	27.6	8.6	53.8
In your opinion, if the PCI were in the government with the DC and PSI, would it be a good or bad thing for Italy?						
A good thing	75.9	46.5	14.9	10.6	13.8	19.9
A bad thing	8.3	13.5	42.6	51.9	74.1	19.2
In some respects, a good thing; in others, a bad thing	11.5	28.4	34.0	16.3	6.9	25.6
Uncertain, do not know	4.3	11.0	21.2	21.2	5.2	34.6

NOTE: Percentages may not add up to 100 because of rounding.
SOURCE: *Bollettino DOXA*, vol. 30 (May 9–10, 1976), pp. 70 and 71. The number of cases is not indicated in the source.

Whatever the causes, it is clear that the PCI has succeeded in persuading part of the electorate that it is different from the Communist parties of Eastern Europe. According to data released by the DOXA Institute, this view was shared in the spring of 1976 by over half the Socialist voters and by one-fifth of the DC sympathizers (Table 8). To be sure, the reservations toward the PCI have not entirely evaporated, and in fact a majority of the centrists and right-wing voters still believe that the PCI has not changed. Thus, the suspicions about the true nature of the party are still an effective deterrent in some quarters, but clearly the anti-Communist barrier is no longer as solid as it once was. At the very least, there is considerable ambiguity among non-Communist voters about the possibility that the PCI might enter into a governmental coalition, as the figures in the lower part of Table 8 indicate. Although relatively few moderate voters express positive feelings toward this move, a considerable percentage of electors are uncertain or have mixed reactions.[15]

The Decline of the Religious Objection. A second element that was common in the anti-Communist appeals of the past had to do with religion. The belief that Communists were against religion and against the church was rather widespread in large segments of the population. The clergy's strong opposition to the PCI in the first part of the postwar period reinforced the hostility of Catholic voters. And DC leaders could be persuasive when they pointed to the fate suffered by religious institutions and believers in Communist countries. In short, for many years the religious element was important in the anti-Communist barrier. In the last decade or so, however, it has become apparent that this objection too has been losing ground. The perceived incompatibility between a "good" Communist and a "good" Catholic has diminished substantially over the years. Toward the end of 1976 a remarkable 28 percent of Christian Democratic sympathizers did not object to the proposition that a Catholic could also be a Communist.[16] They form a segment of the Catholic electorate that displays weak loyalty toward the DC and is the source of the dissenting votes for the parties of the left in the mid 1970s. The emergence of this segment, and the appearance of Catholic intellectuals in the lists of the PCI in 1976 are the consequences of secularization, a phenomenon that has significantly affected Italian society in recent years. The steady decline of religious practice has progressively depleted the once huge reservoir of Catholic votes. Secularization does not automatically produce Communist voters, but by removing some of the obstacles of the past, it expands the area in which PCI can seek to attract support. The fact that young women are no longer bound to the clerical tradition of the past fits the trend.[17]

The Organizational Factor. Many students of Italian Communism have emphasized the significance of the party's distinctive organizational traits that set it clearly apart from other political forces.[18] There is a large number of card-carrying and dues-paying members. Total membership for 1971 reached the 1.5 million mark; at the end of September 1976 the recruiting campaign, still underway, had pushed the figure to 1.8 million

15 Evidence of doubts and ambiguity is also to be found in a July 1977 survey reported in *La Discussione* (August 8, 1977), p. 2.

16 The figure is taken from *Bollettino DOXA,* vol. 31 (February 3–4, 1977), p. 18.

17 Sani, "Generations and Politics in Italy."

18 Among others, see Sidney Tarrow, *Peasant Communism in Southern Italy* (New Haven: Yale University Press, 1967); Francà Cantelli and others, *L'organizazione partitica del PCI e della DC* (Bologna: Il Mulino, 1968); Giorgio Galli, *Il bipartitismo imperfetto* (Bologna: Il Mulino, 1966).

members.[19] The Communist Youth Federation, which had suffered serious losses in the late 1960s, has done rather well in the 1970s. Members, old and young, are organized in some 12,000 local sections scattered throughout the country but with a heavy concentration in the northern regions. In addition, organizational units of the party operate among migrant workers in a number of European countries. The PCI has a higher proportion of active members than other parties. Although it is difficult to estimate the number of these militants, there is little doubt that the party can count on a large core of loyal supporters who devote their time and efforts to party work, during and between electoral campaigns.

Above the grass-roots level is an impressive administrative machine, a veritable bureaucracy, with layers at the provincial, regional, and national level. This organizational apparatus is complex, highly specialized, and appears to be quite effective in stimulating and supervising party activities. The PCI has built an excellent communication network. Its daily, *L'Unità,* claims the highest circulation of any Sunday newspaper, and the third largest among the daily press. Two other newspapers, one in Rome and one in Palermo, though formerly independent, are aligned with the party's positions. The PCI weekly, *Rinascita,* is widely read by intellectuals and has doubled its circulation in the last five years. The party also controls an active publishing house and a number of specialized publications.

So far the PCI has been a highly united and cohesive party. Perhaps the outside observer is likely to overemphasize this trait, but conflict within the PCI seems to be far more contained than is the case in other parties. The organization of factions is forbidden, and their divisive consequences are thus eliminated. Debates within the party have certainly become more common and lively in recent times, but for the moment there is little visible dissent from the officially sanctioned party line. Undoubtedly the mechanism of democratic centralism has its drawbacks, but it has enabled the leadership to create and enforce a high level of consensus. This advantage might very well explain why the organizational formula has been adamantly defended against a number of attacks by political adversaries. Furthermore, the PCI has been able to channel its influence through a number of organizations which, although formally independent, have, in fact, been very close to the party: segments of the unions, the cooperative movement, cultural and recreational associations, and the like.[20]

---

[19] This information and the data presented below are drawn from *Almanacco PCI 1977.*

[20] For a documentation of the phenomenon from the early postwar years until the mid 1960s, see Agoupik Manoukian, ed., *La presenza sociale del PCI e della DC* (Bologna: Il Mulino, 1968).

Given these characteristics, it is not surprising that a large majority of Italian electors are impressed with the strength and the effectiveness of the PCI. Over 90 percent of the Socialist voters agree that the PCI is an "efficient" party. A large majority of DC, PSDI, PRI, and PLI voters admit, perhaps grudgingly, that this is indeed the case. The same applies, but to a lesser degree, to the capacity of the PCI to "maintain order" which is recognized by a substantial number of non-Communist electors.[21]

The significance of the organizational factor goes beyond the creation of a favorable party image. Organizational structures and manpower allow the party to carry out a considerable volume of activities, not only during electoral campaigns but between elections as well. The widely attended *Festival dell' Unità,* a mixture of recreation, culture, and politics, is held every year in many communities and is a good example of the party's organizational capacity. Organization and the availability of a core of militants allow the party to be present in a variety of grass-roots arenas such as the *consigli di quartiere* (neighborhood councils), the *consigli scolastici* (school councils), and the *consigli di fabbrica* (factory councils). These arenas provide opportunities to establish contacts with the population, raise issues, explain the position of the party, and attract support. Not surprisingly, throughout the postwar period, there has been a strong correlation between the organizational capability of the PCI (as measured by party membership) and its electoral strength.[22] One plausible interpretation of this finding is that membership drives help consolidate electoral support, and the human resources thus harnessed are utilized for a further expansion of the support base.[23] Recent gains in the electoral strength of the PCI were in fact accompanied by an increase in the number of members as well, and there is a good correlation between the percentage of increase in the party's strength in these two dimensions, as shown in Figure 2. In general, increments of both voters and members have been higher in regions where the party was weaker, whereas in its strongholds the percentage of increase has been lower. But of most significance is the correlation between the two rates of growth.

Political Socialization and Communication. Contemporary Italy has changed in many respects since the years of the reconstruction and the economic miracle. In my view, one of the most significant differences

21 The findings are from an unpublished study conducted in 1975 by Giovanni Sartori and Alberto Marradi.

22 For evidence of this, see Giorgio Galli and others, *Il comportamento elettorale* (Bologna: Il Mulino, 1968); and for recent times, Bartolini, "Insediamento culturale e distribuzione dei suffragi."

23 For alternative interpretations of the relationship between party membership and electoral strength, see Tarrow, *Between Center and Periphery,* and Bartolini, "Insediamento culturale e distribuzione dei suffragi."

FIGURE 2

PERCENTAGE OF INCREASE IN PCI VOTES AND MEMBERSHIP IN EIGHTEEN REGIONS

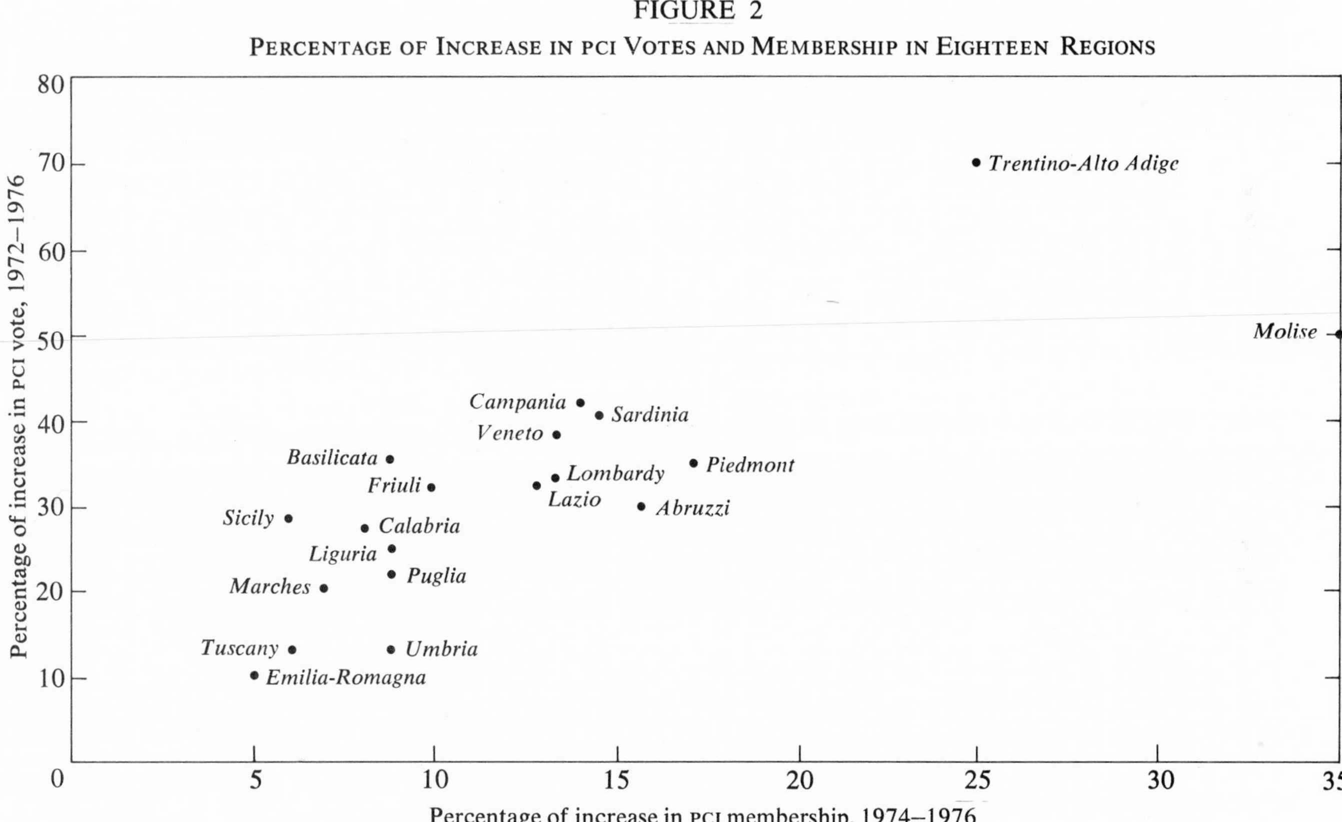

concerns the political culture of Italian society. From the 1940s until the late 1950s, the modal, dominant culture of Italy was relatively impermeable to Marxist ideas. Catholics and moderates controlled the state-owned radio and television network, most of the press, the printing industry, the institutions of higher learning, the judiciary, the bureaucracy, the armed forces, and the police. The ideas, beliefs, myths—in short, the culture—that sustained and legitimized that power structure was not a cohesive whole; it contained elements that ranged from conservatism to reform, and it was badly split by the clerical-secular cleavage. But the dominant culture had a common denominator: rejection of Marxism. Side by side with this dominant culture existed what might be called a leftist culture. It was vital but self-contained and, at least at first, it did not penetrate the major institutions of society. For all practical purposes this minor subculture, though capable of reproducing itself and perhaps even expanding marginally, remained largely cut off from the public structures of political communication and political socialization. An analysis of the changes that have intervened in the last fifteen years or so is beyond the scope of this paper, but clearly the mid 1970s have brought fundamental differences.

If there is a dominant culture today, it has little resemblance to that of the past. The Catholic moderate bloc, if it ever was a bloc, is on the defensive. Most intellectuals identify with leftist causes even when they do not identify with the positions of leftist parties. Factions with leftist sympathies have surfaced—partly as a consequence of structural changes and the introduction of participatory institutions—in the bureaucracy, the judiciary, the armed forces, and the professions.[24] Equally startling are the changes in the mass media: moderates and Catholics no longer have a monopoly of the "independent" press; leftist sympathies are clearly apparent in the editorials of the leading magazines; the reform of the radio and television networks has opened these channels of communication to voices once excluded from them.[25] Similar developments have taken place in secondary schools and within the universities: thirty years ago, leftist academics were a minority, today they constitute an overwhelming majority.[26] Although the precise distribution of political

---

[24] On the distribution of political orientations within the judiciary, see Carlo Guarnieri, *Politica del diritto,* vol. 6 (November–December 1976); also Giorgio Freddi, *Tensioni e conflitti nella magistratura* (Bari: Laterza, 1977).

[25] These changes in the structure of political communication have been acknowledged by Communist observers. See, for example, Luca Pavolini, "La stampa e la democrazia," *Rinascita* (August 27, 1976); and Celso Ghini, *L'Italia che cambia* (Rome: Editori Riuniti, 1976), p. 516. In the summer of 1977 the PCI scored important gains when several important posts within the state-controlled radio and television company (RAI-TV) went to personnel close to the party.

[26] Data on the predominance of leftist leanings among academics are presented in Pierpaolo Giglioli, "Barons and Bureaucrats: The Italian Academic Estate" (Ph.D. diss., Department of Sociology, University of California, Berkeley, 1977).

tendencies within the student body is not known, there seems to be little doubt about the predominance of leftist leanings.

I have used the generic terms *left* and *leftist* on purpose. What is involved here is not so much partisan preferences in the narrow sense of the word but rather a general identification with a certain part of the political spectrum, a sense of belonging to a political family, and the broadly shared use of a certain terminology. Although there is little systematic evidence of this trend, wide segments of informed public opinion appear to be making use of symbols and terminology that have an overall leftist flavor.[27]

The impact of these changes on political communication and political socialization is clear. The content of political messages has shifted. Social segments that were once insulated from the flow of communication from certain quarters are now exposed to new messages. The stereotypes or basic filters that people used to interpret and discriminate among political stimuli are no longer fully effective, and new ones are gradually being absorbed. In brief, the new and different climate of opinion has increased the probability that certain appeals will reach a larger audience and that they will be persuasive. As in the case of secularization, the changes in the structure of political communication do not automatically enlist support for the Communist party, but the expansion of the area with generic leftist sympathies offers the PCI a wider territory for recruitment.[28]

Looking Ahead

How solid is the electoral support that the PCI has acquired in the 1970s? What reasonable conjectures can be made about the strength of the PCI in the years ahead?

Assessments of future trends in mass behavior are difficult for a number of reasons. The overall level of support for a party is the sum of different components, the strength of which can fluctuate in opposite directions. It is difficult to sort out short-range from long-range factors and assess their joint impact. Inevitably, there is a great deal of uncertainty about the mass consequences of the coalition alignments that are now in the making. The international context and the constraints emanating from it complicate the picture further. No one knows when and under what circumstances new elections will be held, or what the social

[27] Journalists have coined a new word, *sinistrese,* to refer to the vocabulary and style that have become fashionable in recent times.

[28] On the importance of the political orientations of teachers, see Giovanni Berlinguer, "Gli intellettuali nella crisi," *Rinascita* (May 6, 1977). He argues that "where Socialists and Communists have paid more attention to mass education, the results can be counted not only in terms of votes but also in terms of the cultural and civic education of the youth."

and economic picture will look like in the years ahead. Finally, it might be unwise to attempt to make projections on the basis of past experience. Two Italian scholars have recently argued that perhaps the most important change to surface from the recent elections concerns a shift in the nature of the vote. According to this view, there has been an expansion of the "opinion vote," that is, choices are influenced more by the issues of the day and by the immediate political situation. Correspondingly, there has been a reduction in the "identification vote," that is, electoral behavior is based less on stable attachments to parties or to camps.[29] If this is indeed the case, predicting future trends is even more problematic. Opinion votes are sensitive to the nuances of political life, to the evolution of party alignments, and to the emergence of new political actors—in short, to conditions that are difficult to anticipate.

Given these uncertainties, the best one can do is to advance some tentative speculations based in part on past experience and in part on relatively plausible conjectures. The projections that, on the basis of the information presently available, seem more realistic to me are:

- The overall electoral strength of the PCI in the near future is likely to remain relatively stable with possible fluctuations on the order of, say, plus or minus 2 percent of the popular vote.
- A moderate, gradual increase in the level of popular support of the party appears more likely than a sudden, dramatic reversal of recent trends.
- The losses that the PCI might suffer are more likely to benefit groups of the radical left than other parties. Voters who might become disenchanted with the PCI are unlikely to turn back to centrist and moderate parties.
- Other things being equal, greater fluctuations in the strength of the PCI are to be expected in the southern regions. Such fluctuation might introduce a more marked element of instability in the overall level of support for the PCI.
- Another potential source of instability are the suspicions and apprehensions about the nature of the PCI that still linger in large segments of the non-Communist electorate. If international or domestic events, and the PCI response to them, were to renew these doubts, the ability of the party to retain support in moderate quarters and to attract another wave of centrist votes would be impaired.

The arguments underlying these conjectures cannot be fully explored here, but a few points can be quickly reviewed. First of all, the PCI should

---

[29] Parisi and Pasquino, "Relazioni partiti-elettori e tipi di voto."

TABLE 9
SUPPORT FOR THE PCI IN DIFFERENT AGE GROUPS, 1975

Age in 1975	*Percentage Favoring the PCI*	*Number of Cases*
65 and over	17.4	132
55–64	23.6	178
45–54	25.6	281
35–44	27.5	258
25–34	41.1	265
20–24	43.5	407
18–19	47.5	181
16–17	52.0	150
All age groups	35.5	1,852

SOURCE: The Sartori-Marradi survey (1975).

continue to be the beneficiary of electoral turnover, that is, it should have fewer losses due to demographic attrition and higher gains among those who will vote for the first time in the next election. In the elections of the mid 1970s, the gain among new voters was particularly important because of the expansion of the electorate. In the future, and especially if the next elections are held before the expiration of the regular term, the impact should be less pronounced but not insignificant. A quick glance at the figures of Table 9 will show why. In 1975 the percentage of PCI sympathizers was considerably higher among the younger cohorts than among the older voters who are gradually going to be replaced. Naturally, it is assumed that the political orientation of the youth will remain relatively stable and that the people born in the early 1960s will have sympathies roughly similar to those born in the late 1950s. Although this extrapolation is not entirely safe, the supposition that the trend is likely to be reversed in the short run seems less plausible.[30] The observations developed earlier on political communication and political socialization make it hard to suppose that in the near future the bulk of the young people will favor center-right parties.

The second point concerns the ability of the PCI to consolidate the support recently gained among dissenting Catholics and other middle-of-the-road voters and perhaps even expand it further. Here the ground is less firm, but insofar as these votes were reform oriented or designed to punish the DC, there seems to be no reason to suppose that these electors

[30] The correlation between age and partisan preference is confirmed by other studies; see, for example, Sebastiani, "Un paese indisfatto e politicamente maturo."

TABLE 10
POPULAR OPINION ABOUT ITALIAN PARTIES AND THE DEFENSE OF FREEDOM
(percent)

Parties Evaluated	*Party Wants to Defend Freedom*	*Party Wants to Limit Freedom*	*Uncertain, Do Not Know*
Communist	39	45	16
Socialist	62	18	20
Christian Democrat	60	25	15
Neo-Fascist	12	66	22

SOURCE: *Bollettino DOXA*, vol. 30 (September 17–18, 1976), p. 142.

will shift back, at least in the short run. A shift back is even less likely if the behavior of the defectors, instead of being a contingent choice, represented a change in their basic political orientation or identification. On the other hand, a further increase in Communist strength at the expense of moderate forces will continue to be impeded by the persistence of doubts about the democratic vocation of the PCI. The image of the Communist party has improved considerably in many dimensions, but strong apprehensions are still diffused in large segments of the population. In 1976 the non-Communist portion of the mass public was not entirely reassured by the PCI pronouncements in favor of pluralism. As the figures of Table 10 make clear, many Italians still do not believe that the PCI has the ability or the willingness to "protect freedom," and many others entertain doubts. Evidently, the inheritance of past statements, positions, and behavior is strong.[31]

On the question of democratic legitimacy, the PCI has won a major battle but clearly not yet the war. In a sense, these lingering doubts are likely to become more salient—and hence have a greater negative impact—as the party approaches the center of power. Recent public opinion data lends strength to the supposition that the prospect of a PCI in governmental position would trigger or reinforce doubts about its future

[31] The PCI can occasionally be embarrassed by the behavior or the positions taken by the Soviet Union: for example, in February of 1977 when prominent Soviet journalists visited Italy, or in the summer of 1977 when a Communist intellectual, Vittorio Strada, was denied a visa to attend a cultural affair in Moscow (the decision was later reversed). At the core of the polemics surrounding these two episodes is the persisting uncertainty in the eyes of many electors as to the autonomy of the PCI in relation to the Soviet Union, as well as doubts about the party's commitment to freedom.

TABLE 11
VIEWS ABOUT THE PCI IN THE GOVERNMENT
(percent)

	Partisan Preference of Respondents					
Questions and Answers	PCI	PSI	PRI-PSDI-PLI	DC	MSI	Not given
Do you believe that the PCI could stay in the government together with other parties?						
Yes, it would stay in the government with other parties	64.0	51.0	22.3	11.3	20.7	20.5
No, eventually it would govern alone	15.8	21.3	53.2	59.4	67.2	28.8
Do not know, cannot foresee, no answer	20.2	27.7	24.5	29.3	12.1	50.6
Total	100	100	100	100	100	100

SOURCE: *Bollettino DOXA*, vol. 30 (May 9–10, 1976), p. 73.

behavior. In mid 1976 vast segments of the electorate felt that after an initial period of sharing power with other political forces the PCI would eventually remain in government alone (Table 11). Perhaps this expectation is mistaken, but the data are rather informative as to the attitude of part of the voters. The anti-Communist barrier has been partially eroded but it has not collapsed. It might actually regain some strength were the PCI to appear close to reaching the goal of sharing power at the national level.

The greater volatility of the Italian electorate in the southern regions is another potential source of instability for the party's strength. Communist gains in the South in recent years have been considerable, especially in relation to the baseline. The advance of 10.3 and 9.6 percentage points in the Communist share of the vote in Sardinia and Campania, respectively, represents a 40 percent increase (see Table 2). Furthermore, unlike the party's record in the North, strong gains were made by the PCI in the South in the very short period of one year between the municipal elections of 1975 and the parliamentary elections of 1976. In Molise the vote for the PCI jumped from 17.9 to 25.6 percent of the total (an increase of 45 percent). In Calabria the increase was 30 percent, in Basilicata 23 percent, and in Sicily 20 percent. Whether the party will be able to consolidate the support of this mass of newcomers remains a question. The fact that the party organization has traditionally been weaker in these regions indicates that the South might be a problem. Relatively low levels of partisan identification and a tradition of patronage politics are likely to increase the potential for instability. The returns of municipal elections held in a few communities in the spring of 1977 indicate that the PCI might have to pay the price of having fueled expectations that it could not realistically expect to fulfill. As a local PCI leader said in the aftermath of the municipal election in Castellammare di Stabia, where the party lost heavily, "People want everything and they want it right away."[32]

Perhaps a more serious challenge to the PCI comes from the left wing of the political spectrum. The very growth of the party has increased its heterogeneity and, hence, the potential for internal tensions. In the past, tensions could be more easily discharged toward the outside. When the party was fully in the opposition, it could more easily focus the blame on the ruling parties and argue that once in power its contribution to policy making and implementation would turn things around. Under those conditions, there was little room for effective criticism from the left. Dissidents might claim that the party had abandoned its revolutionary ideals, that its opposition was too soft, that their overtures toward the middle classes amounted to a surrender to capitalism. But it was not too hard to dismiss these charges as coming from "sectarian," "infantile," and "adventure-prone" critics. As the party moves closer to the seat of power, however, it becomes increasingly difficult to placate the critics and to reassure the rank and file. In the delicate phase of transition from being the opposition to having an open role in the government, the PCI must be cautious in its moves and moderate in its demands lest the fragile equilibrium collapse. At the same time the party must not leave itself open to the criticism that it has been "tamed" by the Christian Democrats. The difficulty of this position and the tensions that ensue are reflected in the party's self-definition of its own nature: *partiti di governo e di lotta*—a party that has governmental responsibilities but is still involved in a struggle.[33]

[32] Quoted in *Corriere della sera* (April 20, 1977). The regional secretary of the PCI for Campania has written about the losses suffered by the party in that region in the spring of 1977: "We must ask ourselves . . . for how long we can continue if the democratic advance of June 20, 1976, is not followed by facts that demonstrate today and not tomorrow that we have finally started on a new road" (*Rinascita,* May 15, 1977, p. 5). The need for the party to show concrete results in the short run is also stressed in a recent article by Asor Rosa, who writes that "this is our strength; it does not diminish but rather increases our responsibility to be equal to it, to respond to it *soon*" ("Più civiltà più politica più forza," *Rinascita,* September 23, 1977, p. 23; emphasis in the original).

[33] In many respects the tensions and dilemmas of the 1970s are similar to those that surfaced in the 1945–1947 period when the PCI shared governmental responsibilities. See, for example, statements by party elites cited in Cantelli, *L'organizzazione partitica del PCI e della DC,* pp. 33–34 and 175–176.

The very nature of the political realignment sought by the PCI (a broad coalition of all major political forces) imposes the burden of sharing responsibility for policies that stem from a bargaining process and necessarily involve the setting of priorities. This requires the acceptance of policies that fall short of the PCI goals and of the expectations of its rank and file. It also implies deferment of some long-sought reforms and changes. The Historic Compromise might very well introduce "elements of socialism into Italian life," as party secretary Enrico Berlinguer has been arguing since 1973.[34] But this might not be enough for those leftist voters who have always wanted, and still want, a radical transformation of the society.[35]

Deflating some of the expectations that the party has helped build up while in the opposition will be painful and possibly detrimental to mass support. In past years the PCI has severely condemned the division of the spoils practiced by governmental parties and has promised to the electorate a "new way of governing." In recent months, as the party began to reap the fruits of its increased strength, it has become clear that it is much easier to theorize about the new way of governing than to bring it about.[36]

For the moment, the leadership of the party appears to be carrying the day: as far as is known, a majority of Communist voters favor the pursuit of Berlinguer's strategy. But there is hardly full consensus within the party, as surveys have shown and as the recent debates have indicated. According to a poll taken in the summer of 1977, about one-fifth of the PCI electorate judged negatively the program agreed upon by the major parties. Furthermore, over 34 percent of the Communist voters expressed preference for a coalition of leftist forces that would replace the DC in power, an alternative that the PCI leadership has consistently rejected.[37] Recent debates within the party and pronouncements by leading PCI officials confirm the existence of uneasiness, reluctance, and disconcertion.[38]

---

[34] Enrico Berlinguer, "Riflessioni sull'Italia dopo i fatti del Chile," *Rinascita* (September 28, 1973).

[35] A number of surveys conducted in the 1970s have documented the existence of widespread popular discontent with the Italian socioeconomic system. Not unexpectedly, higher levels of dissatisfaction were found among voters of the MSI and of the PCI. In 1974 almost half the Communist respondents agreed with the statement that "the system is radically wrong and has to be changed entirely" (*Ricerche demoscopiche,* vol. 7, nos. 1–2 [1975], p. 4).

[36] In the summer of 1977 external as well as internal critics took the PCI to task for having participated in decisions over appointments in banks and in the state-controlled radio and television system. According to the critics, the decision process had not differed from standard practice in the past for dividing the spoils among the parties.

[37] Data reported in *La Discussione* (August 8, 1977).

[38] "PCI: i malesseri della base," *Espresso* (September 11, 1977), pp. 6–8.

Whether these internal tensions will be resolved, and with what consequences, remains to be seen. What is certain is that there is a considerable potential for conflict. In the early 1960s the Socialists underwent an experience that in many respects was similar to the one facing the PCI in the late 1970s. The PSI eventually obtained access to power, but in the process it lost the left wing of the party.[39] Communist leaders are well aware of the risks implicit in their support of a governmental coalition, but they argue that the political situation today is entirely different from that of the 1960s.[40] To be sure, the PCI is not the PSI. It has leadership of a different caliber, a tradition of unity that has withstood several tests through time, and, above all, an organizational strength that the Socialists never had. But not even the PCI has the magic formula for reconciling the pursuit of its traditional goals with the realities of sharing power in a Western democratic system.

In the short run the challenge to the PCI from the new left might not have serious consequences at the mass level. One should not exaggerate the significance of open attacks against prominent Communist figures recently mounted by leftist youth groups.[41] The visibility of these forces is entirely disproportionate to their electoral strength. Furthermore, the radical left movement is badly fragmented, poorly organized, and lacks credible leaders. Under these conditions it is doubtful that a radical left alternative can attract the support of a large number of dissatisfied Communist voters. In the longer run, however, the possibility of an erosion of the PCI support base cannot be dismissed.

---

[39] At the beginning of 1964 the left wing of the Socialist party seceded and founded a splinter party (PSIUP).

[40] For example, Gerardo Chiaromonte, "Come andiamo alla trattativa," *Rinascita,* (May 6, 1977), pp. 3–4.

[41] Among the prominent party officers attacked are the union leader Luciano Lama, who was insulted by students at the University of Rome, and the mayor of Bologna, Renato Zangheri, who was openly charged by the movement of being a "servant of the capitalists" during the riots and demonstrations that took place in that city in the spring and fall of 1977.

5

The Italian Communist Party and Changing Italian Society

Joseph LaPalombara

Three decades ago, on the heels of political and military disasters wrought by fascism and a compliant House of Savoy, Italy sent the monarchy packing and instituted a republic. It was a remarkably courageous act. For one thing, the country was narrowly divided on the issue, with majorities in the North and South voting, respectively, to abolish and to sustain the monarchy. In addition, the republican choice meant that for the third time in less than eighty years Italy would be experimenting with a new form of national government.

The experiment could scarcely have found less auspicious beginnings. At the end of World War II the country verged on total economic collapse. During the fascist interlude, a generation of Italians had come to political maturity with little knowledge of and no experience with republican institutions. Unlike Japan and Germany, Italy would not have an army of occupation with political advisers more or less strongly guiding the direction of constitution making, electoral regulations, and political institution building.

In Italian politics immediately after the war, disorientation reigned. Major parties that existed in the 1920s quickly reemerged, along with some new ones. Not only did these parties represent ideological extremes but, in the arena of political rhetoric at least, they began to compete for ideological space, thus giving rise to what some have called a party system of "polarized pluralism."[1] The republican constitution itself was put

[1] The description of Italy's political party system as one of "polarized pluralism" is Giovanni Sartori's, who worked out its meaning in a series of articles. His most recent general articulation of this concept, and its application to Italy as well as to a number of other countries, will be found in his *Parties and Party Systems: A Framework for Analysis* (Cambridge, Mass.: Cambridge University Press, 1976), chap. 6. The most interesting application of the Sartori model in an empirical study of Italian political institutions is that of Giuseppe Di Palma, *Surviving without Governing: The*

together at a time when the confusion, animosities, accusations, fears, and recriminations engendered by the advent and collapse of fascism had not yet been sorted out. Far from being a tightly woven fabric, the Italian Constitution is a mesh of compromises, mutual guarantees, and high-flown aspirations without any explicit implementing force or institutions.[2]

Given these beginnings, the most astonishing aspect of the Italian Democratic Republic is not its declining governability but rather its sheer survival. In the midst of all the hand wringing about Italy, it is easy to overlook this achievement, as well as many others too numerous to mention here.

Italy in Crisis

I do not wish to make little of declining governability, however, particularly in a country that once before experienced a major change in regime in the midst of political chaos and governmental paralysis. Even if the Italians' catastrophic orientation to political life is taken into account, the symptoms of crisis are portentous. They include high levels of inflation and unemployment; an unfavorable balance of payments, made structural by heavy dependence on petroleum imports; high labor costs accompanied by low productivity; archaic bureaucratic and educational institutions that defy rational reorganization; growing intellectual unemployment and student unrest; and fiscal, financial, and political scandals that truly boggle the imagination.

Italian newspapers—echoed elsewhere in the West—write alarmingly about these conditions. While the British ponder whether their system can be as sick as Italy's, Italians ask whether their country isn't really the Continent's Britain. The answer is no to both questions. Italy's situation is and will indefinitely remain much more complicated and difficult to handle than is Britain's. Two points are germane. First, several of the basic *institutions* of Italian government now seem to be unworkable. Second, Italy alone in Western Europe is currently experiencing extreme and apparently growing degrees of terror and violence.

Not all of Italy's violence is political, but all of it weighs heavily on

Italian Parties in Parliament (Berkeley and Los Angeles: University of California Press, 1977), chap. 6.

Sartori's formulation is not without its imperfections or challengers. See, for example, Sidney Tarrow, *Peasant Communism in Southern Italy* (New Haven: Yale University Press, 1967); Donald L. M. Blackmer and Sidney Tarrow, eds., *Communism in Italy and France* (Princeton: Princeton University Press, 1975); Giorgio Galli, *Il bipartismo imperfetto* (Bologna: Il Mulino, 1966); and Luciano Pellicani, "Verso il superamento del pluralismo polarizzato," *Rivista italiana di scienza politica,* vol. 4 (1974), pp. 645–674.

[2] For a brief but illuminating discussion of this aspect of the Italian Constitution, see Di Palma, *Surviving without Governing,* pp. 105–114.

the policy and its future: massive jailbreaks; violent confrontations—sometimes shootouts—between demonstrators and police; political kidnappings and assassinations on a large scale; intimidations (real or imagined) of prospective jurors by terrorist groups; provocations by politically extreme groups (widely suspected of receiving assistance from outside Italy); the recent abduction, "trial" and murder of Aldo Moro; growing clamor for law and order. All of this, when added to what else ails the Italian polity, is exactly the concoction that breaks down regimes.[3]

The Italian crisis involves a growing imbalance between the apparent need for governmental action and the willingness or capacity of the leaders and institutions of government to respond. The government of Italy is clearly overloaded. This being so, the dynamic of crisis government becomes circular: many institutional failures become the direct cause of new problems, or the aggravation of old ones.[4]

The electorate plays a role here too. If the crisis centers in the judiciary or military bureaucracy, it is somewhat removed from the influence of the electorate. But if the problem lies with the legislative or the executive branch, it will be profoundly influenced, one way or another, by the preferences voters express at the polls. This is of course an oversimplification. Nevertheless, Italy is a representative democracy, and what happens within it and to it is directly connected with the outcome of elections.

For some years now, and most dramatically on June 20, 1976, the Italian electorate has been at work making obsolete the formula of government that has carried the republic along for thirty years. That older formula rested on a number of assumptions, among which are:

- That the Christian Democratic party (DC) acting alone but preferably jointly with one or more other parties, would maintain hegemonic control of the machinery of government. This pattern was established by DeGasperi in 1948 when he opted for coalition government, but it was not strictly required because the DC held legislative majorities.
- That the parties at the political extremes would never become the government and never formally participate in a coalition government.

---

[3] Acute insights into the causes and patterns of the disintegration of democracies are provided in Juan Linz and Alfred Stepan, eds., *Breakdown and Crises of Democratic Regimes* (forthcoming).

[4] One of the most dramatic examples of this cause-and-effect circularity is the nagging issue of the reform of higher education. Thus far, almost everything the government has done (or ignored) over the last fifteen years has made this problem politically more volatile. It is a good case of a government experiencing the disruptions it invites.

- That, while the Communists (PCI) would not be expected to become a part of government, they would nevertheless be accorded considerable influence within it. Neither the DC nor the PCI expected the latter to behave like the "loyal opposition" in the British sense. The idea of governmental decisions by majority rule and the idea that today's minority would become tomorrow's majority (and vice versa) were *not* commonly accepted.
- That the electoral appeal of the PCI would peak below 30 percent and then either stabilize or decline. Further, that the Communists and Socialists (PSI) would not together obtain a majority of votes and seats in Parliament.
- That a number of minor but significant secular parties would lie between the Christian Democrats and the political extremes. These parties—the Republicans, Liberals, and Social Democrats, and later the Socialists—were expected to attract votes that might otherwise slip over to the extremes. They were also to act as buffers between the DC and PCI in order to avert either a direct confrontation between the two or an agreement between them to govern Italy together.
- That the costs of maintaining this unusual hybrid would not become so high that its contradictions and anomalies would need to be corrected on short notice.

For thirty years the Italian government hobbled along on such premises. In the nature of things it could not be a very dynamic system. If the Communists were restive about it, there was little they could do as long as the voters continued to provide a basis for Christian Democratic hegemony. Furthermore, the system gave the Communists a piece of the action; they were not completely frozen out as an opposition; they achieved considerable influence over some policies; they were widely represented in local and regional governments. They actually fell into collusion with the Christian Democrats in the maintenance of the system. There developed between these two major parties a symbiosis that Di Palma appropriately calls "surviving without governing."[5]

[5] See Di Palma, *Surviving without Governing,* especially chaps. 3, 5, 6; and see also his more recent "Parliament from Uncertain Compromise to Historic Compromise," paper presented to the Seminar on the Italian Crisis, Turin, Fondazione Luigi Einaudi, March 24–27, 1977. The system Di Palma describes produces many misleading indications that it is performing well and according to clear rules. But, for example, a surge of parliamentary output of important legislation need not imply that a decision has been reached. Nor should a spate of decrees lead to the inference that executive control of policy is more coherent and purposive. On these points, see Alberto Predieri, ed., *Il parlamento nel sistema politico italiano* (Milan: Comunità, 1975); and F. Cazzola, A. Predieri, and G. Priulla, *Il decreto legge fra governo e parlamento* (Milan: Giuffrè, 1975).

The old system is now in decay; the assumptions on which it was based no longer hold. The Communists, much to their own surprise, now exceed 34 percent of the electorate, and no one's crystal ball is clear enough to show where or when this growth will level off. The left itself is close to 46 percent of the electorate. This unprecedented level is heady stuff for those Socialists who now insist that the strategy to be pursued is not the Historic Compromise but the Socialist Alternative to give Italy a Communist-Socialist government. So far at least, PCI is having none of that.

At the same time, the secular parties have collectively suffered catastrophic declines. The Liberals seem on the verge of extinction; the Social Democrats are at their lowest ebb ever; and the Republicans still hold on to a modicum of influence, although they represent only 3 percent of the electorate.

The DC was able to hold on to its plurality in the last elections because it attracted votes from the minor parties and from the Monarchists and neo-Fascists on the extreme right. Of the 17.2 million votes that went to the so-called center in 1976, 14.2 million belong to the DC; of the 17.1 million votes that went to the left, 12.6 million belong to the PCI. Together with the Socialists (PSI), these two parties make up about 83 percent of the Italian electorate. (See Table 1 for a clearer picture of these electoral proportions.) This alone suggests that the political future of Italy turns strongly on the accommodations or understandings that can be worked out among these three parties.

Each party is of course groping for some acceptable formula, and I will return to this problem in my concluding observations. For the moment, it is necessary to recognize that the PCI is knocking insistently at the door of formal power. It believes that it is entitled to power and is destined to get it one way or another—probably before the decade is over. Many people believe this step is inevitable, although many of them also view such a transformation with considerable trepidation.[6] Indeed, trepidation is apparent within the PCI itself, reflecting the fact that this step would carry considerable risks for the party as well.

Very much in the minds of PCI leaders these days are questions about *how* to share power, *when* to take each step along the route to power, and what the *consequences* will be to the party. These queries are certainly not new. But they are given dramatic and urgent salience by electoral results that the Communists themselves did not anticipate. Be-

[6] The best data and analysis on general attitudes toward PCI and its coming to power is supplied by Giacomo Sani, "Ricambio elettorale e identificazioni partitiche," *Rivista italiana di scienza politica,* vol. 5 (1975), pp. 516–544; and his "Generations and Politics in Italy," paper presented to the Seminar on the Italian Crisis, Turin, Fondazione Luigi Einaudi, March 24–27, 1977.

TABLE 1

DISTRIBUTION OF VOTES AND SEATS, CHAMBER OF DEPUTIES, 1972 AND 1976, BY POLITICAL PARTY

Party[a]	1972 Election				1976 Election			
	Votes	Percent	Seats	Percent	Votes	Percent	Seats	Percent
DP	224,313	0.7	—	—	557,025	1.5	6	0.9
PCI	9,068,961	27.1	179	28.4	12,614,650	34.4	228	36.3
PSIUP	648,591	1.9	—	—	—	—	—	—
PSI	3,208,497	9.6	61	9.7	3,540,309	9.6	57	9.1
PR	—	—	—	—	394,439	1.1	5	0.6
Other left	235,175	0.7	—	—	26,748	0.1	—	—
Total left	13,385,537	40.0	240	38.1	17,133,171	46.7	296	46.9
PSDI	1,718,142	5.1	29	4.6	1,239,492	3.4	15	2.4
PRI	954,357	2.9	15	2.4	1,135,546	3.1	14	2.2
DC	12,912,466	38.7	266	42.0	14,209,519	38.7	262	41.6
PLI	1,300,439	3.9	20	3.2	480,122	1.3	5	0.8
Other center	187,757	0.6	4	0.8	208,466	0.6	3	0.5
Total center	17,073,161	51.2	334	53.0	17,273,145	47.1	299	47.5
MSI-DN	2,894,722	8.7	56	8.9	2,238,339	6.1	35	5.6
Other	50,128	0.1	—	—	62,923	0.1	—	—
Total	33,403,548	100.0	630	100.0	36,707,578	100.0	630	100.0

SOURCE: *La Stampa*, May 23, 1976; *Corriere della Sera*, May 23, 1976; data provided by Alberto Spreafico.

[a] The list of abbreviations in the front of the book identifies each party.

cause of this, the electoral setback suffered by PCI in the geographically limited local election of 1978 provides that party with an opportunity for sober reflection. Beyond the party's own strategy, changes at work in Italian society seem destined to strengthen the PCI beyond its own fondest hopes. Reviewing some aspects of PCI's postwar orientation to Italian society as well as some of the major social changes will help to clarify the situation.

The Strategy of the Italian Communists

PCI's major postwar preoccupation has been how to come successfully to power in Italy.[7] The countless dimensions of this problem have been discussed endlessly, sometimes with abstruse and arcane hairsplitting over the meaning of Lenin and Gramsci or the requirements of an updated Marxism in the Italian context. Often, the differences of opinion within PCI can run very deep. These divisions are much more apparent today when the prospect of sharing formal power is palpable and when the party itself is much more open about some of its internal dissension.

If the mark of a democratic socialist party were simply and only the renunciation of violence as the means to power, then the PCI qualified on that score as early as 1944. It was then that Palmiro Togliatti returned to Italy from the Soviet Union, bringing the concept of the "New Party." Although this was a party prepared to renounce violence and to substitute Gramsci's idea of "working-class hegemony" for the "dictatorship of the proletariat," it was still to be considered a Marxist-Leninist party.

PCI's insistence that Gramsci's ideas are still valid is a source of considerable disquietude. Many people find it difficult to reconcile Lenin and Gramsci with the support and maintenance of liberal democratic institutions. Italian Communists find this disquietude somewhat irritating; they lose no opportunity to underscore that Lenin himself insisted that Marxism was not to be used as a straitjacket to limit the theory and practice of revolutionary change.[8]

Togliatti's prescriptions were relatively clear, and they have been continually elaborated upon, during his lifetime and after. The most important of these prescriptions for the PCI may be summarized as the following imperatives:

- Renounce violent seizure as the means to obtain power in Italy.

---

[7] On the PCI strategy, see Donald L. M. Blackmer, *Unity in Diversity: Italian Communism and the Communist World* (Cambridge, Mass.: M.I.T. Press, 1968); and Arrigo Levi, *PCI—La lunga marcia verso il potere* (Milan: Etas Kompass, 1971).

[8] For some recent examples, consult the special section in *Unità,* April 24, 1977, commemorating the fortieth anniversary of the death of Antonio Gramsci.

- Avoid at all cost a direct confrontation with the Catholic Church. Eschew anticlericalism; seek an accommodation with the Catholic hierarchy.
- Avoid sectarianism and isolation in politics and society. Seek points of communication, accommodation, and common action with other groups, including segments of the middle class.
- Play a major role in shaping the institutions of the democratic republic. Be prepared to accept these institutions, to operate within them, and to defend them against attack and erosion.
- Avoid contributing to the reemergence or growth of a strong right-wing political movement.
- Press for fundamental social and economic transformations and bring the pressure of public opinion and popular organizations to bear in favor of them. Do not be too specific, however, about the content of these reforms before the party comes to power.[9]

These imperatives provide the foundation for much of PCI's behavior during the last three decades. To be sure, that behavior has not always been consistent. Furthermore, the PCI strategy was greatly complicated in the years of the cold war. Over and over again in those years the PCI revealed a degree of identification with the Soviet Union that seemed at odds with its claims of autonomy, polycentrism, and the "Italian way" to the socialist state. The question of PCI autonomy is still very much on the table, if not in Italy then certainly elsewhere in the West where there is concern about the international implications of the PCI in power.

During the years of the Marshall Plan and the advent of international agreements like the North Atlantic Treaty Organization (NATO) or the European Common Market, PCI's domestic and internal strategy was often conditioned by outside events. The party could not easily follow its own organizational code, given its ties to the international Communist movement and the complicating circumstances of highly tense and strained East-West relations. Despite these complications, the PCI was able to adhere remarkably well to the strategy laid down by Togliatti. Elements of that strategy were themselves conditioned by the international power configuration at the end of World War II. However much Italians may have feared it (or some Stalinists desired it), the probability that PCI would follow the February 1948 Czechoslovakian scenario was very low indeed.

[9] On this specific and important point, see Stephen Hellman, "The PCI in Transition: The Origins of the Historic Compromise," paper presented to the annual meeting of the American Political Science Association, Chicago, September 1976.

The New Party strategy was also a reflection of PCI's sober ruminations on its earlier failure to contain the spread of fascism. The parties of the left had been unable to assess the potential of fascism correctly and could not come together in time to defeat it. The strategy was deeply influenced as well by the writings of Antonio Gramsci. If the "dictatorship of the proletariat" is to be replaced by "working-class hegemony," as Gramsci insisted, an extraordinary amount of Communist preparation would be required to achieve leadership in every possible sector of culture and society. Thus the PCI sought alliance with other groups and classes and developed the important concept of *presenza*—its presence in the basic social, political, and economic institutions of society. Moral authority and guiding political leadership cannot be achieved without this presence; nor can the democratic institutions of the republic be fully legitimized without it.[10]

This basic operational code of the PCI has guided its orientation to Italian society. It would be easy to pile up evidence in support of this assertion; a few examples will have to suffice.

The Catholic Church. Togliatti set the pattern for relations with the Catholic Church when, under his direction, the PCI accepted the Lateran Pact of 1929 and permitted the Concordat to be enshrined in the Italian Constitution. Over the years the Church hierarchy, not PCI, posed the "Christ or Communism" alternative, an appeal that has failed to impress more than one-third of the electorate in an overwhelmingly Catholic country. The Church itself has backed away fom its own rigid posture, although there was some attempt to reassert it in the 1976 campaign. Some observers would in fact argue that without Church opposition PCI would now be the leading party in Italy.

The PCI has responded by insisting on the inviolability of freedom of conscience. It has left the more virulent forms of anticlericalism to the minor secular parties and to the Socialists. It has insisted that the need for fundamental reforms of Italian society can and must be divorced from religious belief and practice. The party has actually championed the integrity of the nuclear family. It was not the Communists who pressed for the law authorizing divorce, nor did the party favor the referendum on divorce. Along with the Vatican it feared that the confrontation might permanently fracture a delicate balance. In any case, PCI believed it would create unpredictable difficulties for the party's relation to its own militants and electorate. In 1974 it failed to realize how profoundly Italian society—and therefore Italian Catholicism—had changed.

[10] For a basic explication of this view, see Luciano Gruppi, "L'esigenza di una nuova guida," *Rinascita,* vol. 33 (December 17, 1976), p. 3.

Nor has the party been at the forefront of the campaign for a liberalized abortion law. With some justification, the laical parties pressing for very liberal legislation accuse the PCI of opportunism and duplicity. On the one hand, it wishes not to antagonize the Catholic Church and will therefore work to bring amendments that would make an abortion law less unpalatable to ardent Catholics. On the other hand, as in the case of the referendum on divorce, it wishes to share with the other secular parties whatever glory may be forthcoming for having helped make Italy more "modern."

That the PCI has not wanted to instigate head-on collision with the Catholic world is eminently apparent in the rationale Enrico Berlinguer provides for the proposed Historic Compromise. If and when an out-and-out collision does occur, PCI will want it to be clear that the provocation is on the other side.

The Middle Classes. The PCI considers class-war postures such as those taken by the French Communists to be hopelessly sectarian, doctrinaire, and counterproductive. Not class war but interclass struggles against exploitative and monopolistic capitalism has been its byword. Working-class hegemony requires that alliances be formed in which the working class and its leaders will show the way to greater equity and justice for everyone.

PCI has had to overcome sectarianism within its own ranks in order to implement this aspect of its strategy. The left within the party has always wondered where these alliances would stop. It has not been reassured by recent tendencies for other wings of the party and for its central leadership to effect a working alliance with the Christian Democrats. The party's history in implementing its alliance strategy has not been marked by internal consensus or enlightenment. For example, it was several years following World War II before the party could crank up an effective campaign for approaching the southern Italian peasantry.[11] Gramsci was an important influence here as well: he had understood as early as Mao the possible value of a backward and even "reactionary" peansantry in accelerating fundamental change. The PCI's success in the South is now underscored by the fact that the party's appeal there is no longer radically less than in other regions. Gains registered in the South in recent years have made the PCI a truly national party and, like the DC, a force to be reckoned with everywhere.

The party has also consistently sought to appeal to small agricultural landowners, artisans, small merchants and industrialists, white-collar workers, and above all the new "middle-class proletarians" that have been

---

[11] See Sidney Tarrow, *Peasant Communism.*

added to the ranks of the traditional middle class. The PCI views the "advanced industrial society" that has developed in Italy as containing large areas of discontent and alienation—important reservoirs that can be tapped for additional voters. To appeal to these categories, the party is aware that it must avoid the entrapments of vulgar Marxism. For this reason it has prevailed on the French Communists to modify their rhetoric and give up such frightening phrases as the "dictatorship of the proletariat." For this reason, too, it has supported Mario Soares in Portugal and has expressed disagreement with the posture and behavior of Cunhal and the Portuguese Communists. More than being embarrassed by marked evidence of Stalinism, even when manifested outside its own ranks, the PCI seems genuinely to believe that the strategy that works in Italy will probably work as well elsewhere in the Mediterranean area.

In its defense of some middle-class sectors, the PCI finds justification in political economy. In Italy's dual economy the less modern sectors display an astonishing amount of dynamism, and small businesses and artisans contribute prominently to production. These sectors not only help to keep the economy above water in these unusually difficult times, but they also absorb unemployment, thereby relieving some of the pressures that threaten to shred the delicate fabric of Italian democracy.

Political Institutions. By and large the attitude of the PCI toward the basic political institutions of the republic has not been one of *tanto peggio, tanto meglio* ("so much the worse, so much the better"). Indeed, it has been a staunch defender of the Constitution, wasting no time at all in underscoring the many ways in which the government has ignored or violated it over the years. The party has been a strong advocate of reforming the national Parliament to make it more effective in initiating and setting policy. In addition the PCI has been the prime force pushing the government to implement the constitutional provision for the establishment of regional governments and the devolution of certain powers to them.

It is easy to belittle the PCI's efforts here, to put them down as cynical, opportunistic, or self-serving. For example, the PCI initially opposed regional devolution of governmental powers but later championed this cause because devolution would give the PCI greater control in the geographical areas where it is the dominant political force. For another example, the PCI concern with making Parliament more powerful may be a response to the successful Christian Democrat campaign to shift many economic powers away from Parliament and into public and semipublic bodies colonized by the Christian Democrats themselves. The Communists are outspokenly critical and unhappy about this shift; if Parliament had more power, so, through it, would the PCI. It may be, as Di

Palma says, that the PCI plays the parliamentary game because it is the only game in town.[12] It is nevertheless important to add that PCI has played the game straight, and in doing so has indeed played a major role in legitimizing democratic institutions.

PCI has also advocated the reform of public institutions such as the judiciary and sectors of the bureaucracy. It has been a major force in bringing about reforms of the penal and civil codes, the law on families, the basic law governing the rights of workers, and other legislation. More recently, it has shown great concern about the need for assuring more effective democratic control over the armed forces and more democratic procedures within the armed forces. It has demanded large-scale renovation of Italy's police system, but it has also come unflinchingly to the defense of the police in the face of the increasing number of disorders that they are called on to quell, at great risk to life and limb. Furthermore, in the face of physical terror and murder, the PCI is capable of reversing itself, as it recently did in campaigning against the abrogation of police powers it earlier condemned as repressive.

Again, one can say that talk is cheap; and the PCI can indulge in the luxury of offering constructive criticism from the outside as long as it does not have the responsibility of governing and as long as it can follow (as it certainly does) the Togliatti stricture against showing too much of its basic policy stance before coming to power. Or one can take the most cynical view of all, that is, that PCI supports Italian democracy because it represents a *necessary* condition for the party's peaceful accession to power, after which freedom will disappear. Although many people, in and out of Italy, deny this underlying assumption about PCI motivation, the assumption is nevertheless there more often than not.[13] Regardless of what its motivation may be, however, I wish simply to establish that on the whole the postwar behavior of the PCI has tended to strengthen and to legitimize the basic institutions of Italian democracy.

Trade Unions and Other Mass Organizations. Trade unions, student movements, extraparliamentary radical groups, and parties to its left—even Italy's aggressively liberal women—constitute extremely baffling dilemmas for the PCI. The growth of parties to its left proves in part that some Italians want to implement the more fiery and revolutionary preachings of the PCI as opposed to its statements of reason and accommodation.

---

[12] Di Palma, *Surviving without Governing.*

[13] For a hair-raising scenario of what disasters might befall Italy were the PCI to come to share formal power, see Giovanni Sartori, "I comunisti al potere, e dopo?" *Biblioteca della libertà,* vol. 11 (July–August 1974), pp. 92–98. See also his chapter in the present volume.

For a short time following the heated-up political climate of the late 1960s, it appeared that the PCI might be able to bring most of the radicalized students (and trade unionists) into line, thereby defusing the kind of volatile behavior that frightens the PCI, precisely because it is outside PCI control.

The party did succeed in reintegrating some of the dissident student groups, and that trend might have persisted except for the rise of large-scale unemployment, especially among intellectuals. PCI leaders are now increasingly unwelcome among student groups, which view the party, with justification, as a force for law and order, opposed to wild political adventures, and in favor of gradual change—all postures that are consistent with PCI's concept of the long march to power. The greatest fear of PCI leaders is that uncontrolled, accelerating terror and violence will provide the ground (or the excuse) for destroying the very democratic system they have long considered essential to their own political ambitions. This is the key reason for their insistence that the government remain absolutely uncompromising regarding Red Brigade demands on the occasion of Moro's kidnapping and murder.

The trade unions may be even more perplexing than the student and radical groups, or women's movements. In an earlier period PCI, following a Leninist concept of the role of trade unions, considered its auxiliary, the Italian General Confederation of Labor (CGIL), to be essentially a "transmission belt" for the political will of the party. For a number of reasons, party control over the CGIL later attenuated, although the topmost leaders of the confederation (which encompasses both Communists and Socialist workers) remain overwhelmingly Communist.

The expansion of trade union autonomy was spurred by a number of concurrent developments, not all of which were anticipated by the PCI. (1) The movement to reunite the fragmented labor movement (something the PCI itself had long advocated) began to pick up steam. (2) The Italian Confederation of Free Trade Unions (CISL) began to assert even more independence from the Christian Democratic party than the CGIL did from the PCI. (3) Important segments of all labor confederations (including the Socialist, Social Democratic, and Socialist-Republican UIL) began to radicalize. The so-called hot autumn of 1969 is a benchmark. In Italy more than anywhere else, the events of the late 1960s have had enduring effects on student movements, extraparliamentary opposition groups, and the trade unions. (4) The trade unions now not only claim independence from party interference, they also insist on acting as separate interlocutors in the political process, with full rights to negotiate with government, organized business, the bureaucracy, and the political parties themselves regarding a broad spectrum of political programs. The PCI is deeply opposed to such corporative tendencies, but to maintain its image it must move with great care to try to moderate extreme demands and to reestablish more effective control over at least its sector of the trade union movement.

The tension between the PCI and CGIL is well known. Luciano Lama, who heads CGIL and is trying to bring the unions more to heel, implicitly acknowledged this in an interview.[14] Trade union autonomy, he cautioned, is acceptable as long as it is limited to a "division of labor" between party and unions. It is *not* acceptable when the unions go beyond this limitation to become the direct protagonists of social transformation. In effect, Lama does not want CGIL to replace PCI or to crowd it. This view is in sharp contrast with those of Bruno Trentin, one of the most popular Communist trade union leaders and a formidable theoretician. Addressing the sixteenth CGIL metalworkers' congress at Bologna on May 15, 1977, he urged that the trade unions rise above their "contractual" (that is, collective bargaining) framework and move ahead to negotiate with major agencies of the state across the broadest possible policy spectrum. Trentin added, however, that negotiations are different from policies and that the policies must be established by the parties. This was Trentin's swan song to the radical, avant-garde metalworkers. His "promotion" to the general CGIL secretariat is widely interpreted as bringing him under more effective control by the central party.[15]

The basic decision to bring PCI more directly into the trade union movement is signaled by Gianni Cervetti, considered by many to be Berlinguer's heir apparent.[16] The difficulty, of course, is that the PCI does not control the Christian Democratic trade unions, and neither does the DC.

The Christian Democrats are destined to experience much more trouble bringing discipline to CISL. Both the party and the labor confederation are ideologically fragmented, and the DC cannot have recourse to anything like democratic centralism. Pierre Carniti (who headed the CISL metalworkers and is as able as Trentin but even more radical in his trade union views) will not tame easily—even though he was "promoted" to the CISL general secretariat in 1976. Benvenuto, the third member of the famous metalworker triumvirate, now heads UIL. It is debatable whether the PSI can discipline him, even if the party wished to do so. An interesting question is what it may mean for Italy's national trade union movement that unusually able leaders like Trentin, Carniti, and Benvenuto are now sitting at headquarters. This is one area in Italian society where the dragon seeds PCI has sown are coming to harvest.

---

[14] *Unità,* December 19, 1976, pp. 1, 11.

[15] See *Unità,* May 16, 1977, p. 2; *Corriere della Sera,* May 17, 1977, p. 1.

[16] See his important speech to the PCI Central Committee, carried in *Unità,* December 14, 1976, pp. 1, 9, 10.

Italian Society and Italian Communists

No matter how single-minded, tightly organized, and well led a party may be, its march to power can never be entirely a function of its wisdom, will, or operational code. Chance, for example, will not be denied. In a more inexorable way, neither will history. What happens in society will test the capacity of a party to adapt, to capitalize on unanticipated opportunities, or merely to survive. Given a power-seeking party of a particular level of skill and determination, factors in the environment, if they are recognized, can make that quest relatively easy or impossibly arduous.

PCI is widely acclaimed one of the most able—perhaps the most able—of nonruling Communist parties. It is often compared with the French Communist party, which appears still locked in the era of Stalin. When the electoral strength of the Communist and Socialist parties is compared, the PCI appears unique. It is more than three times as strong as the Italian Socialist party, and in the years since 1946 the relative strength of the two parties has been radically reversed. This transformation is surely one of the most interesting, most important, but least explored aspects of postwar Italian politics.

To a surprising degree, the PCI seems to have been caught somewhat flat-footed by a number of social transformations in Italy that help account for its unusual electoral prowess. These transformations, which scholars have documented in great detail, cut across every aspect of Italian society. Only a few of the more important ones will be mentioned here.

Industrialization and Urbanizaton. No country in Europe has seen anything quite like the changes in the basic economic and demographic contours of Italy since 1945. At the end of World War II almost half the Italian labor force was in agriculture; today that sector accounts for only one-sixth of the labor force. The modern industrial sector advanced so rapidly in Italy and its competitive position in world trade became so formidable that in less than two decades the country moved from near destitution to seventh place among the world's most productive and prosperous nations.

Hand in hand with these changes went population movements of unprecedented magnitude. In a near ruinous depopulation of the Italian South, the young and able-bodied departed, leaving behind the very young and the very old to languish. Massive movements of persons from the countryside to the cities were only in part related to industrialization. In the South, cities grew not because industry was developing there but, rather, because people were in search of the services and other amenities of urban centers. In all cases, Italy's cities were not equipped to provide any such thing. The resultant conditions made these urban centers ripe for political radicalization.

Secularization. More rapidly than anyone anticipated, Italy has developed the values of a secular society. The signs have been there for years: the decline of religious practice, the lack of recruits to the priesthood and other religious orders, the softening of anticlericalism, and the attenuation of religious cleavage. Of particular relevance are changes in church-related organizations. First, the once-rich network of Catholic organizations controlled by the Vatican and bishops is clearly in decay. Second, existing Catholic organizations are more independent of the clergy, less easy to control, than was the case in earlier years. Third, some of the Catholic organizations are among the most radicalized groups in Italy and are pursuing policies that are often much to the left of anything the PCI has ever seriously advocated. Others are dissenting Catholics absolutely unprepared to follow direction from the church hierarchy and equally unprepared to give their support to the Christian Democrats.[17] The erosion of this organizational network denied the DC a very strong base of electoral assistance. More important, these groups in the past served to educate younger people in the Catholic and Christian Democratic way.

The Church itself in recent years has contributed to these secular trends. Ecumenism, the liberalization of church doctrines and regulations, and the encouragement of debate and dissent all served as a release valve for many Italians. The bitter comment among many Italians that the real trouble with PCI began when the Pope granted an audience to Khrushchev's son-in-law is a shorthand summary of the Church's contribution to PCI's electoral fortunes.

Educational patterns are also deeply significant here. If the Christian Democrats have colonized the largest banking, insurance, and industrial organizations in the public sector, the left has certainly colonized the schools. Whatever else may be going on in Italy's elementary and secondary schools, the basic values inculcated there are secular. Beyond this, however, is the certain evidence that the most radical students are found not in the universities but in the *liceo,* the upper secondary schools for university-bound students.

[17] The growing independent-mindedness of Catholics reached a dramatic peak in 1976 when a number of prominent Catholics, including the well-known writer and intellectual, Raniero La Valle, and other prominent Catholics agreed to run as "independents" under the PCI banner. PCI allotted 10 percent of its candidate slots to these independents. Through this gesture, it hoped to give some evidence of its pluralism, to improve its credentials for participating in a government of national emergency, and perhaps to communicate to Catholic voters that involvement with Eurocommunism and commitment to the Catholic faith are not antithetical nor incompatible. In any case, the PCI gave very little in return since it did not intend to include these nonparty deputies in the PCI parliamentary group, to say nothing of party councils. See *La Stampa,* May 22, 1976, p. 1; *Corriere della Sera,* November 17, 1976, p. 2.

The universities themselves have undergone some noteworthy transformations. In the early 1950s fewer than 200,000 students were enrolled in Italy's universities; today there are around four times that number. If nothing else were going on at the universities, if they were not the breeding ground of dissension and political extremism they have become (often with good reason), they would still be providing many more Italians than earlier with a much more open, objective, instrumental view of society and polity.

Social Class. Class distinctions are less rigid than before, even though mobility rates have not changed radically. Discourse across class lines is made easier and is in turn translated into an increased disposition of persons to vote for parties that do not "correspond" or do not seem "natural" to their class. Class, in short, is now less a determinant of an Italian's party preference than it once was. Furthermore, the more important deviations are among left-leaners from classes that would be expected to support center or right-wing parties. If one could once count on a middle-class Catholic's *not* voting for PCI, that is a significantly less safe bet today.

What Italians learn about politics and society, where and when they learn it, and how that learning proceeds have thus undergone profound change. Not only have the more traditional teaching institutions like the family, Church, and school been transformed, but they also encounter much more competition. Some of it comes from neighboring groups, new militant organizations, or mass movements. Some is from revolutionary changes in the communications media. Italians may not read very much, but they are among the most avid moviegoers in the world. They are also addicted to television, a medium whose political implications in Italy were understood from the start by Amintore Fanfani. There is little doubt that the Italian mass media in recent years have been a major factor in bringing about modified perceptions and evaluations of the Italian Communists.[18]

[18] The treatment of PCI by the Italian press has some disquieting aspects. Except for those newspapers that are clearly right of center, identified with the Christian Democrats, or instruments of the radical left, the press has come to treat the Communist party as something of a sacred cow. Assaults by Communist bully boys against political opponents are ignored or played down; the interventionist role of the U.S.S.R. in the Middle East and Africa goes without comment; the party's own extreme intolerance toward its critics is relatively ignored. It may be that the Italian press is trying to make amends for its treatment of PCI during the years of the cold war. The unkindest interpretation, but heard often enough in Italy, is that journalists are past masters at playing the game of the *tessera anticipata,* which means jumping on the bandwagon early enough to cash in on it later. Significantly, in a recent editorial on the question, "Does the Negotiation with the PCI Threaten Liberty?" (*Corriere della Sera,* April 29, 1977, p. 1), the anonymous editorial writer went out of his way to say that the paper had not handled PCI with kid gloves.

Taken together, the factors I have reviewed suggest that the vote for the Italian left, including the Communists, will continue to grow. In part this growth results from people switching from one party to another. But Italy has had relatively little of this sort of floating vote, and switchers can also switch back.

PCI growth also results from new patterns of party identification and support on the part of new voters. As young people enter the electorate and older voters die off, it is possible that the basic electoral alignment will change and remain changed for a very long time. If it is true that what is learned and experienced about politics in one's younger years, and not just one's chronological age, is the prime determinant of party loyalties, there is then strong ground for concluding that the problem of PCI and its march toward power will not go away, however much some might wish that it would.[19]

Italian Communists and Italy's Future

Enrico Berlinguer and his colleagues are well aware of their party's strength, although the electorate in 1975 and 1976 undoubtedly upset their timetable. Some people believe that, had the PCI understood what electoral strides were in store for it, Berlinguer would never have suggested the Historic Compromise in the fall of 1973. This proposal indicated that even if the left were to secure over 50 percent of the votes, it would refuse to come to power alone but would seek a broad alliance of popular forces and democratic parties to govern together to resolve basic problems.

The Historic Compromise was a bombshell that required explanation, and Berlinguer was careful to provide it.[20] He noted that 90 percent of Italy's Catholics are influenced by the Church and that 40 percent of them support the DC. Many of the latter are members of the working class without whose support and collaboration the basic reforms PCI desires for Italy cannot be effected. Furthermore, he argued, it is unlikely that this working-class base of the DC will wither away or be attracted to the left. Beyond this, Berlinguer raised the specter of Chile and its organized

[19] For the basic social factors associated with political attitudes and voting behavior, see Sani's works, cited in note 6 above, and Samuel H. Barnes, "Italy: Religion and Class in Electoral Behavior," in Richard Rose, ed., *Electoral Behavior: A Comparative Handbook* (New York: Free Press, 1974), pp. 171–226.

[20] Berlinguer has many times elaborated on the Historic Compromise. The first piece appeared in *Rinascita,* October 5, 1973, and other commentary on it has appeared in an avalanche of publications. A very good collection of materials is contained in the special issue of *Biblioteca della libertà,* September 1974. See also the important article by Hellman, "The PCI in Transition."

reaction to a leftist government. Rather than risk a similar reaction, prudence required a less drastic and frightening formula in Italy where the danger would be particularly acute because of the imbalance between PCI and PSI electoral strengths.

There is no evidence whatever that the electoral results of 1975 and 1976 have caused Berlinguer to change his mind. On the contrary, on the heels of both these elections he was quick to reiterate that the PCI wants to govern not alone, not with just the Socialists, but in coalition with the parties of the so-called constitutional arc. If he has soft-pedaled the Historic Compromise, it is partly in deference to the Italian Socialists who greatly fear it, partly in deference to those in his own party who distrust it.[21] The fact remains, however, that whether called Historic Compromise, Government of National Emergency, or something else, the issue of formal PCI participation is now on the table. Indeed it was partly resolved in 1978 when Giulio Andreothi's reconstituted government was certified by PCI, as well as DC and other, votes in Parliament.

The possibility of PCI becoming part of the government raises much consternation about the effects this would have on both national and international affairs. One question is where PCI loyalties would lie in the event of strained relations or a confrontation between the NATO and Eastern Bloc countries. To be sure, Berlinguer has said some reassuring things about existing alliances to which Italy is tied, but PCI has been intransigently opposed to NATO until very recently indeed. It was only two years ago that Berlinguer indicated that PCI would make no move to have Italy leave that organization.[22] During the campaign of 1976 PCI echoed this basic point and went on to spell out a considerably modified view of Italy's foreign policy. Interdependence was acknowledged, as well as (more subtly) the PCI belief that NATO would help maintain both the inter-

---

21 For those who still believe the PCI is a monolith, the party's debates and agonies concerning the Historic Compromise should be instructive. Umberto Terracini, one of the party's founders, makes no bones about his opposition to the Historic Compromise as a concept unworthy of a Marxist revolutionary party (*Il Messaggero,* January 15, 1976, p. 1). Those in PCI who are opposed to the Historic Compromise fear that an agreement with the DC will "denature" PCI. Recent meetings of the party's Central Committee have been characterized by lively confrontations between leaders like Umberto Terracini and Luigi Longo, on one side, and Giorgio Amendola on the other. Berlinguer has his work cut out here. See *Corriere della Sera,* November 17, 1976; and Luigi Bianchi, "La prudenza di Berlinguer e la 'fretta' di Amendola," *Corriere della Sera,* September 23, 1976, p. 2. For a highly sensitive treatment of this issue and others, and how they impinge on the PCI's agonizing over strategy, see Peter Lange, "Notes on PCI and Possible Outcomes of Italy's Crisis," paper presented to the Seminar on the Italian Crisis, Turin, Fondazione Luigi Einaudi, March 24–27, 1977.

22 For Berlinguer's basic statement on NATO, as well as other important comments on Italian foreign policy, see A. Tata, ed., *La politica internazionale dei Comunisti italiani, 1975–1976* (Rome: Editori Riuniti, 1976).

national and the internal domestic equilibrium against possible interventions from Moscow.[23]

So far PCI has provided only words, although no one should minimize how profoundly they differ from words of the past. Nevertheless, those Italians and others interested in deeds remain perplexed, particularly when what Berlinguer may say today one of his colleagues (Lombardo Radice, for example) may deny tomorrow, insisting that if the choice is between Moscow and the capitalist West the PCI will naturally opt for the former. Beyond this quibble is the persistent day-to-day pattern of PCI policy on a wide spectrum of international problems in which East and West are involved. PCI treatment of the problems of the Middle East and of Africa convinces some that identification with the U.S.S.R. remains very strong indeed. It could not be otherwise, as Giorgio Amendola, a leading advocate of this party's opening to the West, has had to point out.[24]

Consternation about whether the PCI would abandon the European Economic Community (EEC) seems immensely less justified. The *engrenage* or meshing of Italy with the rest of the EEC runs too deep.[25]

[23] Robert Putnam, "Italian Foreign Policy: The Emergent Consensus," in Howard Penniman, ed., *Italy at the Polls* (Washington, D.C.: American Enterprise Institute, 1978), pp. 287–326, suggests that it is in PCI's self-interest to maintain NATO, but leaves unanswered many questions of the impact on NATO of PCI in power in Italy. For example, both Alberto Ronchey and Aldo Rizzo specifically note the differences between PCI generalizations about NATO and the stand its official organs take on concrete issues. See *Corriere della Sera,* March 3, 1976, p. 1, and September 23, 1976, p. 1; *La Stampa,* October 10, 1976, p. 1.

[24] In February 1977 an editorial by Alberto Ronchey, "Waiting for the PCI," provoked an interesting exchange with Giorgio Amendola. Ronchey asked about the PCI's seeming contradictions—its attachment to Lenin and pluralism, its identification with NATO and the U.S.S.R., its commitment to democracy for Italy but democratic centralism for itself. Amendola replied that the PCI is prepared to assume governing responsibility on the basis of agreements among parties as to program, but that it doesn't have to make itself more "presentable" to others. He reminded Ronchey that the DC needs the PCI in order to be able to govern at all, and he expressed anger over the suggestion that PCI's denial of Gransci's ideas is a necessary condition for its acceptability. Amendola pointed out that the PCI has criticized the Soviet Union many times, as well as other East European regimes, but he added: "We do not want to transform criticism into agitation, and thereby break the relationships of fraternity and solidarity that tie us to the Soviet Communists, and to an international movement that no longer has a recognized center at Moscow or anywhere . . . but which nevertheless brings together a number of universal experiences in the battle for peace and socialism." As for democratic centralism, the PCI is simply not going to fall into the trap of permitting itself to be rent by factions, which is why the DC fears entering into an alliance with the PCI. See *Corriere della Sera,* February 6, 12, and 13, 1977, for the signed articles by Ronchey and Amendola.

[25] One does not have to be a World Federalist or believe in a European superstate to recognize that the *engrenage* of economic interdependence is exceedingly binding. Even the British, late and reluctant comers to the EEC though they have been, are beginning to understand this.

Equally deep are Italian feelings about the Treaty of Rome and the concept of Europe. Despite what is said at Brussels about Italian noncompliance with EEC regulations and directives, no country has remained as steadfastly committed to the ideas of Jean Monnet or Artiero Spinelli. Even those Italians who support the PCI have come around to strong favorable views of the EEC. As Robert Putnam correctly notes, in this area PCI leadership may well be chasing after its own members and voters.[26]

Apart from consternation about international affairs, a more immediate concern to the average Italian is what life would be like in Italy if and when the PCI becomes a formal part of the government. If there are millions of Italians who might view that prospect with equanimity or even enthusiasm, there remain millions more who clearly do not. Of course negative feelings about PCI have been greatly attenuated in recent years.[27] It could not be otherwise given the kinds of things I have reviewed in this paper, and given the critically important factor of international détente. But individuals—men and women in public life, in the intellectual and academic communities, in industry, the trade unions, and the professions—worry about what might happen "after." They do not refer to Stalinism; few serious-minded Italians believe that PCI in power would quickly force out other parties and install an East European type of regime. People are worried about jobs, property, pressures to conform, arrogance, control of the mass media, political dissent, the police, and orchestrated elections. They are clearly also worried about a reign of international terror that might be unleashed against Italy if the Communists are brought into the government. It should be added that the Communists worry about that too.

Of more basic internal concern are the apparent ambiguities in what PCI leaders themselves say about their party and about their orientation to the Italian political system. What does it mean, for example, to say that once the parties of the working classes are elected to power it would be unthinkable for them to give it up again?[28] How can a party claim simultaneously to be a Leninist party, committed to the revolutionary transformation of society (however peacefully or gradually) but also a force for law, order, and the preservation of democratic liberties in society?

PCI leaders show impatience and irritation with questions such as

---

[26] For an interesting discussion of this aspect of PCI and Italian foreign policy, see Putnam, "Italian Foreign Policy."

[27] Samuel H. Barnes and Giacomo Sani have collected interesting data on the transformations of attitudes toward the PCI and reactions to the prospect of PCI sharing governmental power. See references to these authors above and in chapter 4.

[28] In *Unità,* January 15, 1976, p. 3; it is difficult to tell whether the writer means to say that no working-class party worth its salt would lose its power *in a free election,* or something else.

these.[29] Sometimes this is entirely justified. Visceral, knee-jerk anticommunism is often at the root of these queries. Even worse, the questions are raised most insistently by the crassest, most cynical political opportunists, whose own commitment to democratic values is very much in doubt. Nevertheless, it is vitally important for PCI leaders themselves to recognize that many of these questions are genuine and sincere and that PCI itself continues to provide ample reasons for asking "Will the real Italian Communist party please stand up?"

As often as not, the reply would be that PCI is what one sees, that its basic character and commitment remain today what they have been in the past. The latest litany may be merely a rhetorical device, designed to reassure those within PCI ranks who are fearful and restive about "revisionism." Indeed, one certain consequence of the recent upsurge in its electoral strength is that the PCI must now cope with supporters whose ideologies and values are considerably more diverse than was ever true of party members in the past. For a Marxist party whose core of followers is scarcely ecumenically minded, pleasing everyone takes on unusual poignancy.

The main issue remains whether the same party can be Leninist, subscribe to democratic centralism and to Gramsci's conception of working-class hegemony, and also be committed to political pluralism. While this is not the place to begin a detailed exploration of this issue,[30] I for one doubt that this is possible. Establishing that this is impossible is increasingly difficult given the confusion that has come to surround the concept of pluralism itself.[31] Like so many other words used in politics and the social sciences, "pluralism" can now be used to stand for one particular kind of political system as well as its exact opposite. In any event, many people in Italy—including many Italian Socialists—are still hoping to get from PCI a more satisfactory answer to the basic question posed by

[29] A good example of PCI impatience is Amendola's exchange with Ronchey, cited above. Another is Paolo Buffalini's piece on "Gramsci, the Italian Way to Socialism, and the Revolution in the West," *Unità,* April 24, 1977, p. 3, which gives a good summary of the major phases in the evolution of PCI's operational strategy. Berlinguer himself can bring discussions about PCI's credibility or acceptability to a pause with comments such as "without us it is not possible for the country to get out of crisis. Rather it will be taken directly to the precipice" (*Il Giorno,* May 17, 1976, p. 1).

[30] I have treated some aspects of how one can develop quite distorted views of conceptual meanings and empirical realities in my "Monoliths and Plural Systems: Through Conceptual Lenses Darkly," *Studies in Comparative Communist Systems,* vol. 8 (Autumn 1975), pp. 305–332.

[31] See Joseph LaPalombara, "Political Participation as an Analytical Concept in Comparative Politics" in S. Verba and L. Pye, eds., *Political Participation in Comparative Perspective* (Stamford, Conn.: Greylock Press, 1978).

Norberto Bobbio some time ago: "How do you accommodate or integrate 'pluralism' in your cultural and political traditions?"[32]

It is entirely possible that events will outrace PCI's own propensity to offer further clarification. Certainly it is unlikely that PCI will have the time to demonstrate by deed (for example, in the centralism within its own structure) that its concept of pluralism is not as alien to Western political thought as some suspect. As I write these concluding lines, PCI is part of Italy's parliamentary majority, and the Communists, Socialists, and Christian Democrats are engaged in the most delicate maneuvers and negotiations to find a commonly acceptable next president of the Republic. Around this issue turn many of the fears and aspirations that Italy's political leaders, as well as the public, express regarding PCI's role in the nation's governance.

These are difficult and weighty matters. If Italy's current political plight is grave, the parties that have mismanaged the country for thirty years are largely responsible. If PCI looks more appealing than ever before, it is in part because it easily stands comparison with the other parties.

The principal actor in Italy's postwar governmental evolution has been the Christian Democratic party. When difficulties reach crisis level, it is easy to make the DC exclusively responsible for political and governmental failures.[33] But if the center-left has failed, the PSI must be willing to accept its share of responsibility. Similarly, if many aspects of Italian politics have worked well, if there are striking postwar achievements that one can identify, these things too evolved under hegemonic DC control.

Having said this, I must add that, for many, Italy's chief political party problem today is not the PCI but the DC. The prevailing picture of the DC is of a party ridden by faction, addicted to clientelistic politics, morally eroded and publicly discredited by scandal and corruption, incapable of providing the nation with coherent leadership, held together by a desire for power and the increasingly watery cement of Catholicism.

Beyond this, two telling points are made. First, even in the midst of the latest and most drastic crisis, the DC seems to put its own welfare (that is, the preservation of the DC) above the welfare of the nation. Second, the DC's propensity to promise its own internal reform and rejuvenation

---

[32] Norberto Bobbio's writings have triggered a great deal of often heated response in the pages of *Mondo Operaio*. Bobbio's four basic articles appeared in *La Stampa*: "What is Pluralism?" (September 21, 1976, p. 3); "How to Understand Pluralism" (September 22, 1976, p. 3); "Marx, a Pluralist?" (November 28, 1976, p. 3); "To Be Free Today" (December 1, 1976, p. 3).

[33] A revealing article on the efforts of the DC to renew itself is Gianfranco Pasquino, "Transformazioni nel sistema di potere della democrazia cristiana," paper presented to the Seminar on the Italian Crisis, Turin, Fondazione Luigi Einaudi, March 24–27, 1977.

is exceeded only by its failure to perform on these promises. Few Italians believe it will be much different this time around. Furthermore, a party that has most consistently wounded a fragile democracy cannot forever keep sounding the alarm and making it appear that the blame lies elsewhere.

Judgments like these may be unduly harsh. Some in the DC are today strongly committed to party reform. Andreotti himself managed to bring about an austerity program of unprecedented severity. This achievement would be inconceivable without the collaboration of the PCI. It is even more difficult to maintain in the face of the loss of Aldo Moro and the resignation of President Leone in the midst of growing political scandal.

Even more foreboding are those elements within the DC which are working toward an early confrontation with the PCI—perhaps even a quick dissolution of Parliament and elections designed to compel the Italian voters to say whether they *really* mean it about supporting the PCI. They are encouraged in this by the results of local elections—involving only ten percent of the electorate—in the spring of 1978. Presumably, a diminution of PCI electoral appeal on a national scale would reestablish the old equilibrium and give the DC more time to reform. This kind of reasoning carries the very highest risk of misadventure. Furthermore, it shares with the Socialist Alternative an overriding defect: it would launch Italy on exactly that experiment in parliamentary government (majority rule, loyal opposition, alternation of majority and minority) which the country is least prepared to accept, culturally or psychologically.

In the short and medium term, the workable solution appears to be the umbrella. Some formula must be found that permits the PCI to stand under it with the others and eventually to participate in the cabinet. If there are concerns about the domestic or international implications of PCI in power, it does not seem to me that these are likely to be most effectively relieved by a system of alternation that might bring the left to power alone in Italy.

The basic issue here is not the preservation of this or that Italian political party. It is the preservation of the system itself.

6

Eurocommunism in Limbo

Enzo Bettiza

When the phenomenon of Western Communism—different from the Eastern version in its political strategy and ideology—first aroused interest on both sides of the Atlantic, commentators did not know whether to call it "Neocommunism" or "Eurocommunism." After a short period of uncertainty, the second term prevailed. It had been coined by a heretic well known to the Russians, the Yugoslav political journalist Frane Barbieri, in Milan's *Giornale Nuovo,* June 26, 1975. Nearly a year later its worldwide use was backed and legitimized by those most directly interested, that is, the Italian, French, and Spanish Communist parties, which assimilated the term cautiously and with great propagandistic skill. Still in quotation marks, the word "Eurocommunism" first appeared in the official lexicon of the Italian Communist party (PCI) in Enrico Berlinguer's speech on June 3, 1976, the day before the first mass joint meeting in Paris of the Italian and French parties. Ramon Tamames, a member of the Spanish Communist party board, and also a possible successor of Carrillo, declared in the magazine *Opinion* that the expression invented by Barbieri would reach the same historical and symbolic peaks as did Churchill's "iron curtain" and Lippmann's "cold war" after 1945.

Origins of the Concept of Eurocommunism

I think it useful and fair to refer to Barbieri himself who, two years later, was prompted to explain the origin of the famous neologism. He said he had turned to the word "Eurocommunism" to counteract other ambiguous expressions currently used, like "neocommunism." Eurocommunism, he thought, was definite from the geographical point of view, and indefinite from the ideological viewpoint. Neocommunism sounded to him ideologically more precise, and therefore too binding, for a flow-ing, elusive event, whereas Eurocommunism neither denied an ideological component, nor exaggerated it.

This explanation indicates that the neologism was intended to be restrictive. If it has since acquired an extensive ideological gloss, its ideological substance is still unknown. The subtle Italian propagandists of Eurocommunism have manipulated the formula with the help of many authoritative French, Spanish, English, and American newspapers, which have granted a remarkable opening of ideological credit to PCI, PCF, and PCE's *declarations* (rather than to their acts). Almost nobody remembers that fifty years ago Karl Kautsky classified social democracy—still in Marxist terms—by making a subtle but crucial distinction between a "revolutionary party," and a "party making revolutions."

For diplomatic reasons, the three Eurocommunist parties are today very reticent in their theoretical reflections about the Russian revolution and revolutions in general. Therefore, I shall try to define these parties on the basis of their *omissions* rather than on the ground of their elusive statements. The Italian, French, and Spanish Communist parties are revolutionary parties in a historical and sociological context far different and far removed from that of 1917 Russia. They have therefore rejected the Russian-style revolutionary pattern, that is, the seizure of power through armed revolt or a *coup d'état*. Nevertheless, these parties have never denied their constant aspiration for a final, not necessarily violent, revolution. In their refined and complex political strategy—full of pauses, silences, and compromises—the revolution will be fully accomplished *after* the long march through society and its democratic institutions, a march designed to end in the peaceful ascent to power. Barring the unexpected, power must not be conquered by force. The conquest has to be made patiently and gradually, in such a way that the preexisting power structure, progressively dismantled from inside, will break open nearly spontaneously.

In analyzing the phenomenon in greater depth, a distinction can be made between a new hypothetical form of Western Communism (that still does not exist concretely) and the reality of a new pathway to Communism in the West, whose best example is the Italian one. The related distinctions are between *pressure* and *aggression*; between *conquest of power* and *ascent to power*; between the old Soviet strategy of *preventive revolution,* which failed in Portugal two years ago, and the new Euro-Latin method of aiming at a *final revolution.* Only in Czechoslovakia in 1948 were the two methods successfully combined in two almost simultaneous moments. There, without the intervention of the Soviet army and seemingly lawfully, Gottwald's Communist party passed from the penetration tactics of the early Kautsky to the "movement war" of Lenin after only a short three-year wait. Another nearly simultaneous interlacing of constitutional legality and revolutionary will also occurred in Chile in 1970–1973. One of the reasons for the failure of the Chilean mixed experiment was that Allende (who was, after all, an amateur, not a technician of Bolshevik-type revolutions) tried to implement illegal radical operations under the cover of constitutional means. He might have succeeded if, instead of representing a minority, he had had 80 percent of the electorate.

In 1977 it is apparent that the Eurocommunists are tied more cautiously than ever to the Kautsky-type, democratic, parliamentary, and electoral strategy. For thirty years this approach has been especially profitable in Italy, where—right next to underdeveloped areas that socioeconomically resemble the Third World more than Europe—there is a society that is incommensurably more sophisticated and articulated than those in Eastern Europe. For many reasons that I shall try to explain later, Italy more than France seems to be the natural greenhouse of Eurocommunism. In the past, Palmiro Togliatti's jesuitical Stalinism was remarkably more advantageous for PCI than was Maurice Thorez's drastic Jacobin Stalinism for the PCF. At present, Berlinguer's sober and soft Eurocommunism keeps on being more useful to PCI than is Georges Marchais's more rough and controversial version for the PCF. In 1946 the party of the Italian left with the greatest electoral strength was not the Communist but the Socialist party. But the march "toward consensus," from Togliatti's soft Stalinism to Berlinguer's disciplined Eurocommunism, has been unceasing.

After the collapse of the Portuguese revolutionary attempt, and in the face of the constant electoral ascent of the French Socialist party, Georges Marchais, whose fortunes are in decline, has little choice. He must either subjugate himself to Berlinguer's cart or abandon the "common program," revert to the Stalinist ghetto (waiting for H-hour), and thus face a double clash with the bourgeoisie as well as with François Mitterand's social-radical amalgam. On the other hand, Santiago Carrillo repeats thirty years later—and in more vulnerable conditions—the same monarchic turn taken by Togliatti at Salerno in 1944. He is deeply interested not only in following the cautious Berlinguerian line but even more in representing its constitutional right wing. For all three—Berlinguer, Marchais, and Carrillo—the negative examples of Portugal and, above all, of Chile are catalysts of the typical "power fear" that seems to emerge from deep inside the Western revolutionary left whenever power comes within reach. (Remember, in this connection, the Hamlet-like behavior of the French Communists during the 1936 Popular Front.)

Let me now confront directly the issue of what is Eurocommunism. Are the legal and peaceful ways employed to slide into power really part of a democratic and "pluralistic" aim? Up to this moment, the natural antagonist of Italian Communism, the Christian Democratic party, has not been able to define the true nature of its opponent. Yet a precise definition of the opponent is urgent, not only for the Christian Democrats but also for Italian society and, I would add, for the whole of Western society as well. A precise definition of Eurocommunism is also needed for the American mass media, which up to now have helped, in naive good faith, to legitimize the image of a new Communism free from all ties with "proletarian internationalism."

Antonio Gramsci and Eurocommunist Strategy

The three most important Western Communist parties will probably continue to improve their technique of painless penetration into their respective societies, provided that the international framework, especially Europe's status quo, is not subjected to traumatic shocks. That is, the three parties will try to combine, always in a tighter and more coherent way, the social democratic tactics of Karl Kautsky with the hegemonizing strategy of Antonio Gramsci, the real theoretician of the final revolution. Almost the reverse of the preventive revolution carried out by Lenin, Gramsci's concept of final revolution is what Euro-Marxists are pursuing when they try to conquer the society before conquering the state. In this grand design the state remains, for quite some time, a secondary objective. By now, however, the state has become an urgent problem for the PCI, though it is less so for the PCF and is not yet a problem for the PCE.

In Gramsci's diagnosis, the recent bourgeois state remains rooted in the Catholic soil of the old Italian tradition—in spite of the *Risorgimento,* which gave Italy a modern laic and liberal ideology. It will therefore be necessary to use this liberal ideology (or part of it) to act on the deepest Catholic subsoil of Italian society. To start, the philosophy of the greatest thinker of bourgeois liberalism, Benedetto Croce, must be modified and overturned—as Marx overturned and modified Hegel's. The resulting ideological product must be put to the party's service in the long-term historical clash between Communism and Catholicism. In Gramsci's world vision—which is more cultural than economic and more antireligious than anticlerical—the Italian-style *Kulturkampf* against Catholicism resembles a prolonged competition between two similar phenomena. In 1919, Gramsci greeted the foundation of the Popular party, the ancestor of the modern Christian Democratic party, as a positive fact for socialism. He described the entrance of the Catholic masses into the political scene as being in the "spirit which makes flesh corruptible" and, concretely, as "Catholicism emerging from a narrow hierarchy and becoming a crowd." He saw this event as the beginning of a "suicide" of the

Catholic world. Two years before the foundation of the Communist party, he was thus already anticipating, in his vision of a suicidal fate of Catholicism, the political premises and mental reservations of the Historic Compromise.

Only after the establishment of the PCI, however, did Gramsci specify his cultural strategy. From then on, his mind pursued with growing consistency the idea that a progressive religious erosion and political debasement within the Catholic world itself would afford the best opportunity for a "national way" to Communism or, as the Catholic philosopher Augusto Del Noce put it, for the transition from the old to the new Church. At a certain point, the state would be fated to fall apart and surrender to the advance of a new Church that would dispel and absorb the old one. Italian Communism, conceived by Gramsci as both the competitor and the continuer of Catholicsm, would only then enter its second and last historical phase: the final revolution.

According to Gramsci, this complex strategy of attaining domination via competition takes place in two settings. In the first the cultural superstructure of the bourgeois state—idealistic philosophy and liberal ideology—must be upturned (in Marx's sense) and carried to its extreme antireligious consequences, with the help of committed radical-progressive intellectuals. In the second setting, Gramsci's party must use the Catholics against the bourgeois state to obtain the slow withering away of both. In Italy it is said that "Catholics have no feeling of the state." This lack of sense for the state has been skillfully and constantly fostered by the PCI in the postwar period, during which the Christian Democratic party has "occupied" the state apparatus and—as can easily be seen today—has actually allowed it to fall to pieces. Gramsci, who died in 1937, was unable to see how his premonitions of the unavoidable political suicide by the Catholics received an almost perfect historical confirmation by 1977. Indeed, by now the crisis of both bourgeois state and Catholic world are perfectly synchronized.

If the slow digestion of the adversary counts more than its immediate destruction, and if the state is the last mouthful to be swallowed, there is little need for the Leninist-type preventive revolution. Furthermore, by now the leaders of the three Eurocommunist parties are convinced that such a revolution would almost certainly be unsuccessful in the Western world. The appropriate course is therefore to become immersed in the national and social complexities of the Western world and to stimulate from within a far-ranging revolutionary development. The society, not the state, is the battlefield on which to engage in a long and wearing trench warfare. But if Gramsci's theories on the prior conquest of the society actually overturn Lenin's revolutionary scheme, is it still possible to talk of an orthodox Marxism-Leninism? Amedeo Bordiga, the founding father of Italian Communism, boasted that unlike Gramsci he had never read a line of Benedetto Croce, and he accused Gramsci of having "idealized" and perverted the nature of Marxism. Maybe he was right. Yet what matters is the existing nexus between Gramsci's theoretical lesson and the politics of Eurocommunism.

As the Italian Communists are now approaching a political agreement with the Catholics, a cultural agreement with the middle classes, and an economic agreement with the entrepreneurs, the Gramscian intellectual component appears more central than ever. If the workers, the soldiers, and the sailors were indispensable in 1917 for the assault on the Winter Palace, the intellectuals have become irreplaceable for bringing to final dissolution the two traditional European cultures—religious and liberal—and for a final conquest of radio, television, newspapers, and publishing houses. Today, a mere glance at certain articles in some major bourgeois organs of France and Italy attests to the enormous practical impact of a political theory that may sound, in my account, abstruse and academic.

"Pidgin-Marxism," according to Gramsci's forecast and expectation, has penetrated deeply into the average Euro-Latin intellectual. In no small part, it has indeed become the "common sense" conventional way of assessing the values, policies, and social situations of the contemporary world. A Milanese Socialist publisher has said that Gramsci's theories sound as if they were elaborated expressly for the mass media; and since what is not diffused by the mass media does not exist in the modern world, their control is equivalent to the making of history, that is, to a true revolution. In this respect, Gramsci was indeed a man who well understood his time. With arguments inspired by a more philosophical and, I dare say, totalizing and Thomistic vision of the world, he gave systematic form to the strategy of possessing the mass media that his contemporaries (such as the Fascist Mussolini, the Nazi Goebbels, the Communist Münzenberg) were already successfully applying to the real world. Gramsci, from his prison in Turi, devoted his solitude to studying organically, in the light of his goals, the manipulability of mass society.

I have touched upon the complex relationship among Gramsci, the Catholics, and the liberal world. Let us now consider his ambiguous and polyvalent way of relating to Fascism. Significantly, Gramsci never reproached Fascism for being totalitarian; on the contrary, he accused it of not being totalitarian enough. Mussolini's compromises with the Church, industry, and the financial world appeared to Gramsci to be static agreements to maintain and consolidate the Fascist regime instead of to further the revolutionary expectations of the original Fascist movement: pacts of stalemate and collaboration rather than dynamic moments of trench warfare in which the trenches must be conquered one after the other.

It is not without reason that a German dissident Marxist, Christian Riechers, maintains that Gramsci and Togliatti historically embody a mediation between the most authoritarian fascism, the leftist one, and Communism. George Lichtheim equally hits the target in pointing out that Gramsci, when he was imprisoned by Mussolini, elaborated a doctrine that was even more totalitarian than that of his jailers. Gramsci was a totalitarian who always used the term in the same laudatory sense given it by the Italian right wing. In his *Notebooks* he underlines the "total" character of Marxism—its unity of theory and practice—and denies that it can really "hold a dialogue" with other competing visions of the world because it is, by its very nature, an instrument of conquest. A Socialist theorist, Massimo Salvadori, goes so far as to call the Gramscian theory of hegemony the highest and most complex expression of Leninism. In Salvadori's view, Gramsci is a sophisticated follower of the most classical Marxist-Leninist totalitarianism, while Enrico Berlinguer's current strategy of the Historic Compromise is perhaps a deviation more than an up-to-date continuation of Gramsci's thought. Del Noce, on the contrary, believes that Gramsci is not a follower but one who went *beyond* Marxist-Leninist totalitarianism, an innovator with a view of his own about totalitarianism as competing, and at the same time integrating, with Italian Catholicism. In this latter view, Berlinguer becomes the natural executor of Gramsci. In my own view, Salvadori is one-quarter right and Del Noce three-quarters right. Gramsci's profound understanding of Catholic geology and of the unequaled skill with which the Church organized a religious consensus throughout the centuries resulted in his recommendation to work from the inside to overturn this enormous historical accumulation in favor of the Communist ideological expansion. All of this leads me to view Gramsci as a sort of Lenin with a doctorate in Eurocommunism. Gramsci's intuition of the importance of the Catholic reality for the Italian revolution can be compared to Lenin's intuition of the importance of the peasant reality for the Russian revolution.

Today Italy and France are witnessing the incubation of a future Western totalitarianism. One of its salient characteristics, already described, is its inseparability from the concept of final revolution. The final revolution pursued by Eurocommunist parties may be contrasted with both preventive revolution and revolution *tout-court*. The slow, illusionist, temporizing tactics of Eurocommunism seem to be directed toward a far-off "final stage": to a deferred totalitarianism rather than to an immediate revolution. Their renunciation of immediate revolution might make Eurocommunist parties appear similar to other social-reformist parties, while their aspiration to a complete but always postponed totalitarianism (in its fullness) could make them seem Utopian parties. But they are neither one nor the other.

Eurocommunism and Pluralism

The fundamental problem is whether Eurocommunism is totalitarian in its present strategic and essential being. It is unclear whether Eurocommunists consider that pluralism (itself a very vague concept) includes party pluralism. And even if they were to accept formal party pluralism, the concession is neither new nor reassuring: a formal party pluralism is already practiced by several para-Soviet countries, such as East Germany and Poland.

The philosophy of pluralism does not in the least affect the PCI's "democratic centralism," which in fact governs the party's internal life and shapes its totalitarian organizational structure. Furthermore, the present "pluralistic" tactics and strategy of the PCI are being presented as having been discovered by Gramsci. During the party's celebration of the fortieth anniversay of Gramsci's death, the *mâitre à penser* of Italian Communism was praised as the inventor and the forerunner of the present pattern. But, as the former Communist philosopher Lucio Colletti points out, this is not true: the ideas of party pluralism, of minorities and majorities alternating in government, of Parliament and the like are not to be found in Gramsci, nor has Lenin's dictatorship of the proletariat been abandoned.

Although all other parties have to be classified by their actions, Communist parties wish to be judged by their declarations. Not even their declarations, however, are clear. Between November and December 1976, the PCI daily *l'Unità* published two articles written by representative Communist intellectuals. The gist of them was: "Pluralism is a state of being, it is not an aim," and "We cannot reduce pluralism to an abstract, democratic, meaningless game." Clearly, on the basis of these declarations nothing is wrong with the present course of action—as illustrated by how the pluralism of the press is understood and respected. The fact is that the traditional Leninist organization of Communist apparatus is unchanged. Thus all the statements on "pluralism," on the democratic alternation of power, and so on are, in fact, contradicted and rejected by an organization which anticipates that the future structure of the entire society will duplicate its own structure.

A strictly soldier-like united apparatus may serve only two aims: waiting for a favorable, revolutionary H-hour or maintaining a totalitarian picture of the future countersociety. And it seems to me that a model of party organization as hateful as it currently is can only harm Eurocommunism unless the ultimate purpose of such a structure is precisely an absolute and irreversible power. The "liberal concessions" of the Communists almost always refer to the future, hardly ever to the present. They are always promises, never facts. To give factual testimony of their liberal good will, the Communists should dismantle now their Stalinist-Leninist apparatus. Otherwise, what will happen tomorrow when the power of the state is added to the effectiveness of the Communist organization?

The inner working of the Italian Communist model is aptly described by the philosopher (and disappointed Communist) Lucio Colletti in his "political-philosophical interview," published in the July–August 1974 issue of *New Left Review:*

> My refusal of this kind of party can be summarized in a formula. The real power situation in the contemporary Communist parties is as follows: it is not the Congress which elects the central committee, but it is the central committee which nominates the Congress; it is not the central committee which elects the management, but the management which nominates the central committee; it is not the management which elects the Political Bureau, but it is the Political Bureau which nominates the management.

Berlinguer himself, despite his promotion of the new Eurocommunist myth, incessantly repeats that his party is, and always will be, a Leninist one. In the speech delivered by Berlinguer in Milan on January 31, 1977, to the workers of the northern organization of the party, one of his most telling sentences was: "We answer a flat no to those who would like to take us to a breaking point with other Communist parties."

The parliamentary tactics of the early Kautsky, now diligently followed by the Eurocommunist parties, differ from the authentic social-democratic strategy of the later Kautsky (as distinct from, and opposed to, that of Lenin) precisely in the contrasting concepts of power. According to the later Kautsky, "Parties and classes do not need to coincide. A class can split into several parties, can remain in a commanding position and still can change the party which rules. The rule of the party, therefore, changes much more rapidly than the rule of the class. In such circumstances, no party is sure of remaining in the government, each of them must accept the possibility of becoming a minority." Lenin, by violently denouncing the "renegade" Kautsky, actually repudiated the conciliation between socialism and democracy and reaffirmed the necessity for a "dominant socialist party" to remain in power forever once it had conquered it. This was the path followed unsuccessfully in 1975 by Alvaro Cunhal in Portugal. The French Eurocommunist party backed him. The PCI did not clearly condemn him and censored the German social democracy's initiatives for Soares. After a while, Cunhal himself gradually turned to the democratic tactics of the PCI, PCF, and PCE. But this did not stimulate Eurocommunism to take a clear stand. Eurocommunism, following Kautsky, is able to work out a democratic way to power, but it remains unable to work out a democratic way of surrendering power.

In a similar fashion, Eurocommunism appears unable to elaborate an exhaustive critical theory of the Soviet "socialist" system. Even though Carrillo is saying formerly unthinkable things about the Soviet Union, neither Berlinguer nor Marchais dare say to their electorates and followers that socialism—not only democracy—was betrayed in the Soviet Union. The attitude toward the Soviet Union is not as secondary a problem as Eurocommunists would have us believe. From their evaluation of Soviet power and Soviet society, one infers the use of Communist power and the future pattern of a Communist society in Western Europe. But the only objections Eurocommunists mention against Eastern despotisms relate to the absence of civil rights. Eurocommunists promise a happier synthesis of socialism and democracy; but the concrete relation they have established with historical communism in the countries of Eastern Europe indicate that for them democracy and socialism are still two different concepts. Socialism as such, even if lacking in democracy, is not debated.

In spite of occasional and often hermetic polemics with the ideologists of the Soviet bloc, Eurocommunists continue to express the intention of being part of the "movement." By continuing to affirm their basic loyalty to the movement, however, they expose themselves to possible excommunication by the Soviets, and this means that they are not protecting themselves against potential Russian blackmail. Why? Presumably because Berlinguer and Marchais well know that the compactness of their parties, so effective in trench warfare within the capitalistic world, becomes fragile when it faces a colossus a thousand times more compact, such as the Soviet power. Even if they reached power with the best intentions of independence, they would not be able to hold out against the Soviet Union if it decided to excommunicate them. They also know that in the long run they would not be able to stay in power without the support of the trade unions, where the influence of the Soviet myth is still powerful.

The last problem to be discussed is the change of the property structures of big business, especially in Italy. With 60 percent of its industrial power nationalized, the Italian economy is already partially socialistic. The huge economic bureaucracy of the state nested in public industries, together with the overabundant intellectual bureaucracy inserted in the mass media, creates a new class that has grown up in the shadow of Christian Democratic power but that is ready to change master to maintain its power. Communists are well aware of this fact. They know they may well find, among the powerful in industry and the mass media and within the new technocratic and intellectual class brought up by the

Catholics, numerous and influential allies. Even here, one can only bow to Gramsci's foresight.

Conclusion

The problem of the democratic credibility of Eurocommunism cannot be solved quickly. Hasty and superficial judgments cannot help solve the squaring of the circle of today's Eurocommunism—something which no longer wants to be an Eastern despotism and still is not a Western social democracy.

For over fifty years, Italian and French Communists have wanted to maintain a Leninist organizational structure while gradually absorbing from Western democratic opinion a more serious and more complete analysis of the Soviet phenomenon. Yet this analysis is permanently postponed. Why? The reason is that since the socialist system in Russia quickly degenerated into despotism and has remained such, any serious analysis of it would inevitably raise the question: How can an identical degenerating process be avoided in Western Europe? After the famous Togliatti interview given to *Nuovi Argomenti* more than twenty years ago, after the secret Khrushchev talk on Stalin's "errors," nothing more fundamental or more organic has surfaced in the theory of the Eurocommunists on Stalinism.

That which must be asked of Eurocommunism is to explain explicitly the reasons for its changes—if there are changes. I believe that we must demand today from Western Communist parties, not a compassionate understanding of their past, but a definite break from it. Great historical turns hinge not only on accumulation but on selection, not only on continuity but even more on discontinuity. I end by quoting again the former Communist Lucio Colletti when, with reference to the PCI, he said:

> If the leaders want their line to penetrate into the body of the party, if they want to be believed inside and outside the party, they must decide to show, once and for all, evidence of changes: to explain in which sense today differs from yesterday; in which sense the new strategy differs not only from Leninism but also from what Gramsci thought. This is the price of serious political operations. Without it, confusion, even though dialectic, will eventually prevail: that is, everything and the contrary to everything.

PART THREE

THE CURRENT STATE OF ITALIAN POLITICS

7

The "Expedient Compromise"

Marino de Medici

The process the Italians call "clarification" continues in Italy as the country gropes for a way out of its economic, political, and social crisis. The most recent stage of this process began in the spring of 1976 when, after repeated failures to form a new government, Italy's political leaders resorted to national elections in the hope of finding solutions to their mounting problems.

The voters were called to the polls in June 1976 to elect a new Parliament. These elections were viewed as a turning point for the Communists, the time for them to make a play for the government now that they had gathered respectability and strength. The desirability of Communist participation in efforts to deal with the economic crisis, especially in terms of eliciting union support for the inevitable budget tightening and wage restrictions, could no longer be ignored. Or so it was thought. The turning point, however, had occurred even before the June elections, in March 1976, when Prime Minister Aldo Moro had met with PCI leader Enrico Berlinguer for a crucial ninety-minute talk.

Although this was not the first meeting between a Communist leader and a Christian Democratic government official, the Moro-Berlinguer encounter appeared to be a major step toward what the PCI called the Historic Compromise. An emergency economic austerity package, which Moro's minority government had proposed earlier to Parliament, needed Communist support or abstention to pass. The Moro-Berlinguer negotiations were unavailing and new elections were called. But an important formula had been broached and it was to be perfected, following the elections, in the new and mesmerizing policy known as *non sfiducia*—"abstention," or, literally, "non–no-confidence."

The upshot was that the PCI, for thirty years an opposition party, became a quasi-government party to the extent that it agrees with the DC, the party with a relative majority, on a program—even one of limited breadth and timing. In a two-party system, one of the two parties presumably will win a majority sooner or later and take over the government. Italy has not been a textbook democracy, but it has changed. The Italian "two-party system" in fact may be only the latest guise of a different political reality, where the Christian Democrats are behaving like a moderate lay party, and the Communists are a mass Socialist party. And now the PCI is as close to being a government party as it can be without reserving the duty to take over by itself until new elections give it a relative majority. The Italian innovation of "government by abstention" is clearly destined to remain in place for the time being. It allows the Christian Democrats to claim that the political framework has not been changed and that promises made to the electorate are being kept, while on the Communist side Berlinguer is able to tell his camp that their accession to power has come closer.

Rising Violence

Yet the most dramatic development in the political life of the country is taking place not in the parliamentary halls of Montecitorio and the Palazzo Madama or in the headquarters of the parties, but once again in the squares and in the streets. It is a turn that does not fit into the classic pattern of confrontation between left and right in Italy, but rather can be looked upon as the "Argentinization" of Italy. The strategy of tension of the early 1970s shook up the traditional order, with varying political consequences, including heated exchanges of accusations and counteraccusations among political and ideological contestants. The violence of 1977, by contrast, is quickly becoming endemic and threatens directly the very structure of the state, posing a much more dangerous challenge to democracy.

It began on March 12, "a nice day to start the revolution," as the fliers said that were distributed among the thousands of students and young people gathered in Rome to protest against just about everything. Early in the day these "guerrillas" attacked thirty different locations in the Eternal City, including the central headquarters of the Christian Democratic party and various local offices and barracks of the carabinieri and police district commands. Shops were assaulted and looted, automobiles ransacked and burned. The fighting lasted for five hours and the damage quickly rose to tens of millions of dollars. A new party had appeared on the Italian political scene, the "guerrilla party."

The fight against the "heart of the state" (in the revolutionary jargon of the ultraleftist movement) had taken a quantitative and qualitative jump. Compared with the earlier bombings and assassinations, the new wave of terrorism was much more like a military operation. On March 11 and 12 in Bologna and in Rome, the Italian "Montoneros" opened fire on the police and the *carabinieri,* killing and wounding an unprecedented number of them. The shooting and the arson, the looting and the sabotage must be considered a frontal attack on the foundations of democratic government.

The question in Italy in the late 1970s is, Which party or movement is the most likely to benefit from the situation? At first glance, no political party or personality should, but the backlash, the demand for law and order, will have its own political consequences. First and foremost, individual rights might be curbed, perhaps temporarily, to control the spread of violence. The "programmatic document" submitted in 1977 by the Christian Democrats for a new round of discussions with the "democratic" parties calls for preventive arrest, wiretaps, and other measures to combat the virulent threat to institutions, individuals, and property. The discussion is heated: Are the present instruments of public order sufficient or should new and drastic emergency measures be adopted to stop the shooting in the streets? The "preventive arrest" proposed by the DC would apply to those who are suspected of planning kidnappings, robberies, and armed actions.

The Communists and Socialists stick to the argument that the present laws are adequate, if firmly applied. To be sure, the preventive arrest proposed by the DC is more limited than that introduced by a center-left government (when Pietro Nenni was deputy premier) and approved only by the Senate. And yet the existing laws do not seem to stem the guerrilla onslaught. After the armed engagements in Rome and Bologna, the extremist Red Brigades aimed its guns at newspapermen in a brazen attempt to intimidate them. On June 2, in Milan, the publisher of *Il Giornale Nuovo,* Indro Montanelli, was wounded by young terrorists. The same day, in Genoa, the deputy editor of *Il Secolo XIX,* Vittorio Bruno, was shot in the legs in a similar assault. The following morning, a young couple, elegantly dressed, alighted from a car in Rome and shot the news director of RAI-TV's first television channel, Emilio Rossi. The attempt occurred just outside the RAI production center. Surgeons removed seven bullets from Rossi's legs. Finally, months later, the deputy editor of *La Stampa* of Turin, Carlo Casalegno, was shot well above the knees and did not survive the wounds. His killing was, in all likelihood, deliberate.

The four journalists represented a wide range of political opinion. Montanelli is a well-known writer of conservative persuasion, Bruno belongs to a center-left newspaper, Rossi is one of the leading journalists of the DC-controlled television channel, and *La Stampa,* Casalegno's newspaper, could be properly described in the U.S. as a paper of liberal persuasion. The Red Brigades do not differentiate; their enemy obviously is the entire system, a system that in their fanatical view must be destroyed. The challenge they bring to democracy has open and hidden dangers; one is that laws restricting individual freedom may facilitate an authoritarian takeover. Democracy is obviously weakened in more than one way by the growing violence in Italy.

And what about the Communist party? It is not a coincidence that some of the most violent demonstrations occurred in Bologna, for a long time the showcase of the PCI. The simple answer would be that now that the PCI is practically involved in governing the country, it, too, is challenged from the left and cannot control the extremist uprising. The Communist party organ *L'Unità* was firm in condemning the outbreak of violence against journalists and yet left open the question whether the purpose of those who shot Montanelli was to abet rightist reactions or to stir up complacency among the more primitive sectors of the so-called left.

Clearly, the extremist movements—not only the Red Brigades but the similarly infamous Armed Proletarian Nuclei (NAP) and the rightist Black Order—do not have a general following and do not enjoy any parliamentary support. But the violence from the lunatic fringes cannot be dismissed as irrelevant or relatively unimportant to the political structure of the country. The most insidious element in the outbreak of violence is the manifestation of weakness of the state. The trial of Renato Curcio, the founder of the Red Brigades, and his thirty associates provided dramatic evidence of this weakness. First, the president of the Turin Bar Association was murdered. The intent of the killing was to inject an atmosphere of terror into the trial, which had to be postponed because prospective jurors became too fearful of retaliation. When the trial finally took place at the end of June 1978, Curcio was sentenced to fifteen years, a penalty that could have been meted out merely for contempt of court. The sentences for the other defendants were surprisingly light.

For all the talk about public order, the tiny Radical party managed to have a referendum called in June 1978 that called for reducing the existing police powers. The referendum, by 77 percent of the votes, sustained—it was all it could do—the existing legislation, the so called Reale laws. The referendum followed the kidnapping and murder of the former premier and then president of the Christian Democratic party, Aldo Moro. Yet, despite Moro's brutal assassination, the ways and means of "restoring order" remained in mid 1978 within the framework of the negotiations of more than a year before.

New Program Negotiations

Restoring order was in fact the central theme in a document drawn up by the Christian Democrats at the conclusion of a long round of bilateral meetings with the representatives of five parties: the Communist party, the Socialist party, Social Democratic party, the Republican party, and the Liberal party.

This lengthy document, which the Christian Democratic party sent out May 28, 1977, to the parties of the "democratic arc," sums up these complex negotiations and presents DC proposals on the four subjects that were discussed: public order, economic policy, local agencies, and reform of the health system, universities, and secondary schools.

The document traces the various steps of the bilateral negotiations starting with the meeting of the DC Central Directorate on April 27. At that time, the DC was forced to react to the initiatives of the Socialist party and gave a mandate to a special delegation to find out whether the two parties could agree on various points of a program. However, the mandate specified that no changes in the present "political setup"—were envisaged. Finally, it called for a "more compact pledge" in order to solve "some important and urgent questions raised in the country" and to bring about "a climate of greater political stability and democratic security." The explosive problem of public order was paramount in the discussions, particularly its implications for the limitation of personal liberties. The DC document takes great pains to point out that there exists "a wide inclination of the parties to reach agreement" in view of the worsening situation which endangers the life, the freedom, and the property of the citizens as well as the functioning of democratic institutions. The solutions advocated by the negotiators include: (1) preventive arrest, to be limited to certain crimes; (2) wiretaps, to be limited to suspected terrorists and kidnappers (a special authorization is required to obtain "elements of enquiry without evidentiary value"); (3) police interrogation, which must be made possible after the arrest but cannot be used as evidence in a trial; (4) subversive command posts, which can be shut down by administrative order, to be formally confirmed by the magistrate; (5) reform of the security forces. While it was recognized that the police must be reorganized, no agreement was reached as to the creation of a police union. The Christian Democrats are on record as favoring a "representative organization" but insist that the "police union" should be independent of the parties and other workers' unions, which are largely controlled by the Communists.

In matters of economic policy, the document deals with the proposed reduction of the public deficit, the vexing and unsolved problem of the cost of labor, the acceleration of investment (in order especially to create new jobs for the young), and the ticklish issue of financing of industries, with a note of caution about the public ownership of industry.

It was then up to the five "abstention parties" to evaluate the fourteen-page "programmatic document" destined to be the basis for one more round of negotiations. The unofficial unveiling of the document—which was supposed to be kept confidential but was widely circulated within a few hours of its delivery to the interested parties—has strengthened the conjecture that its main purpose was to bring about the minimal agreement necessary to preserve the current legislature. The secretary of the DC himself, Benigno Zaccagnini, did not hide such purpose, but said that an attempt was underway to find an equilibrium that would enable the continuing of the legislature. A reason for this was found in the general recognition of the "delicate moment," in the "fragility of the democratic texture," and in the singular character of the political balance that emerged from the 1976 elections. This singular balance called for smoothing out the classic prerogatives of the majority and the opposition, and for rejecting the rule of the assembly, according to Zaccagnini.

The first reaction came from the Socialists and was, by and large, noncommittal. The Socialists seemed to be saying that they were asking for another government and yet did not want to precipitate the crisis of the DC *monocolore* ("single party government") whose life depended upon the abstentions. Furthermore, the PSI said that it intended to bring forth the negotiations by developing positive relations with the Communists and searching for a better understanding with the PSDI and PRI. But the main thrust of the Socialist position is hardly ambiguous: to avoid a break with the Christian Democrats by asserting the need, in one clean breath, to work on a solid majority around a program and a new government that would constitute a guarantee for all the parties. Tactically, then, both the Christian Democrats and the Socialists could claim success. The DC has not shunted the pressing requests from many sides to give a new direction to the government policies, but it has succeeded in preserving a certain margin of maneuver for the Andreotti government. In particular, the DC has held its ground against the Communists, by making clear that Communist cooperation would be useful but should not go beyond informal collaboration on specific subjects at specific moments. The first reaction from the Communist camp was cautious: the DC, it promptly pointed out, had circulated "a draft for internal use" since a universal agreement would have to be formulated by means of "collegiate" and not just "bilateral" consultations. The smaller parties, as always, had reservations. The Republicans found the process too long and the prudence overdone. The Liberals termed the DC document "interlocutory," while manifesting their apprehension over the possibility of a direct entente between the PCI and the DC.

At the conclusion of what appeared to be one of many stages of negotiations between the Christian Democrats and the Communists, Alfredo Reichlin, a Communist journalist and member of the Central Committee, pointed out that only a year before the DC was swearing that under no circumstance would it negotiate with the Communists; now, however, the DC leadership had begun to take stock of the reality of an even deeper crisis of the economy, of the state, of the very moral and civil order, a situation in which no one of the great popular forces can govern alone. The solution that the Communists formally suggested was nothing new, but gradually became more compelling: open the door to some form of participation for the PCI. The emergency climate, of course, would make it easier for the DC to open the door, and more important, for the Communists to enter the halls of government.

The Economic Crisis

In the economic area, it is the annual report of the governor of the Bank of Italy—issued every year on May 31—that reminds Italians of the priorities the country finds so hard to accept. In the 1977 report Paolo Baffi warned of the need to follow an economic policy that would favor investment over public and private consumption. The main instruments of this policy, Baffi said, were the containment of wage increases, the reduction of the public deficit and the channeling into saving of a higher quota of income from the private sector. The good news in his report was that the increase in the national income had been larger than anticipated, 5.6 percent. The bad news was that the deflator of the gross national product had risen to 18 percent, and the yearly balance of payments deficit had reached 2,300 billion lire, $2.6 billion over the existing deficit of approximately $19 billion. Some progress had been made in moderating the increase of the cost of labor, which went up only 10 percent compared with 35 percent the previous year. It was meager solace, if confronted with increases of only 1 to 2 percent in major industrial countries like the United States. It was a low voice and yet dramatic condemnation of unrealistic demands aggravating the economic and financial situation of the country. The political turmoil had a lot to do with it, but the governor of the Bank of Italy could not point his finger to political culprits. He could only admonish, choosing his words carefully, that too many political leaders were too concerned with tactical choices and contingencies instead of long-term strategies and structural revisions. Beyond the present difficulties and structural weaknesses, the message of Baffi was quite clear: Italy must continue to build its economy on the premise of continued participation in international exchanges. The open market character of the economy constituted a necessary condition for renewal and expansion, the governor concluded. In the 1978 report the picture was somewhat brighter with respect to the balance of payments, and somewhat gloomier with respect to the public deficit. But the message was essentially the same, for the problems remained the same. The unions had moderated their tactics and demands, but the Alfa Romeo cars were still being sold—practically on the state budget—at a $1,000 loss per car.

The Moro Slaughter

The kidnapping of Aldo Moro, and his subsequent horrendous "execution," dramatically showed how vulnerable Italy is and how precarious its political balance. On March 16, 1978, a well-rehearsed commando of the Red Brigades abducted Moro as he was being driven to the Chamber of Deputies for the parliamentary debate on the vote of confidence for the fourth Andreotti government. The attack, aimed at the "heart of the state," speeded up the parliamentary process of approval of the Andreotti cabinet, the fortieth government in Italy since the end of World War II. In the view of many observers, the ambush by the Red Brigades, in which five escort agents were gunned to death, gave substance to the Communist claim to be admitted into the government as a direct force for social and political stability in a national emergency. The long captivity of the Christian Democratic leader, the stream of defiant communiqués of the Red Brigades, the poignant pictures of Moro, the letters of the man "sentenced to death," and finally the killing and the delivery of his body in a street very near the PCI and DC headquarters were a traumatic experience for the country. And yet Moro's assassination finally gave unanimity and strength to the nation, and, in turn, this created a backlash in the administrative elections of May 14 and 15. The Communist party paid for its "ideological matrix" with the Red Brigades, and the Christian Democrats increased their vote. The PCI loss of over 9 percent was seen by many as a confirmation of a reversal of voting trends, but the Communist setback did not alter the political equation. Two months after the Moro assassination and one month after the elections, President Leone suddenly resigned after increased criticism for possible personal gains at the time of the Lockheed sales to the Italian Air Force. After many votes and political maneuvers, an old Socialist, former Speaker of the House of Deputies Sandro Pertini, was elected president of the Republic. His election was welcomed by the country at large as a good choice but the age of the new President (eighty-two) was perceived as the main element of a temporary solution to gain time.

However that may be, the violence, and especially the "kneecapping," continued. Five days after the Moro kidnapping, the Italian cabinet decreed new antiterrorist measures along the lines of the general agreement that had been reached in July 1977 by the Christian Democrats, the Communists, and four other parties. One of these parties, the PLI, bolted the new "programmatic majority" and voted against the Andreotti cabinet. The vote in the Chamber of Deputies was 545 in favor and 30 against, with 3 abstentions. One of the new antiterrorist measures mandated life imprisonment for kidnappers whose victims are killed and a term of thirty years otherwise. But this show of determination by the political parties in supporting a law-and-order program could hardly dispel the uncertainty created by the efficiency of the urban guerrilla group.

The New Majority

The Italian political alchemy has brought about a brand new response to the country's vexing problems in 1978. The philosophers' stone which Italian leaders have long been striving to produce is the solution to a burning dilemma: how to accommodate the Communist demands for more power without letting them into the command room of the government.

The latest product of such alchemy is the device of a political majority without direct Communist participation in the cabinet. In practice, the minority Christian Democratic government will be closely monitored by the new majority, which includes the Communists. But this larger measure of Communist control over the government's life should be supplemented by other means so as to make clear to everyone that the PCI is now part of the democratic majority or, to put it bluntly, that the PCI is a quasi-partner of the Christian Democrats in the management of the nation.

The foundations for this de facto partnership were laid in July 1977 when the programmatic accord was signed, but the social and cultural conditions had been secured long before that, probably more than three years before. The difference between the formula agreed upon in July 1977 and the new arrangement that emerged in January 1978 is that henceforth, in order to ensure a working majority for the government, the Communists will not have to abstain on government bills before Parliament but will be able to vote yes. Thus, in January 1978 the Communists joined four other parties in a new governing majority. One of the issues on which the Communists will cast yes votes is foreign policy, and the implications of this development will confer even more urgency on the problems of the Carter administration in facing the spread of Eurocommunism.

The American Response

Since June 1977, the Italian Communist question has commanded the attention of the National Security Council and the Department of State. On June 18, in an interview with *Il Tempo,* Secretary of State Cyrus

Vance restated the preference of the Carter administration for the democratic forces in Italy. The administration's desire not to interfere in the internal affairs of any country, emphasized Vance, "does not mean that we are indifferent to who is elected and who serves in the government of any country." This was the first step in the administration's attempt to focus its policy toward the growing influence of the Communists in Italy and in other Western European countries.

Finally, in the statement issued by the Department of State on January 12, 1978 (see the Introduction to this volume), the United States attempted to clarify its position in order to dispel, in the words of an administration official, the "misinterpretations" which certain political circles and commentators had attached to the previous statements. The position of the United States had not changed, the statement said. And it explained: "We do not favor such participation [that is, Communist participation in Western European governments] and would like to see Communist influence in any Western European countries reduced." The State Department spokesman concluded: "The United States and Italy share profound democratic values and interests, and we do not believe that the Communists share those values and interests."

The official statement of January 12 gave rise to yet another round of polemics in Italy. Leftist leaders and commentators saw it as a shift of policy by the Carter administration, although the Communist party press, which throughout the administration's first year kept a more cautious stance, did not take this view. The same papers which had welcomed the original pronouncements of the new democratic administration as evidence of a less negative attitude toward Italian Communists were quick to attribute the January 12 statement to the pressures of conservative circles and to the influence of former Secretary of State Kissinger. In June 1977 Kissinger had chosen the conference on Eurocommunism sponsored by the American Enterprise Institute and the Hoover Institution to point out the basic incompatibility of Communist parties with Western European social and political institutions. (See chapter 11 of this book.)

PCI Advances in 1978

Despite the American response, the long march of the Italian Communists toward power continued and reached yet another milestone in February 1978, when the Christian Democratic party's directorate granted Giulio Andreotti, the outgoing premier and the premier-designate, greater latitude to make concessions to the PCI's leadership. The fall of the government had indeed been caused by Enrico Berlinguer's decision to deny support to the DC's minority government. This cabinet had governed Italy for a surprisingly long time—eighteen months—and in fact had been able to make remarkable economic progress, especially by reversing the huge balance-of-payments deficit.

Berlinguer's decision was in part prompted by the behavior of the Socialist and Republican parties, which had called for a new government that would include the Communists in the national emergency. However, other factors also led to the PCI's move. Among them was the pressure from the PCI's own rank and file for quicker and more substantial results from the party's cooperation with the Christian Democrats. The push from the party's grass roots for a larger voice in government was balanced by the unexpected pronouncement of the secretary general of the CGIL, Luciano Lama, who admitted the practical impossibility of defending the wage levels of the Italian workers while providing jobs for the unemployed. In a rather candid interview at the end of January 1978, the Communist labor leader called for sacrifices by the workers. By doing so, he lent further legitimacy to the Communists' claim that by entering the government they would help to solve Italy's problems. The Communists' line—"Italy cannot be governed without us"—was then given additional credibility both by the Lama interview and by the Socialist and Republican call for a definitive role for the Communists in the government.

The search for a new formula, then, had to encompass the Communist condition of a new majority—"a majority clearly stated and negotiated"—and yet safeguard the Christian Democratic minimum requirement that the "political framework not be altered" by admitting the PCI into the government. Once again, the crisis impinged upon the parliamentary system in that a way out could be found only by camouflaging a political accord through the so-called programmatic accord of a new majority, outside the Parliament.

In sum, the events of 1976–1978 have shown (one is tempted to say conclusively, but nothing is final in the country of Machiavelli and Pirandello) that the Italian parliamentary system does not work according to the classic rules of parliamentary democracy. Italians have invented new formulas and slogans with a passion. The political game evolved from "parallel convergences" to "more advanced equilibria," and now is moving from "programmatic convergences" to "a more active abstention." To an outsider, it is a theater of the absurd. To Italian insiders, it is what makes a dialogue possible. The danger is that the new grand coalition will do away with the orthodox majority-minority interplay. The Italian-style parliamentary system not only would obliterate the principle of opposition but also could bring suppression of political dissent.

Beyond the question of whether the new coalition should be called a programmatic majority, as the Christian Democrats stress, or a governmental majority, as the Communists claim, the evidence of a dramatic evolution in Italy's political arena was shown by a photograph taken on the evening of March 16, 1978. The picture showed red Communist flags and white Christian Democratic flags side by side in a massive demonstration to protest Moro's kidnapping. Since Moro's funeral was, at the request of his family, a private funeral, that was indeed a historic picture of a historic compromise.

8

The Christian Democratic Party Today

Massimo de Carolis

Before expressing my personal opinion about the state of the Christian Democratic party, I must establish the limits of my analysis. I belong to a generation that never had any relationship with the Catholic political movement before or during the Fascist period. No matter how much I appreciate the political and historical studies on the Catholic movement in Italy, my views are grounded on the direct experience of seventeen years of active political life. Moreover, I cannot even claim to follow or interpret the official party line, for the simple reason that the DC has never had a well-defined theory. Indeed, it seems to me that no explicitly formulated Christian Democratic orthodoxy exists.

The Party under De Gasperi

The current crisis of the DC is part of the crisis of Italian Catholicism, which, in turn, is the crisis of a social structure unable to keep up with the rapidly changing state of the country.

In the 1950s, Italian Catholicism witnessed the rapid decomposition of the peasant society in which it had been rooted for centuries and from which it had drawn its values and it conceptions of man and history. In the political arena, the demise of this way of interpreting and guiding society goes further back. At the beginning of the century, Luigi Sturzo developed a full-fledged political theory by transferring traditional middle-class values into Christian Democratic terms. But there were insurmountable limitations that would have prevented the party from gaining a political majority even if the Fascist dictatorship had not occurred. The break between the Catholic Church and the state that followed the unification of the country had brought about a reciprocal rejection. Sturzo's party was strongly conditioned by that rejection and at the same time was tied to community-oriented experiences that were disappearing.

Sturzo assumed a model of communal relationships contrary to the typical conflicts of industrially advanced democracies.

The policies of De Gasperi after World War II cannot be viewed as a direct continuation of Sturzo's Partito Popolare. De Gasperi's pragmatism was soon translated into a classical liberal-democratic scheme. This became especially evident in his economic policy, which isolated and brought to an end the last residues of Christian social thought. The DC's collaboration with the minor parties of the center was used by De Gasperi to eliminate the radical element linked with Dossetti. In doing so, De Gasperi accepted the profound transformation the Catholic political movement underwent between 1946 and 1948, which made the DC a party quite different from Sturzo's Partito Popolare. The transformation was reflected in the sharp difference between the 1946 and the 1948 election results: the DC share went from 35.2 percent up to 48.8 percent. Italy is known to be a country with a singularly stable electorate; sharp swings in votes for or against a given political party have taken place only twice—in 1948 for the DC and in 1975–1976 for the Communist party. Both cases reflected a change in the party's constituency, that is, the acquisition of new social classes.

When Italy was liberated in World War II, the Christian Democratic leadership was the same as the Catholic leadership. The leaders who had emerged during the long night of fascism in various Catholic associations, closely linked with the Church, were transferred into the political arena, where they gave birth to the party. The local elections of spring 1946 first and the elections of June 2 showed that the DC could claim the majority believed to belong to the Socialist-Communist bloc. The Catholic leadership became aware of a strength it had not suspected (even if the Popular Front had won pluralities in the key regions and the major cities). This 1946 constituency was what we would now call the center-left. It was made up mostly of middle-income employees, small farmers, and blue-collar workers from the southern and the so-called white areas—yet the total strength of the DC was significantly less than it is now.

Between 1946 and 1948, the coalition government with the Communists was terminated and political campaigns became radicalized. As a result, members of the anti-Communist middle class converged in the Christian Democratic party, even if they did not share its Catholic background. In less than two years, the DC won an absolute majority of seats in Parliament. The leadership remained, however, the same; the confluence of the new social classes (that were neither anti-Catholic nor "confessional") took place at the grass roots level and did not affect the leadership. Even today, the DC leadership comes almost entirely from a strict Catholic orthodoxy. But the party, which was conceived as an even more "Christian" party (as the name was meant to convey) than the Partito Popolare, had drastically changed. In it had converged two profoundly different elements: on the one hand were the Catholics, who were oriented toward the masses, and on the other were the liberal-democratic middle classes.

De Gasperi stabilized these elements through a series of political decisions. He chose not to characterize the party as confessional (against the opposition of the Catholic left); he entrusted the Liberals Einaudi and La Malfa with the responsibility of the economic policy; and he supported cooperation with the minor parties of the democratic center. And for many years the inner contradictions of this policy were kept in abeyance.

The Dorotei Come to Power

The country's industrial transformation called for experimentation with new alliances. In the early 1960s the Dorotei group, as the legitimate heir to De Gasperi's pragmatism, formed a coalition government with the Socialists, which could be viewed as an attempt to respond to that transformation. In the most critical moment of the transition, the Dorotei, by breaking away from Fanfani in 1959, signified a political choice that confirmed the rise of the second-generation leadership. The new leaders were oriented less toward the "people" and Catholicism and more toward technology and modernization. Moro's speech at the 1962 Naples Congress contained the most far-reaching strategic design ever conceived by the DC after De Gasperi. The decision to nationalize the electric companies—however wrong on technical grounds—was not merely the price that had to be paid to the Socialists, but rather the beginning of a new political trend. That decision resembled the one that led the Kennedy administration into a showdown on prices with the steel companies. With that decision, the DC leaders opposed the leaders of the country's private sector. The DC leaders claimed their own autonomy and maturity; and, with the Dorotei, a strong public-economic leadership immediately became competitive with the private sector.

From the vantage point of the late 1970s, the center-left appears to have been a choice that looked right on paper, or a Machiavellian decision aimed at institutionalizing a political alliance, rather than the result of a profound acceptance of the country's new needs. The total failure of the center-left coalitions resulted above all from the failure of the DC, and Italian Catholicism in general, to follow up the new course with a new culture, which could confront the Socialist culture.

Catholic culture shows its weakness by being often divided between, on the one hand, a passive conservatism unable to respond to developing social trends and, on the other, a progressivism that rejects Western civilization and pursues, in a utopian way, mankind's ultimate liberation. Most of all, the Catholic culture has not acquired a method and a language suited to the new political rapport.

This Catholic culture might be characterized as being axiomatic rather than problematic. It is a culture more suited to sustaining its initiated adepts than to acquiring new and free areas of influence. As a consequence, it has declined along with traditional Catholicism, as being Catholic has become a free personal choice rather than a widespread social phenomenon. In the political field, this means that being Catholic has become an ideological choice in the framework of a society that is now secularized. The current secular way of thinking has solidified to the point of excluding the Catholic culture from the most exciting intellectual milieus, where it is simply not understood, rather than rejected.

The lack of democratic alternatives to the DC, on the one side, and, on the other, the almost automatic consensus achieved thus far had progressively brought the Christian Democrats to consider the need for a connection with public opinion and social forces of only minor importance. The DC leadership has thus become a small, coopted group of people who rotate among cabinet posts. It is hardly capable of direct communication with the most modern segment of its constituency.

The Turning Point and the Party Renewal

The local elections of June 1975 broke a thirty-year period of Christian Democratic power in most local administrations and made the DC aware that it had lost its connection with the country. The vote of 1975 means the following:

- Italy has changed.
- The national values and the prevailing modes of behavior are not, for the most part, shared by the DC.
- The institutional structure (still run by the DC, especially at the central level) no longer corresponds to the social reality.
- The "system" does not produce any new consensus among the youth for the DC.
- The cultural hegemonizing force in Italy is, progressively, the Communist party.

These tendencies were not confirmed (indeed they were somewhat counteracted) in the 1976 political elections, especially—it seems—as far as the young generations are concerned. But the DC held on at the expense of the minor parties of the democratic center and of the right, without arresting the impressive progress of the Communist party.

The 1976 elections made the DC aware that it could not recover from its crisis merely by improving its organization or by reinforcing its traditional policy. On the contrary, its recovery presupposes a radical renewal that I interpret as a need for *modernization.* The DC can save itself if, and only if, it can be transformed from the party of the Catholic middle class in a predominantly agricultural country into a modern mass party that represents in a unitary, cross-class fashion all the social components of an advanced industrial society. Such complex political undertaking calls for clear-cut choices. But the DC today is hesitating to make them.

First, it would be necessary to soften the party's confessional bent. Given the "radical" leanings of modern Italian society, an essentially Christian political force has neither the necessary strength to rally a majority nor the necessary driving force to put together a solid coalition government. This raises the question of the DC's relationship with Italian Catholicism; but perhaps this is merely academic, in that the Christian inspiration of the DC in recent years has been more confined to words than actually realized in consistent legislative or executive actions.

Second, it would be necessary to give up, once and for all, the temptation (still very strong within the Catholic left) to line up with the Third World. A clear choice must be made in favor of the West, and the model of growth of the advanced industrial democracies must be explicitly accepted. A Catholic-populist component of the DC has always been inclined to converge with the Marxist left in its critique of capitalist society. In the last ten years, the influence of such a convergence on governmental actions has brought the country below the level of rationality and efficiency necessary to keep it within the West. It is particularly in this connection that a profound transformation of the party's prevailing cultural models is needed.

Third, the democratic forces must respond to the Communist strategy of the Historic Compromise with a political line of equal strategic amplitude, offering a democratic alternative to the hegemony of the PCI. De Gasperi's idea of the democratic solidarity—the complex system upon which the Italian political life should be founded—depended on the driving force of the DC vis-à-vis the minor parties of the democratic center; inner contradictions have exploded that policy, and mistrust of the DC is now evident among its old allies. The Andreotti administration that emerged from the 1975 elections, supported by a so-called "abstention of no confidence," results from a state of necessity and cannot be viewed as a solution. It has opened a transition period that could be used to reconstruct a new democratic bloc, without which the Historic Compromise with the Communist party is the only middle-range alternative. And there is no doubt in my mind that the Historic Compromise is being proposed by the Communists with the final goal of gaining hegemony, amid the current division of the democratic parties, over the country's new political shape.

A democratic alternative must be rooted in the country's consciousness and political culture, rather than in its present structures. Such an alternative cannot be constructed, however, by simply reorganizing and updating the old principle of democratic solidarity; it cannot be attempted by the DC without a radical transformation of the party itself in a liberal-democratic direction. If the Catholics persist in an ideological use of their religion, then they can have only a minority role. The central issue is the modernization of the DC, as distinct from "renewals" based upon the ruinous philosophy of a "return to the beginnings." Contrary to this philosophy, the DC must be transformed in its very way of being. It is only under this coalition that the DC will become receptive to the values and needs of an advanced industrial society and could again become the political axis of a democratic front—not only at a parliamentary level but above all at the cultural and social levels.

A comeback of the DC and other democratic parties could be occasioned by the PCI's first strategic mistake in thirty years, namely, its decision to found a model of development on a policy of permanent austerity. Such a policy is irreconcilable with the Italian position within the Western world; and such a decision is also revealing in that it shows that the PCI's notion of pluralistic democracy would remove Italy from the Western bloc.

The Ambiguities of the "Constructive Confrontation"

Faced with problems of such gravity and urgency, which call for meditated, yet swift decisions, the DC has remained idle. A new phase of "constructive confrontation" was initiated in the wake of the 1976 political campaign, which was conducted in direct contraposition to the Communist party. This new attitude presupposes a prudent and wearisome search for a new balance each day, that in turn prevents the DC from proposing a global political strategy to the other parties and to the country. Moreover, the search for a meeting ground with the Communists strains the relationship with the smaller democratic parties, provoking upset reactions that may wipe out whatever was left of the democratic solidarity.

By adopting the policy of constructive confrontation with the PCI—instead of proposing a democratic alternative to communism—the DC has again yielded to one of its internal "currents"—the one that interprets democratic pluralism in terms that are closer to the Eurocommunist than to the Western liberal-democratic vision of the world. Like the Catholic polemicists of past centuries, this wing of the DC considers liberalism the same as anarchism; it sees no value in political conflict or differentiation of political positions, and it understands pluralism essentially as a step toward attaining unity. Such a conception is dangerously close to the position of Italian Communism at the present moment.

The PCI's acceptance of the Western democratic model is, in my opinion, purely verbal. Democracy in the Western sense is a complex system of ethical-political values, requiring more than the recognition of the value of essential civil rights. And the PCI is still highly ambiguous in regard to political problems of fundamental importance. The PCI expresses the most advanced illiberal political doctrine: a modern version (the only possible one in a Western country) of the old design to subjugate the entire national society to the permanent hegemony of a single mass movement.

In building its image, the PCI has exploited the shortcomings and mistakes of the democratic parties and, well assisted by the mass media and the intellectual milieu, has spread a series of totally unjustified myths. For example, there is a myth about the administrative soundness and correctness of the "red" local administrations. In reality, these administrations are largely dedicated to the most disgraceful methods of patronage and clientelism (the so-called *sottogoverno*), and their systematic acts to limit personal freedom come close to resembling typical totalitarian methods.

In any event, the contradictions of the "constructive confrontation" are so serious that it will be wiped out, at some point, by the choices the government will be forced to make. At that moment, the invitation of the Communist party will have to be either accepted or refused by the DC. Those who believe that the DC can offer a substantial alternative to the Communists and that the PCI's invitation will eventually be rejected must also foresee a hard political fight in the country.

New Tendencies within the DC

The country's swift transformation from 1972 to 1977 has caused a crisis over the DC's traditional structure. The old DC is left with only two political strategies: Moro's and Andreotti's. They both move from a realistic recognition that the past is past, that the old system and its political class cannot endure. But they tend to freeze the party's internal dialectics, because they do not envisage the possibility that new energies may emerge from the party itself.

Four new political movements may be recognized within the party. Two of them are characterized by their reference to the Italian socioeconomic situation and could be defined as nonconfessional. The other two are characterized by their reference to Catholic traditions, and are thus at odds with the former ones.

The two political trends with confessional content are: (1) the

"Democratic Catholics" gathered around party secretary Zaccagnini; (2) the group called "Communion and Liberation." The Democratic Catholics aim at an impossible conciliation between an "integral" Christian identity and the management of power; the second group recognizes the impossibility of that, chooses fidelity to Catholicism, and moves toward the formation of a party sect whose clear, if perhaps unconscious, vocation is to be a minority group.

Of the two nonconfessional trends, one is typified by the technocratically oriented group gathered around Senator Umberto Agnelli; and the other, by the group that aims at reconstructing the "Democratic Alternative." The former is vitiated by its limited objective, namely, to salvage the economic system, and above all the management of industry, by setting aside the solution of the political problem (in other words, by dodging the Communist issue). By contrast, the Democratic Alternative recognizes that in Italy the fundamental issues are the Communist issue and democratic solidarity—and that they are strictly interconnected.

These new trends raise problems that differ from those raised by the old so-called currents. These currents managed, as a whole, to institute an almost miraculous mechanism of counterweights and complementary forces. Instead the new trends are mutually exclusive because of the contents of their programs. There is still little self-awareness of all of this. Yet the new trends represent challenges to the party's roots, if not to the very presence of a Catholic party in a modern industrial society. This is not surprising since these trends developed from the explosion of the democratic galaxy.

Each of these political trends cannot be assimilated, then, to the old "currents"; rather, they represent the potential core of a future party. This interpretation is sustained by the fact that constituencies of the new movements come not from within, but from without the party. This was also true of the old left-wing currents within the party, who were quite properly accused of working for the enemy. The difference is that the left-wing currents used outer support simply for internal strife. Instead the four new political trends find their support directly in Italian society and regard themselves as its political expression in lieu of the official DC. In particular, the Communion and Liberation group leans on the local church hierarchies; the Democratic Catholics find their strength in the Catholic movement and in the Vatican milieu; the technocratic trend appeals to the private sector; and Democratic Alternative makes a direct appeal to public opinion and autonomous unions for a mass mobilization around its political program.

It is difficult to foresee which one of these four trends will impress its identity upon the party, and it is not clear whether any of them will jeopardize the party's unity. My hope is that out of this travail may come a renewed ability by the DC to interpret the social reality of a country that has profoundly changed since World War II. What the coming time requires, more than new policies, is a new political culture. The Christian Democrats should understand that a political leadership without culture is essentially a leadership without future. As such, it is condemned to extinction.

9

The Problem of the PCI

Lucio Libertini

The Italian Communist party (PCI) is an important component of what is now habitually called Eurocommunism. I therefore wish to state precisely, as a contribution to this debate, some of the positions of the party. I speak on a personal basis, but I know that I am expressing the general consensus of my party.

(1) Some observers and political leaders have stated that PCI participation in the government might alter the balance of power in Europe in favor of the U.S.S.R. We Italian Communists do not believe this to be true. A central element of our strategy is precisely not to alter the balance of power in Europe and, thus, to facilitate détente, multilateral agreements on European security, and the pursuit of peace. In the second place, all of this is in consonance with our approach, which is directed at the independence of Italy and at the autonomy of our party. Both objectives are strictly related to the development of détente; everyone can understand this. For these reasons, we loyally accept NATO and because of the same consideration we do not wish to be either anti-Russian or anti-American.

(2) What can and must change is the internal Italian situation. Our country is facing a profound economic, social, and ideological crisis. If production is increasing, it is only due to our rate of inflation, which amounts to 20 percent a year; on the other hand, our foreign debt exceeds $18 billion, while the domestic public debt is greater than the aggregate national income covering a period of fifteen months. If inflation were to decrease considerably, under present conditions there would be an explosive increase of unemployment as well as a stoppage in the development of production.

In order to cure this crisis, it is necessary to modernize the system of production; to eliminate parasitism and the widespread waste of resources, to be selective in public spending and consumption; to set up a modern fiscal system based on progressive taxation of everyone's income; and to develop, above all, the regions of the South, where unemployment is concentrated. All this requires a policy of austerity directed at the equitable sharing of sacrifice and at the rational utilization of resources.

Without the Communists, there is not at this time a parliamentary majority capable of implementing this policy. Moreover, without the Communists, there is no absolute majority in the current Parliament. The only alternative lies in the dissolution of Parliament. This would mean new elections, which might intensify the current crisis. It is probable, in any case, that after the elections the Communists would become even more indispensable in order to constitute a majority. The problem is not only one of parliamentary arithmetic. It is a political and a social problem as well. In today's Italy, the Communists represent a very large part of the working class and of the political forces. A policy of austerity and modernization requires the support and participation of these forces.

If some should think—and I believe there are some—that a different solution can be found through the elimination of democratic institutions, it is imperative that they be told that they are mistaken. The vast majority of the Italian people do not desire new adventures and are determined to defend democracy, regardless of the divisions among the parties.

On the other hand, today there is not even a leftist majority. But, in any case, we discount the possibility that a weak leftist majority might be able to govern Italy, because the present crisis is too great, and because it would be very dangerous to split the country in two. The reasons are both internal and international. We do not exclude the alternation of parties in the future, but the concrete situation with which we are now faced makes government based on compromise and national unity more realistic.

(3) A new economic policy does not require additional nationalization. The extent of public property is very great in Italy, and it is certainly greater than in the other European countries. The real problem entails its reorganization and its concrete management in consonance with well-balanced development and full employment.

We believe that past experience has demonstrated both the failure of total economic planning, which degenerates into bureaucratic paralysis, and the nonexistence of a market based on perfect competition, which would supposedly ensure an equilibrium and would utilize resources in an optimal manner. The market is dominated by an oligopolistic structure, and if this mechanism is left to its own devices it generates imbalances and waste. Democratic planning is therefore necessary—the kind of planning which defines and guarantees the extent of entrepreneurial initiative. We know that the perspective of effective democratic planning is a new frontier, still unexplored. Reality, however, lays down this historical challenge.

(4) We do not believe that the multinational corporations are the creation of the devil. On the contrary, they are an essential structure of capitalism in its present phase of development. At the same time, they are representative of an objective trend toward unification of the world markets. This trend, per se, is neither capitalistic nor socialist.

On the basis of this evaluation, we are not considering the elimination of multinationals from our country. Even less would we wish to discourage foreign investments. A policy of autarchy and isolationism would be sheer folly. We want to negotiate realistically the presence of multinationals in the Italian economy; this means giving and receiving effective and reliable guarantees. The following problem is quite important: we can no longer accept that multinationals, especially in certain sectors, be allowed to sell in our country products manufactured substantially out of Italy.

In connection therewith, I wish to cite by way of example electronics and data processing, essential factors in the development of the world economy. In these sectors, it is useful that a law be passed in Italy making it mandatory for large corporations to produce in our country a specific percentage of the goods they wish to sell on our market. I remind you that similar laws now exist in the United States, Sweden, and Japan.

A second condition concerns the labor force. Italian Communists consider the mobility of workers as necessary and are prepared to organize it and support it through state intervention. But the mobility of the workers must take place from one place of work to another and *not* from employment to unemployment.

We do not want additional Lockheed affairs. We want clear and honest negotiations in accordance with the law.

(5) Everyone can observe that these positions are variously connected with the growth of pluralistic democracy. We are fighting for pluralistic democracy; for complete freedom of judgment and criticism; for the guarantee of individual human rights; for a new and more active parliamentary role. We are fighting against every form of dictatorship. We wish to expand democracy, not to compress it. And we wish to extend democracy to include the actual participation of the masses by suppressing the condition of inferiority to which most social strata are subject.

In our judgment, the passage to socialism will be irreversible, just as the passage from feudalism to capitalism has been irreversible. But it is a question of historical trend, which must be verified. From the political and juridical points of view, we favor the alternation of Socialist and non-Socialist parties of the government. This means that whenever the Communists become a minority, they will peacefully take up the opposition role and will accept this rule of the democratic game.

In this case, it is a matter of principle. Our position in this regard is different from that of other Communist parties in the world. Polemics and discussions on this topic are permanently going on between us and these parties. Socialism must advance by active support and participation of the popular masses; it cannot be established or protected artificially by means of a police state.

During this century, the left has never posed a threat to democracy in Italy. Threats—and fascism itself—have come from the right. Democracy has been defended, installed, and broadened with the decisive support of the Communists.

(6) We earnestly hope that the responsible forces in the United States—both economic and political—are capable of understanding the situation which has emerged in Italy. Our country has many capabilities, many human resources, and it can play an important role within the context of international cooperation. We wish to increase its dignity and its validity as an international interlocutor.

To cause difficulties for the process of renewal of Italian society is tantamount to aggravating the Italian crisis, increasing contradictions in Europe, and damaging international détente. At the same time, it must be said that even if the great powers are vested with substantial responsibility, the international community cannot be managed exclusively by those powers to the detriment of other peoples. We strongly believe that it is necessary to fight against every form of imperialism.

The firm choice of the Italian Communists is for cooperation and friendship among all peoples; for cooperation and friendship with the American people.

(7) Our party has not invented this policy in the course of one morning. I must stress this point. Our policy is the result of an elaboration developed in the course of many years: it began with the thoughts of Antonio Gramsci and became more recently enriched by historical experience. The number of our activists and voters has greatly increased along this orientation, which has deep roots.

We do not expect to impose our views upon other Communist parties, but we do not want to renounce our convictions; we shall not give up the conviction that socialism and democracy are tightly and reciprocally tied.

We do not make up a faction of the international Communist movement, because we believe in the independence and autonomy of each party and in the free debate among Communists without preestablished and outdated positions.

There certainly are today many points of convergence among the major Communist parties of Europe. This is a positive fact, which derives from specific conditions. But it is not possible to establish an absolute identity relationship between a geographical position and such orientations. In this sense, the definition of Eurocommunism is not exact.

We are not interested in orthodoxy with respect to the classics of Marxism. Marxism is critical thought which evolves with reality. It is not a dogma. Therefore, we shall never wage a war of citations against anyone, nor shall we dispute over one phrase or another of Marx.

But it is true that, beyond the historical boundaries and the contradictions of this theoretic system, we believe we can recoup an essential aspect of Marxist thought: the idea that socialism is a more advanced level of democracy. We must inherit and enrich the democratic patrimony inherited from the bourgeois revolutions. The fundamental objective is to reduce state coercion and increase self-government.

PART FOUR

THE FUTURE AND ITS IMPLICATIONS FOR AMERICAN POLICY

10

Calculating the Risk

Giovanni Sartori

The advantage of the last speaker is that he becomes wiser as he listens. The disadvantage is that he may be left with nothing to say. The drift of Italian politics from the early 1960s to the present day—we may say from the opening to the Socialists to the opening to the Communists—has been exhaustively overviewed and discussed. I am thus left at the thin edge that separates the past from the future, that is, at the juncture where one asks what will happen, and what will be the consequences of what happens. Nevertheless, as Leibniz said, *on récule pour mieux sauter*: in order to jump we must take a few steps back.

In the 1950s Italy was booming economically and appeared a stable or stabilized democracy. Indeed, the last election held under the formula of the "center governments" was the only general election in thirty years that showed a halt in the growth of the Communists: the PCI, which had obtained 22.6 percent of the total vote in 1953, won 22.7 percent in 1958. However, the success of the center formula was a success in "containment." The problem of "integrating" the PSI, the official Italian Socialist party, into the democratic consensus remained, and that process was started in the 1960s. Today everybody acknowledges that the center-left coalition was a total failure; but what failed and why are seldom explained. The failure lay not so much in the fact that the center-left governments accomplished little; this was easily predictable and had in fact been predicted. A heterogeneous coalition is almost by definition a quarrelsome and inefficient coalition. The center-left was a failure for the more central—and far less remembered—reason that its outcome totally belied its aims. There is no doubt as to why the opening to the left was advocated: its declared aim was to divide the left's front, to isolate the PCI, and thereby to reinforce and democratize the PSI. Similarly, there is no doubt about the outcome: it was almost the exact opposite of the design.

The PSI was neither reinforced nor integrated as was hoped and predicted. To be sure, the PSI was integrated into the spoils system; but, unlike their German counterparts, the Italian Socialists have never renounced Marxism as their basic world view. Some fifteen years ago I described the Italian Socialist party as standing halfway between the negation and the acceptance of the political system, and, more precisely, as a party of "feeble acceptance." It seems to me that the PSI remains today very much what it was then and, let it be added, what it has been for more than fifty years: a bundle of contradictions torn by factional outflankings even more than by contrary souls.

In 1922, on the verge of the downfall that brought Benito Mussolini to power, Paolo Bonomi (the leading Social Democrat of the time) made a last, desperate appeal to the Socialists. The party responded that it could promise only "external and conditioned support." Bonomi departed, Luigi Facta entered, and Mussolini followed. If one reads the intraparty debates of the critical period that preceded the advent of fascism, cancels the names and the concrete references, and modernizes the language slightly, it is almost impossible to detect whether a given speech was delivered in 1922 or in the 1970s. The actors have changed, but the arguments are the same.

As for the other expectation from the opening to the left, instead of reinforcement there has been a progressive enfeeblement of the Socialists. The disproportion between PCI and PSI has grown by leaps and bounds. In 1963, in the first center-left election, the PCI vote rose to 25 percent of the total, while the PSI remained, with a small loss, at its previous 14 percent level. In 1976, the PCI was up to 34 percent, and the PSI down to 10 percent. The gap has thus grown from eleven to twenty-four percentage points. Moreover, the PCI was never isolated; quite the contrary, it became uncontainable. The "containment" of the 1950s became the "penetration" of the 1960s. All in all, a political design has seldom been so quickly and so cruelly disappointed.

The Error of the 1960s

Why were the predictions about the outcome of that "opening" so wrong? I still think—even in retrospect—that the policy was in the cards, and that with better players—indeed merely with decent players—the game was by no means a losing one. Quite the contrary, the chances of winning were high. As I recall the debates in the early 1950s, few of the most influential spokesmen objected on grounds of principle or of risk. Much of the debate was about the economic cost and, especially, about the timing and the conditions that would best secure the success of the experiment.

"Experiment" is indeed the word that conveys how the opening to the left was then perceived by most of us.

There is a straightforward explanation of what went wrong with the experiment. It was killed at its very inception by the amazing stipulation that the center-left coalition was "nonreversible." Once done, it could not be undone; it had to perform, regardless of how it performed. This meant, in practice, that the governing parties of the time, especially the DC, divested themselves of their leverage over the PSI. The "pulling in" of socialism had no pulling force to it.

Was this provision the result of sheer stupidity? Not quite. In part it was intended as an ideological constraining; but it also resulted from crude factional maneuvering. Factions of the DC left happily deprived their party of its leverage, in order to acquire for themselves leverage over their party. In any event, an experiment under a nonreversibility clause is no longer an experiment: it becomes an erratic happening that entirely escapes monitoring. This is how what appeared to be a safe risk at the inception of the center-left coalition turned out to be an unsafe risk, and indeed, from today's vantage point, a badly miscalculated one. And this is the lesson of the 1960s that I propose to carry over to the predicament of the 1970s.

To be sure, the assertion that the PCI involves a far greater risk than the PSI does not require buttressing from the experience of the 1960s: it stands on its own merits. Nonetheless, a revisit to the 1960s is highly instructive. For many people, perhaps unknowingly, seem to assess the opening to the PCI with the same arguments and yardsticks that were applied to the opening to the PSI—as if it were a same kind of move, albeit on a more ambitious scale.

It is evident, for instance, that the integration of the PCI is often treated exactly like the integration of the PSI, with complete disregard not only for the enormous differences between them but also of what the center-left confirmed once again—namely, that a "democratic integration" is far more easily promised than accomplished (in Italy, let it be recalled, the attempts at integrating socialism go back before World War I to Giovanni Giolitti). More important, I am struck by the growing frequency with which the Historic Compromise is being propounded in the 1970s as an experiment—exactly as the opening to the left was in the 1960s. As I hope to have shown, even the so-called experiment of the 1960s turned out not to be such: it was distorted, and indeed disnatured, by a mere "mental clause" (for the nonreversibility of the center-left coalition was not imposed by the distribution of power in Parliament). Can it escape us that the Historic Compromise will be reversible, if actuated, only if the PCI decides to undo it?

The "Minor Risk" Logic

Let me spell out the underlying lesson we should have learned from the 1960s. When the stakes of politics are high—as they are in Italy, as well as in all other countries of "polarized pluralism"—then a *risk perspective* is the appropriate perspective. But how does one calculate a risk? The suggestion offered here is that the calculus of a risk necessarily involves a *minor risk logic*. Let me explain with reference to the case at hand.

The PCI currently proposes itself for a governmental alliance, and there is no doubt that a risk is involved. The question is: How should we interpret both the statements and the actual behavior of the PCI? We are advised, at times, to interpret them without imputing motives and purposes. That advice involves a maximum risk. If verbal behavior is not to be interpreted in the light of what may have prompted it, we are left with words taken at face value; and I can think of nothing more dangerous (at least in politics). Similarly, since behavior is never intentionless, if we do not explain it with reference to plausible interests and rewards, choices and constraints, the sure thing is that we are not explaining it at all. Instead, we add blindness to uncertainty, or we smuggle as "facts" our own hidden imputations and preferences.

The logic that I am recommending does take, then, the risk of imputing motives and intentions to words and to actions—after all, this is how an explanation explains. However, it minimizes the risk of a misinterpretation that carries the weight of a miscalculation by seeking a *minimally sufficient explanation,* as distinguished from a complete explanation. The criterion of a minimally sufficient explanation is whether or not it provides a *sufficient reason.* The scholar's inclination is to explore all the conceivable possibilities. This yields greater completeness but it multiplies the probability of error. The strategy of the minimally sufficient explanation is to minimize the maximum loss. The scholar enjoys being an adventurous player—after all, he plays for others and at the expense of others. But the "risk calculator" must be a safe player.

Eurocommunism: A Quest for International Legitimacy

The question now becomes: Why has the PCI not forced its way into the government since the 1976 election? As phrased the question assumes that the PCI could enter the government anytime it really wanted to. So, why does it not want to?

The explanation need not be farfetched. The PCI well understands the imperatives of economy. It has long administered cooperatives and local governments, as well as its own colossal party budget; it has entrepreneurial experience and capacities; and, last and foremost, it is haunted by what happened in Chile to Allende. International stranglehold? Maybe. However, Portugal in only one year, between 1974 and 1975, wrecked its economy all by itself, unaided by international or capitalistic plots. Chile and Portugal are accustomed to poverty, and their populations are on the order of 9–10 million. Italy has 55 million inhabitants; it has tasted the glow of prosperity; and its level of expectations approaches that of the affluent societies. If the Italian Communists are haunted by the Chilean economic collapse, they are dead right, for the magnitude of an Italian economic catastrophe would be immeasurably greater. Italy's agricultural output falls short of being able to feed a fifth of its inhabitants; the country has no oil, no gas, no coal, no minerals; it lives off industrial transformation, and the giants of the Italian industrial system, with very few exceptions, are by now in shaky condition.

Without international economic credibility and support, Italy would become unable to purchase what it desperately needs for survival in a matter of some twelve months. I am not assuming, let it be stressed, any international conspiracy. A boycott would make things worse, but, in the long run, no different. Capital owners—whether individuals, banks, or multinational corporations—abide by the "law of nature" that, when imperiled, they seek safety in fleeing. Thus, any perception of Italian Communism as a danger is already a sufficient reason for the Italian balance of payments to collapse.

So, the PCI waits. It does not force itself into the government because any forcing would arouse fears that would frighten away both internal and external capital. A related question is: What does it wait *for*? Here the surmise is substantiated by mounting evidence that the PCI is keenly, if not anxiously, engaged in seeking international credibility and, even more, *legitimacy*.

The word "Eurocommunism" was coined, casually and in utter innocence, around 1975 (see the discussion in chapter 6). Its immediate success is by no means fortuitous but attests to the game in town. I shall not enter into the obscurities of what Eurocommunism *is*. What is far less obscure is what it is *for*. Simply put, Eurocommunism is the word that symbolizes a quest for legitimacy. Its supporters are, in fact, legitimizers; and its detractors are, in effect, combating the legitimation. Hardly anybody denies that European Communism in general, and Italian Communism in particular, has changed. But has this change gone as far as to imply that a Communist party no longer is, in reality, a Communist party? This is the question. And a label whose referent is merely geographic has this convenience: it encourages a question for which it provides no clue. Again, it is no accident that Eurocommunism is preferred (by the Communists themselves) to "neocommunism." The latter term implies, despite the "neo," that Communism remains Communism (thus conflicting with the quest for legitimacy) while on the other hand acknowledging more change than the Communist parties are prepared to acknowledge (on other fronts, and with respect to their true believers). "Eurocommunism" implies nothing, and by the same token allows limitless speculation.

Moderation and "War of Position"

The PCI, then, waits, and we have a sufficient—if, perhaps, incomplete—explanation of why it is waiting. We still have to look into *how* it is waiting. There is little doubt that in the last few years, and especially since the 1976 elections, the PCI's behavior has been characterized by responsible moderation. In particular, the DC government owes its survival to the "constructive opposition" (in the visible arenas) and to the bargained "collaboration" (in the invisible ones) of the PCI. Does this behavior—which is real, not verbal—attest to the true nature of Eurocommunism? More pointedly, does it imply that the PCI is by now "integrated" into the system and, through another inferential leap, a "democratized" party? This is indeed a crucial, if not *the* crucial question, but before an answer is attempted two preliminary points should be settled.

I would emphasize the novelty of this recent behavior, as against the view that it simply represents a crescendo of a longstanding trend. That view flies in the face of the fact that the Italian state has, by now, been almost destroyed. Without delving into a state of disruption that surely has no equivalent in Western Europe, it is hard to believe that a total dysfunction results simply from the ineptitude of the DC. The PCI is often described, especially by foreign observers, as having promoted, over two decades, the democratization of the institutions (such as the schools, the university, the judiciary, the police, and the army). But from nearby, this appears to be an entirely different process—one of ruthless infiltration. (Curiously, these foreign observers seldom credit the PCI with the democratization of the press and the other media, though exactly the same kind of "democratization" has occurred there.) In my view, then, the PCI's game never is "played straight."

There is indeed a longstanding coherence and continuity in the strategy of the PCI; but it can be understood only by reading Antonio Gramsci. While I place little trust in occasional speeches, articles, and *ad hoc* interviews, I do take seriously the doctrine—the real socializing instrument. So I take very seriously Gramsci's strategic advice, which hinges on the distinction between *war of movement* and *war of position.* The war of movement is the frontal attack and seizure. The war of position—Gramsci's original contribution—consists of a systematic undermining and infiltration aimed at "hegemony" over the civil society, that is, over its controlling ganglia. The PCI was shaped by Togliatti to follow the so-called Italian road to socialism, precisely in the manner of Gramsci's war-of-position party; and the long march of the PCI across the institutions and networks of Italian society is precisely a marching toward Gramsci's hegemony. Note that if the war of position is won, the war of movement becomes unnecessary: the state will fall by itself. But note especially that the war of position is still a *war*.

Gramsci had witnessed the defeat of the working class in a frontal war, that is, of a class war conducted in the orthodox fashion. With his concept of hegemony, Gramsci called for a post-Malthusian strategy of cross-class war. Indeed, a Communist party that remains a class party hinders its own expansion and at the same time antagonizes the excluded class, or classes. Thus, under Gramsci's doctrine, it was natural for a PCI that had reached its class borders to become a catchall party. The objection might be: can a cross-class, catchall party still be a "war party"? The reply, as authoritatively given by Carl Schmitt, is yes, obviously. In contrast to a peaceful and legalitarian conception of politics, Schmitt projects the vision of *politics as war*. By this, he intends not recourse to arms or actual violence, but the perception of "the other" as an enemy. When politics is so conceived—as it has been conceived in all times—politics becomes Gramsci's war of position: a matter of gaining control of the territory of the enemy, and dealing with its population as one deals, in occupation, with enemies. This is why the PCI cannot be said to play the game straight. This expression is appropriate to a peaceful-legalitarian perception of politics, but meaningless or deceitful when applied to a warlike one. With this essential proviso, it can be granted that one of the side effects of the PCI's war of position has been to legitimize the parliamentary game; but this is a meager reassurance. Having seen it happen with fascism, Gramsci well knew that when the state falls, a parliament can be reduced to a sham almost overnight. Moreover, the Marxist doctrine has in store a formidable arsenal for delegitimizing a parliamentary game, if there were ever a need.

We are now ready to confront the question, How should we interpret the current moderate and constructive behavior of the PCI? My reply is again a very simple one: the moderation of the PCI is *a function of its proximity to state power.*

This interpretation flows from the war-of-position strategy, whose basic tenet is first to undermine in order to occupy, and then to sustain what is being occupied. Moreover, if the PCI's ability to reign is contingent upon external legitimacy (and help), then a responsible moderation becomes the more essential as the PCI approaches power. Finally, demolition for the sake of demolition is not only a practice that is alien to the nature of the PCI; it would also be, under the circumstances, shockingly irrational. Whether rightly or wrongly, the PCI expects to inherit the Italian Republic, not only with its ministries, but also with its enormous problems and liabilities. From this perspective, the rational course of action (and the PCI leadership is very rational) is to keep its inheritance in the best possible condition. In the final analysis, by being collaborative the PCI collaborates with itself.

The arguments presented above in support of the assertion that the "good behavior" of the PCI is a function of its proximity to power are no more than a minimally sufficient explanation. This interpretation may well be incomplete, and the PCI's good behavior may reflect a "new soul." If, however, the behavior of the PCI since 1976 reflects a perfectly rational self-interest (in the sense that it would be highly irrational to behave otherwise), then it cannot reveal what is happening in the PCI's soul. Maybe the soul explorers have hit upon the truth, but the level of uncertainty in their explorations is—given the magnitude of the stakes—far too high.

Coalitions With and Coalitions Under

If the PCI enters the government, what is the import of this event? It will be noted that I say *if,* not *when.* We may be able to predict trends or sequences of self-generating events, but surely not their timing and tempo, and the quest for international legitimacy is a major delaying factor. Moreover, predictions, when believed, have a reflection effect, or feedback. For these and other reasons, a prospective analysis is best stated in *if . . . then* terms.

The question may be divided into two subquestions: If the PCI ascends to the government, (1) What is the import of the occurrence as such? and (2) What will happen next?

In order to assess the import, it is essential to perceive the fundamental difference between *participation in* and *control of* a coalition. If this distinction is missed, then everything else is missed. The Historic Compromise is most often described as a "coalition government with Communist participation," with little consideration whether it makes sense to conceive of the PCI as a mere "coalition partner."

Let us begin by establishing that the Italian case has no precedent. In the late 1930s, in the aftermath of World War II, and again in the 1970s, Communist parties did indeed enter "bourgeois" governments. But these were all cases of partnership without control. The more recent instances occurred in four Western countries: Chile, Iceland, Portugal, and Finland.

In Chile, during the Allende period, the Communists, with about 15 percent of the total vote, were doubtless unable to monitor the course of events. Instead they were the victims of the infantile malady that swept the Chilean left.

Iceland, with an electorate of little more than 100,000, is not only a minor but also a peculiar case, for the country's overriding concerns are fishing rights and the American military base. A Communist-controlled Popular Alliance entered a coalition government between 1971 and the summer of 1973 with two ministries (out of seven); the Communist electoral strength was estimated to be in the 15 percent range; and the coalition collapsed under a heightening inflation that was nearing 60 percent.

Portugal provides an even less significant instance. In 1974 and 1975 Cunhal, the Communist leader, did influence the government headed by General Gonçalves, who was clearly riding Cunhal's tiger; yet at the April 1975 elections the Communists mustered a bare 10 percent of the vote and obtained, under the subsequent Azevedo government, just one ministry (Public Works).

Finland offers the only truly significant case. The Finnish Communist party entered a coalition in 1966 and again in 1970–1971 (for eight months), and it was almost forced by President Kekkonen to enter the coalition government of 1975. Its average electoral turnout is 20 percent, with a peak strength of 23 percent in 1945 and 1958, and a low of 17 percent in 1970 and 1972. Not only has the party failed to expand, but it has long been bitterly split between a "liberal" and a Stalinist wing (which currently votes against the party's own cabinet members). The Finnish Communist party owes its participation in these coalitions to Finland's lack of autonomy vis-à-vis the Soviet Union, not to the fact of being a needed coalition partner. Thus, nobody in Finland debates whether the party can be "trusted." The matter is irrelevant; and in fact the party is not trusted, and has never been given a free hand with the crucial portfolios. Not even Finland, then, comes anywhere near to being a comparable precedent to Italy.

In the debate on the Historic Compromise, trust is indeed a crucial concern, because the PCI in government will be not a participant *without* control, but rather a participant *in* control. At the outset we may speak of a coalition in which the PCI is "first among equals." But the import of the event as such is that the PCI will be not a *partner in,* but the likely *master of,* the coalition. And this is the crux of the matter.

There are many yardsticks for measuring the force of a party. Thus far I have used the most expedient one: the electoral yardstick. On this measure, the PCI has arrived at one-third of the total vote, the Finnish Communist party musters about one-fifth, and the French Communist party has declined from the one-fourth it had during the Fourth Republic to about one-fifth in the Fifth Republic. If only by a narrow margin, then, the PCF ranks, electorally, as the second largest Western Communist party. And since France not only displayed a popular front coalition in the late thirties, but tried again at the same formula—under the name of *Union de Gauche*—in 1978, it is appropriate to add France to our list of comparisons. Whether or not the French union (and disunion) of the left will ever pass the post is immaterial, for our question reads: *If* the PCI were to enter the government in Italy, and *if* France were to have a new popular front government, how would the two situations compare? The pertinent yardsticks would be: (1) Who controls the unions; (2) How strong are the Socialists; (3) Where do the influential intellectuals stand; and (4) The constitutional differences between a parliamentary and a presidental system.

Only by the first criterion would there be a resemblance, but only a feeble one. The PCI's control over the Italian labor force also extends over the Socialist workers, whereas the French Socialist workers constitute a respectable force of their own. By the second criterion, the Communists are much stronger than the Socialists in Italy (even more than is revealed by their respective vote shares of 35 and 10 percent), whereas the opposite is true in France (and French Socialists do not have the inferiority complex of their Italian counterparts.) By the third criterion—the crucial one for Gramsci—the PCI has hegemony over Italy's cultural networks, whereas the French intelligentsia is often anti-Communist and by no means under the spell of the PCF. Finally, by the fourth criterion, the two cases are far apart: in the French presidential system, a parliamentary victory of the left would lead only to a stalemate (unless implemented by a successive and, under the circumstances, unlikely presidential victory). All in all, then, France currently compares to Italy as a low, or in any event, lower risk; and Italy, not France, is and remains the test case of Eurocommunism.

The foregoing also suggests how the force of the PCI is to be measured at home, that is, in Italy. By now it is uncertain how much control the PCI has over the Italian general confederation of labor and, through it, over the whole of the "confederal" labor force; but the PCI does remain well in control of a large majority of workers, while the DC has lost its leverage over its former Catholic unions. On the other hand, we already know that the PSI is a poor competitor, and often a convenient outrider, for the PCI, and that the PCI has largely won the "cultural" war of position. We are thus left with the problem of assessing the force of the PCI in comparison with the force of the DC in a global fashion. Electorally the DC remained ahead, even at the 1976 elections, with 39 percent, compared with the PCI's 34 percent; and the interval may well revert to some ten percentage points. The fact remains that the electoral distance is a poor indicator, for on all substantive grounds the relationship between the two parties is like that between iron and clay.

The PCI demands "democracy" everywhere and for everybody else, but it never practices any kind of democracy in its own house—thus failing the best test of where its soul really stands. The party remains as strongly centralized and as hierarchic as ever, all the way down the line. This entails that it can easily change course, that it can reverse tomorrow what it does today, and that its mobilizational capability is enormous. At the other extreme, the DC is a confederation of factions that have long been far more concerned with serving themselves than the party's fortunes. Even if the DC's factionalism is not pressed to the point of suicide, the fact remains that the party can maneuver very slowly, if at all, and has almost no mobilizational power. Also, the PCI's electorate is either identified or encapsulated within strong clientele-type networks, and in any event kept under steady media bombardment. The DC's voice in the media is inaudible, and the party owes its plurality to a frightened electorate, holding on to the DC as long as it holds the PCI out. The government is, thus, the only remaining trump up the DC's sleeve. At the very moment that the DC embarks the PCI in a government, both its electorate and its clientele will be in danger of disbandment. This is, then, the import of the event uneventfully called "coalition government with Communist participation."

To summarize, even if these estimates of the forces of the PCI and the DC are challenged, the Historic Compromise still cannot be viewed as a "coalition experiment" like others, that is, of a normal or tested kind. A coalition among equals is different from a coalition among unequals; and a coalition among ideological neighbors is a far cry from a coalition among ideological foes. The magnitude of the risk is not grasped, therefore, by saying coalition *with* the PCI, but by saying, coalition *under* the PCI.

What Will Happen Next?

Having discussed the correct formulation of the risk, we can now begin to explore the future. My scenario of "possible futures" will be confined, however, to a first and second act.

At the outset, the only firm element of the plot is a dyarchal coalition—with all the minor parties, including the PSI, relegated to façade roles—engaged in a tug-of-war. The tug-of-war is a certainty because it is embedded in the very nature of a PCI-DC dyarchy. No matter how much the party leaders may want to soft-pedal their divergences, the PCI and the DC inescapably represent, for their respective activists, electorates, and clienteles, contrary and alternative coagulation poles. Even if we grant (for the sake of conjecture) that the PCI is a democratic party, yet its *Weltanshauung* still shares nothing, or very little, with a non-Marxist liberal-democratic vision of the world. The ideology that nurtures and makes a Communist Marxist is, at base, as it has always been: it holds that capitalism is the ultimate cause of all ills; that true liberty comes only with economic equality; and that the goal is total victory, the crushing of the exploiters by the exploited.

In the second place, the war of position is a zero-sum game: it consists of seizing a position that somebody else loses. Therefore, on grounds both of ideological beliefs and of survival, the dyarchy hinges on two poles that are mutually repulsive. Actually, the dyarchy endures only to the extent that each team pulls away from the other. If one team yields, or marches in the direction of the other, then the dyarchy becomes a monocracy—period.

My earlier estimate indicated, however, that only one of the two parties, the PCI, is (as Pareto would put it) a "lion." Hence the deployment of the plot will have one director, not two. While in the first act the DC will desperately attempt to resist, the question is: How fast, and how far, will the PCI press its attack? And here begin the uncertainties.

The rational path for the PCI would be to perform very unobtrusively—while attending, at the same time, to the conquest of the remaining positions. This course of action is strongly recommended by the need for legitimacy and the related international and national economic imperatives. It is the path dictated by the Allende lesson. Powerful counterforces may, however, make the rational route impracticable. These counterforces—that I shall call constraints of heredity—are of two sorts: cumulations and expectations.

With respect to the *cumulations,* the PCI inherits the formidable array of ills it produced or aggravated during the long period of its nonconstructive opposition—when it conquered by disrupting. As the PCI ascends to power, the country is almost ungovernable and replete with "bombs" ready for explosion (such as the inflation of useless and unemployable university graduates).

The other element—*expectations*—is seldom recalled. Yet it is obvious that the PCI has sustained its long march across the institutions by means of the adversary expectations it generated. The worker has been told that he would no longer be exploited by the capitalist; the peasant, that the landowner is a parasite and that he is entitled to the land. As the catchall tactics come to the fore, the promises grow in range and incompatibility. Let it also be emphasized that a Communist party does not deal in "ordinary promises"; that it so happens that its promises are taken very seriously; and, therefore, that with victory the expectations bill comes due very forcibly.

If we assume, as it is plausible to assume, that the PCI will try to pursue the rational, slow-moving, and reassuring course of action, then the first act of my scenario will last as long as the above described contrary forces do not prevail. The longer it lasts, the better for the PCI, and also for the country. But the first act may be very short; it may be drawn to an early end, to use Nenni's favorite expression, by the "force of things," that is, by what I have called the constraints of the heredity.

The Moment of Truth

In the second act the force of things would prevail over the rational course of action. But why should there be a second act at all? Why should we exclude, that is, the possibility of a pure and simple evolution and progression of the rational course of action? Well, the second act will be the "moment of truth"—and this moment, I predict, must come.

Let it be noted, to begin with, that the dyarchial tug-of-war period will be marked not only by irresolution and reciprocal vetoes, but also by a very costly inflation; for the PCI will have to placate the expectations of its clientele, as will the DC, by yielding to demands. The economy may remain healthy because on entering the government the PCI may well obtain a honeymoon from the unions, higher productivity from the workers, and a deferral of the expectations. But honeymoons are just honeymoons, and deferral means what it says. Actually, one pressing expectation, shared by the country at large and hardly amenable to postponements, is the expectation of "resolution," of an end of the long era of irresolution. When the resolutions come, however, they will unveil the real master. And this is the moment of truth.

As the PCI loses the convenient alibi (for its rational course of action) that it is a mere part of a coalition government, all the knots will become tangled into a Gordian knot. Take, for example, the hyper-left that has long been menacingly swarming in ever-growing numbers (under the past irresolutions) across cities, schools, and universities. Not only the ultras will trigger the expectations—encouraging occupations of homes, lands, and factories—but they become a "provocation" (from the left) that a Communist party seated in the house of power cannot tolerate. In any event, unlawfulness, disorder, and violence have reached a point at which they can be curbed only by an iron fist. The PCI will also find itself increasingly (and, I venture to add, unsustainably) pressured from its own quarters, that is, by the expectations of its believers. If it gives in, the economy is doomed. But in order not to give in, it must again have recourse to an iron fist—and, from this angle, to an iron fist that is undistinguishable from a dictatorship *over* the proletariat. All in all, the moment of truth seemingly leaves the PCI with no choice. Its only choice is to draw the sword and to use it, both for cutting the Gordian knot of the "cumulations," and for dishonoring, as is necessary, the "expectations bill."

The scenario can and should be deployed in far greater detail than I have just given.[1] Let me bring it, however, to a close by addressing the problem from an entirely different angle. My scenario is an optimistic one insofar as I have implicitly assumed that the PCI, in its heart of hearts, would prefer to perform nondictatorially. This surmise has three grounds: first, that Italians are Italians (even when they are Communists); second, that "changes" have occurred; third, that a Communist dictatorship is highly disrecommended, under the circumstances, by "rational" imperatives. Nevertheless, we should also recognize what is a near impossibility, namely, that a Communist party save a crumbling democracy through democratic means. Aside from the fact that "democratic means" cannot be an important value for a Communist (as the structure of his own house attests), not even the truest and most experienced democrat knows quite how to avert a breakdown with democratic means. So, are we not asking from a Communist party something that lies between the absurd and the miraculous?

However that may be, my unfinished scenario suggests that, once in orbit, the deployment of the Historic Compromise will hinge less and less on good intentions or rational oughts. In the final analysis, the "soul"—even if democratic—becomes totally irrelevant. The force of things takes over and unleashes a chain reaction, a *chaining of events,* that imposes its own course.

Maybe it has been noted that, throughout my argument, soul searching explorations based on exegetic analysis have been absent. The neglect is deliberate, on two counts. In the first place, exegesis is treacherously unreliable, at least when the messages are selected, as they in fact are, on the basis of their novelty. What about the other messages, the reinforcing ones that are not new? When Nenni spoke as an orthodox Marxist in the 1950s—when he was the undisputed leader of the official Socialist party—we said: these are mere words that should be disregarded, for the real Nenni is not to be found in his maximalist rhetoric. Today, when Berlinguer does not quite sing the Eurocommunist tune, we say the same thing: this is for mass (or other) consumption, not the real Berlinguer. The point is not, of course, that we should not watch over what is said, how it is said, and what is no longer said; but we should, by now, be on guard and realize for how long we have been deceived by swimming in a sea of naiveté. And the warning is that single, isolated messages may

[1] The more detailed scenario in four acts (that are, therefore, differently sliced) will appear in Italian, *Lo scenario del compromesso storico,* in "Quaderni di Biblioteca della Libertà," n.ro 11 (Turin: Centro Einaudi, 1978).

reveal less than the aggregate message conveyed every day in the headlines of the party press.

My second reason for neglecting soul searching explorations is that my scenario suggests that the constraints of the situation will dictate—regardless of intentions—the course of the events. An objection might be that the exegetic exercise does enjoy at least one advantage over the scenario technique, namely, not sharing in the fallibility of games played "against the future." It seems to me, however, that the text decipherer projects himself into the future just as much as the scenarist. When he judges an assertion to be credible, he is actually predicting that at some future point in time these words will become deeds. We are all surmising. The difference is whether our bets are best placed on words or, instead, on a chaining of circumstances.

The International Aspect

The last question is, Can something be done? If the Italian case were only an Italian case, the question would be better addressed in Rome than in Washington. Yet the Historic Compromise will be—if enacted—of very great consequence in the international arena. If the experiment were to succeed in Italy, it would in all likelihood chart the course also for France and, in the longer run, for Spain and Portugal. Putting it somewhat dramatically, if Italy were lost, Europe would be lost—with West Germany plunged into a Berlin-type predicament. But what is exactly meant by "success"?

For the sake of argument, let us assume that Italy will end up with Communist-controlled coalition governments whose substance is a Communist rule under coalitional façades. What then would be deemed success and, conversely, what would be perceived a failure? This is no small question. It can be disposed of briefly, however, by recalling that in a world pervaded by mass media "the media are the message," and that in most of the West the media are currently far more ideologized than, say, twenty years ago. Somewhat differently and more specifically put, today the media personnel increasingly display proleft sympathies; and to the extent that this orientation currently leads to advocating the legitimization of the PCI, to the same extent those who favor the Historic Compromise today are already committed to its "success version" tomorrow. That is, I realize, a harsh judgment. Yet the drift of Italian politics—surveyed at this meeting—from one "opening" to another has been the working of influential elites which have been invariably wrong in whatever they designed and predicted, and yet have managed to appear always right—either by applauding whatever happens, or by disguising it, and in any case by forgetting their earlier prophecies. The point is, then, that "success" will hardly be established by the facts of the matter. The advocate of the "PCI solution" will always hold that it is the best possible solution. Hence the risk is poorly calculated by assuming that if the Italian experiment fails, no dire consequences will follow for the rest of Europe. True—if the media were not the message. But far less true in a world whose media message is—in these matters—ideologically willed and ideologically blinded.

The central question may not be, however, about the destiny of Europe, but rather about the potential threat of Eurocommunism to the Soviet empire. I shall not enter this intricate question, except for noting that we are surely dealing, here, with a double-edged knife. If Eurocommunism may well be, for the Soviet Union, an ideological disturbance or even menace, the fact remains that the ascendance of Communist or Eurocommunist parties renders Western Europe an easy prey not only on military, but even more on belief grounds, for it attests to the crisis of the belief system upon which liberal democracy rests. To perceive Eurocommunism only as a menace to the Soviet Union, and not as a menace to what the West stands for, strikes me as an ominous symptom—and as a miscalculation on a grand scale.

The last argument that I wish to consider is that since the Historic Compromise is inevitable, it is in the interest of the United States to be friendly and to dispose the PCI to friendship. Since this is a simple argument, it can be simply discussed and challenged.

First, the Historic Compromise is made inevitable by declaring it inevitable. I have never declared it such, and have stressed all along that the international context plays in this matter a decisive role. Italy is an autonomous entity when it votes. Nonetheless, Italy has a very low economic autonomy. The PCI confronts, in this respect, a dilemma that resembles the squaring of the circle: reconciling capitalism and Communism. If the capitalists flee, an economic disaster of unprecedented magnitude is certain. But for how long can the PCI abide by Lenin's New Economic Policy? The Italian industrial system is already largely state owned, and ripe for a socialist transformation, that is, for being converted to a socialist economy. Unfortunately, Italy cannot afford the low productivity that marks all the socialist economic systems. So, either in the immediate or in the longer run the economic problem is bound to become, for the PCI, an explosive, dramatic problem. Second, gratitude has never been important in politics. In particular, the Communists are realists who understand and respect, by their own token, forcefulness. What they respect less is feebleness or, being intelligent, stupidity.

My advice comes down to this: the minor risk lies in not igniting the fuse. In the 1960s, the alleged American "interference" in the opening to the left merely consisted—we have been authoritatively told—of showing a green light that was largely of Arthur Schlesinger's fabrication. Currently, even that little could be too much. There are some things that can be said on behalf of Italians: their astounding resilience, their ability in floating and remaining afloat, their inventiveness in patching up, and their resourcefulness in making the provisional endure, in buying time. Italians distinguish among (1) my problem, (2) your problem, and (3) their problem. Maybe the PCI cannot afford to wait. But an Italian would say, or might say, that this is their problem.

11

Communist Parties in Western Europe: Challenge to the West

Henry A. Kissinger

The cohesion of the industrial democracies of Western Europe, North America, and Japan has been for thirty years the bulwark of peace and the engine of global prosperity.

This unity has been the keystone of our foreign policy in every administration from President Truman's to President Carter's. The first permanent peacetime security alliance in American history was with the democratic nations of the Atlantic Community; it was soon followed by our commitment to the security of Japan. Since then, the agenda of cooperation among the industrial democracies has spread from collective defense to common action on energy policy, economic recovery, the international economic system, and relations with the Communist countries and with the Third World. This cohesion rests not simply on material considerations of wealth and power but on a common moral foundation as well—on the shared conviction that the consent of the governed is the basis of government and that every individual enjoys inalienable rights and is entitled to constitutional liberties.

It is ironic that at the moment when the industrial democracies are most cohesive in their opposition to external threats, at a time when our cooperative efforts cover a broader range than ever, the unity developed with so much effort and imagination over a generation should be jeopardized by an internal danger—the growth of Communist parties and the danger of their accession to power in some of the countries of Western Europe.

In Italy, in the parliamentary elections of June 1976, the Communist party obtained 34 percent of the vote, strengthening its position as the second largest party and as a powerful rival of the Christian Democratic party, which has governed Italy throughout the postwar period. The Communists' growth since the 1972 election has been primarily at the expense of the Democratic Socialist groups, and is part and parcel of an increasing and dangerous polarization of Italian politics. The Communists have already achieved a virtual veto over government programs in the Italian Parliament.

In France, in the presidental election of April 1974, a coalition of the Communist and Socialist parties came within one percentage point of victory on the final ballot. A majority for this coalition in the parliamentary elections, which must take place by March 1978, would bring Communist leaders into key ministerial positions. It would do so, moreover, in conditions of constitutional crisis, for the constitution of the Fifth Republic has not yet faced the test of a president and a prime minister from different parties.

In the Iberian peninsula, where hopeful steps are being taken towards democracy, Communist parties have fought with ruthlessness and disciplined organization to increase their already considerable influence. Portugal is a member of NATO; Spain is strategically crucial and tied by special agreements to the United States. Communist participation in the government of either country would have serious consequences for Western unity and Western security.

And these Communist challenges do not exist in isolation from each other. There is no doubt that a Communist breakthrough to power or a share in power in one country will have a major psychological effect on the others, by making Communist parties seem respectable, or suggesting that the tide of history in Europe is moving inexorably in their direction.

Most of the causes of this phenomenon are indigenous to the individual countries. And by the same token, the response to this challenge must come in the first instance from European leaders and voters who are persuaded that democracy is worth the effort. America cannot make their choices for them or decide the outcome of free elections.

But America *must* recognize the significance of what may lie ahead. We must not delude ourselves about what the accession of Communist leaders to executive power will mean to the most basic premises of American foreign policy. We must not confuse either our own people or those in allied countries who take seriously our judgments about the gravity of the threat. We must not weaken their resolve either by treating a Communist victory as inevitable—which it is not—or by imagining that a Communist electoral victory would be an accidental, transitory, or inconsequential phenomenon. The ultimate decisions are for the voters of Europe to make. But they—and we—would be indulging in wishful thinking if we all did not acknowledge now:

- that the accession to power of Communists in an allied country would represent a massive change in European politics
- that it would have fundamental consequences for the structure of

the postwar world as we have known it and for America's relationship to its most important alliances

- and that it would alter the prospects for security and progress for *all* free nations.

The Communist Parties and Western Democracies

Those who take a less grave view of these prospects often claim that the European Communist parties are independent of Moscow, that they have been effectively democratized or assimilated, and that they therefore pose no international issue in the broader East-West context.

It is true enough that the centrifugal and polycentric tendencies in the Communist world are one of the most striking developments of our age. These schisms, moreover, are made doubly intense by the passions of a quasi-religious battle over what is true dogma and what is heresy. Symptomatic is the fact that the Soviet Union has used military force in the postwar period only against other Communist countries—in East Berlin, in Hungary, in Czechoslovakia, and on the Sino-Soviet border. The Sino-Soviet conflict may indeed be the most profound and potentially explosive current international conflict. Nor is there a serious observer who disputes that the Communist parties in Western Europe have in fact occasionally demonstrated some degree of independence from the Soviet Union.

But this hardly exhausts the issue. For we must ask: In what sense and on what issues are they independent? And what are the objective consequences for the West of their policies and programs?

We are entitled to a certain skepticism about the sincerity of declarations of independence which coincide so precisely with electoral self-interest. One need not be a cynic to wonder at the decision of the French Communists, traditionally perhaps the most Stalinist party in Western Europe, to renounce the Soviet concept of dictatorship of the proletariat without a single dissenting vote among 1,700 delegates, as they did at their party congress in February 1976, when all previous party congresses had endorsed the same dictatorship of the proletariat by a similar unanimous vote of 1,700 to nothing. Why was there not at least one lonely soul willing to adhere to the previous view? Much was made of this change as a gesture of independence. Now it turns out that the new Soviet constitution, in preparation for years, drops the phrase "dictatorship of the proletariat" as well.

Throughout their existence, the guiding principle of the Communist parties has been their insistence that a minority had to seize power as the vanguard of the working class and impose its views on the rest of the population. This disdain for democratic procedures—whether it is presented in the traditional form of the "dictatorship of the proletariat" or wrapped in Gramsci's more elegant phrase, "the hegemony of the working class"—is precisely what has historically distinguished the Communist from the Socialist parties. I find it hard to believe that after decades of vilifying Social Democracy and treating it as their mortal enemy, especially in every Communist country, Communist parties have suddenly become Social Democrats. Whether or not they are independent of Moscow, Communists represent a philosophy which by its very nature and their own testimony stands outside the "bourgeois" framework of Western constitutional history. The Communist movement appeals to a different tradition and uses a largely misleading vocabulary.

To be sure, the French, Spanish, and Italian Communist parties have all recently declared their resolve "to work within the pluralism of political and social forces and to respect guarantees and develop all individual and collective freedoms." Enrico Berlinguer and Georges Marchais pledged their devotion to national independence and political pluralism at a conference of Communist parties in East Berlin in June 1976.

But can we take these declarations at face value? After all, Marchais has listed Bulgaria, Poland, and East Germany as countries having a "pluralistic" party system. As recently as 1972, French Communist doctrine was that "there can be no return from Socialism to Capitalism." And a few weeks ago, to the great irritation of their Socialist allies, the French Communists estimated the cost of the economic program of the two parties at over $100 billion. The Communist program—by definition—calls for the radical transformation of society; by the very nature of their beliefs Communists will be driven to bring about institutional changes that would make their ascendancy permanent.

Moreover, are these professions of the national road to Communism and of devotion to democratic principle really so new? Let me offer some quotations from European Communist leaders.

- *First:* "The crux of the matter, and we Marxists should know this well, is this: every nation will effect its transition to Socialism not by a mapped-out route, not exactly as in the Soviet Union, but by its own road, dependent on its historical, national, social, and cultural circumstances."

That was from a speech by Georgi Dimitrov, leader of the Bulgarian Communist party, in February 1946.

- *Second:* "We take the view that the method of imposing the Soviet system on [our country] would be wrong, since this method does not correspond to present-day conditions of development. . . . We take

> the view rather that the overriding interests of the . . . people in their present-day situation prescribe a different method . . . , namely the method of establishing a democratic anti-Fascist regime, a parliamentary democratic republic with full democratic rights and liberties for the people."

That is from a proclamation of the (East) German Communist party in June 1945.

- *Third:* "The great national task facing the country cannot be solved by either the Communist Party or by any other party alone. The Communist Party holds that it does not have a monopoly, and it does not need the monopoly, to work among the masses for the reconstruction of the new [nation]. The Communist Party does not approve of the idea of a one-party system. Let the other parties operate and organize as well."

That is a statement by Erno Gero, Communist party leader of Hungary, in November 1944.

- *Fourth:* "In [our country] there is a division of functions, and State power is based on parliamentary democracy. The dictatorship of the proletariat or of a single party is not essential. [Our country] can proceed and is proceeding along her own road."

That is from a speech by Wladyslaw Gomulka, Communist party leader of Poland, in January 1946.

- *Fifth:* "The Communist Party seeks to attain Socialism, but we are of the opinion that the Soviet system is not the only road to Socialism. . . . The coalition of the Communists with other parties is not opportunistic, a temporary limited coalition, but the expression . . . of all strata of the working people. . . . We seek at present to make certain that our new democratic parliamentary methods . . . be expressed in constitutional law. If you want the view of the Communists, I can only say that they will be the strictest guardians of the new Constitution."

That is a statement by Klement Gottwald, Communist party leader of Czechoslovakia, in January 1947.

- *Sixth:* Marchais speaks of "Socialism in the colors of France." But in 1938, George Orwell described French Communist strategy as "marching behind the tricolour."

In short, what the leaders of the Western Communist parties are saying today about their affection for the processes of democracy is not significantly different from what East European Communist leaders declared with equal emphasis in the 1940s—just before they seized the total power which they have never relinquished since.

Certainly Communist parties are willing to come to power by democratic means. But could they permit the democratic process to reverse what they see as the inevitable path of "historical progress?" Would they maintain the institutions—press, parties, unions, enterprises—that would represent the principal threat to their power? Would they safeguard the freedoms that could turn into instruments of their future defeat? No Communist party that governed alone has ever done so, and the vast majority of those democratic parties which entered coalitions with European Communists are now in the indexes of history books rather than ministries or parliaments.

The Italian Communist party, to be sure, left the government in 1948. But the situation today is greatly changed. In 1948, the Communist party was far smaller, with little regional or municipal power. It had to contend with a younger and more united Christian Democratic party, a strong Socialist party, and a determined Western Alliance alarmed by Stalin's adventures in Greece and Czechoslovakia. Today, Italian Communists participate in the governments of most major cities and regions, have enormous trade union strength and substantial support from intellectuals and the popular culture, and have reduced the strength of the Socialists to a fraction of what it was three decades ago.

The French Communists were similarly removed from the government in 1947, following the intensification of the cold war. But, just as in the Italian case the following year, the popular revolt against the Communists took place within the framework of a united West with a clear perception of an external and internal threat to its survival. By contrast there are now too many people on both sides of the Atlantic who have permitted themselves to be convinced that European Communism is only Social Democracy with a Leninist face.

We cannot know, with certainty, whether a fundamental change has occurred in these parties' traditional goals and tactics. But their internal organization and management speak against such a view. It is not democratic pluralism but the stern Leninist precept of "democratic centralism" which continues to guide the internal structure of all European Communist parties. This is a doctrine of iron discipline, not a principle of free and public dialogue. It is a system of dogma, of a "party line," of authority and obedience, of suppression of dissent and purge of dissenters. There are too many recent instances of resorts to violence, attempts to censor newspapers and broadcasting, and efforts to control the functioning of universities to be optimistic about their character.

Only in *Western* Europe and the United States are there still illusions about the nature of Communist parties. In Eastern Europe boredom, intellectual emptiness, inefficiency, and stultifying bureaucratism have been obvious for decades. Countries which used to be leading industrial powers have been reduced to mediocrity and stagnation; nations with long democratic traditions have seen the destruction of civil liberties and democratic practices. The countries of the West would mortgage their future if they closed their eyes to this reality. Societies that try to avoid difficult choices by making comforting assumptions about the future win no awards for restraint; they only speed their own demise.

Communist Parties and the Atlantic Alliance

It is sometimes asked: If the United States can deal with Communist governments in the Soviet Union, China, Eastern Europe, and even Cuba or Vietnam, why can we not accept and learn to deal with Communist parties seeking power in Western Europe? Is not the Soviet Union uneasy about the prospect of new Communist regimes that they may not be able to control?

These questions miss the central point. There is a crucial difference between managing conflict with adversaries and maintaining an alliance, when the prospects for stable East-West relations depend vitally on the cohesion of the Western Alliance. And even if some West European Communist parties should prove more difficult than the better disciplined satellites of East Europe, and thus pose new problems for Moscow, they would pose far more serious problems for the West.

For the key issue is not how "independent" the European Communists would be, but how Communist. The dynamics of the Communist parties and the program on which they would be elected suggest that their foreign and domestic policies are not likely to be consistent with the common purposes of the Atlantic Alliance.

The solidarity of the great industrial democracies has maintained global security for thirty years. Western collective defense provided the shield behind which the United States, Western Europe, and Japan developed the institutions of European unity and of the progressive world economic system. All these relationships would be severely jeopardized if Communists came to power in allied governments. Specifically:

The character of the Alliance would become confused to the American people. The signatories of the North Atlantic Treaty pledged in 1949 that "they are determined to safeguard the freedom, common heritage and civilization of their peoples, founded on the principles of democracy, individual liberty and the rule of law." If Communists entered governments in allied countries, the engagement to help maintain the military balance in Europe would lack the moral base on which it has stood for a generation. The American people would be asked to maintain their alliance commitment on the basis of two highly uncertain, untested assumptions: that there is a new trend of Communism which will in time split from Moscow, and that the West will be able to manipulate the new divisions to its advantage.

Both of these propositions are open to the most serious doubt. No major Communist split has ever been generated or maintained by deliberate Western policy—in fact the Soviet Union's disputes with Yugoslavia and with China had been festering for months and even years before the West became aware of them.

But even such a split—which would surely take years to develop—would hardly diminish the danger to current allied relationships. By the time it occurred the damage to the NATO structure would probably have become irreparable. And the character of the Atlantic relationship would be totally transformed, even should the United States, for its own reasons, eventually decide to support a revisionist Communism. While the United States can never be indifferent to the extension of Soviet hegemony to Western Europe, the permanent stationing of American forces in Europe could hardly be maintained for the object of defending some Communist governments against other Communist governments. Such a deployment could be justified only on the crudest balance of power grounds, which would be incompatible with American tradition and American public sentiment.

This is not a personal recommendation as to a desirable policy, but a judgment of stark reality. Significant participation by Communist parties in West European governments will over time undermine the moral and political basis for our present troop deployment in Europe.

The effect on Alliance cohesion generally would be disastrous. The Western Alliance has been held together by a system of close consultation based on shared goals and compatible philosophies. President de Gaulle cherished France's independence from the United States, but in major crises, over Berlin or Soviet missiles in Cuba, he stood firmly with his allies. By the same token, Communist governments in Western Europe, however independent of Moscow they may be on intraparty issues, can be expected to demonstrate their basic Communist convictions on major international issues.

If Communist parties come to power in Western Europe, significant divergences on foreign policy would be bound to develop between Europe and the United States and between European states in whose governments Communists participate and the others.

In February 1976, Italian Communist leader Berlinguer stated to a

London *Times* interviewer that "the Soviet Union's peace policy is in the general interest of mankind." The Italian party newspaper denounced NATO last year as "one of the fundamental instruments for American manipulation of the politics and economy of our country and Western Europe," and urged that "the relations between the countries of Western Europe and the two superpowers must be rediscussed." A leading member of the Italian party's central committee was asked in a recent interview with Radio Free Europe: If the French and Italian Communist parties were in power, what would they do in the event of "a grave international crisis between the Soviet Union and the West?" He answered: "We would choose the Soviet side, of course." Such "support" of NATO as is expressed is explicitly tactical, and rests upon a distortion of détente. It is coupled with the proposition that a Soviet threat against Western Europe is inconceivable. No European Communist party suggests that it wishes to be part of a Western Alliance to withstand Soviet aggression. And, indeed, how could Leninist parties dedicate themselves with any conviction to a military alliance whose primary purpose was and remains to counter Soviet power?

To be sure, these parties have had their differences with the Soviet Union, but in practically every case it has been on a matter of relations *within* the Communist movement. They have rarely, if ever, diverged from the Soviet position on an international issue. The Italian Communist party has hailed the Cubans in Angola as "freedom fighters," condemned the Israeli rescue of hostages at Entebbe as an "intolerable violation of Uganda's national sovereignty," applauded Soviet policy in Africa, and denounced American diplomatic efforts in Southern Africa as an attempt to "save the neocolonial and military-strategic interests of imperialism."

At best, West European Communist parties can be expected to steer their basic policies closer to the so-called nonaligned bloc and in an anti-Western direction. Yugoslavia—whose independence from Moscow on East European issues is by now traditional—has emerged as a champion of anti-Western and anti-American positions on most international issues outside of Eastern Europe. Why should we expect that Communist parties in Western Europe would be more friendly to us than the most independent East European state, which has been engaged for nearly three decades in an open dispute with Moscow and whose government the Kremlin has sought repeatedly to undermine?

The strong role our allies play in defending Western interests in many regions of the globe—such as President Giscard's courageous actions in Zaire—could not be expected from a nation where Communists share in governmental power. In the Middle East, in Southern Africa, in relations with the Third World, on Berlin, on arms control and European security, the parallelism of views that has existed between the United States and its European allies would almost certainly be eroded. On the contrary, active opposition, especially in regions of traditional European cultural and political influence, is probable. In our common efforts to improve the world economy and stimulate progress in both the developed and the developing worlds, in the OECD, in the conferences on international economic cooperation, and at heads of government summits, divisions would soon be apparent. How could Atlantic unity possibly be maintained in such circumstances, even on the security issue?

The military strength and unity of NATO would be gravely weakened. The Communist parties of Western Europe pay lip service to NATO. In fact, it is hard to visualize how the present NATO structure could continue, with its exchange of highly classified information, its integrated military planning and political consultation, if Communists had a significant share of power.

The participation of Communist parties in West European governments would force a major change in NATO practices, as occurred temporarily with Portugal, which had to exclude itself from classified discussions within the organization when its own political future was in doubt. These parties are unlikely to give NATO defense a high budgetary priority. Communist parties would surely use their power to diminish the combined defense effort of Western Europe and inevitably sap our own will to pay the costs of maintaining U.S. forces in Europe.

Furthermore, if Communists participate in a significant way in the governments of key European countries, NATO may turn by default into a largely German-American alliance. This specter could then be used in other West European countries to undermine what remains of Atlantic cohesion. With NATO thus weakened, while the Soviet Union continued to increase its strategic and conventional strength and maintained its grip on the Warsaw Pact, the essential equilibrium of power between East and West in Europe would be fundamentally threatened, the freedom of many European countries, allied or neutral, to chart their own future would be diminished in direct proportion to the growth of fear of Soviet power. Eventually, massive shifts against us would occur, not because a majority freely chose such a course, but because the upsetting of the overall balance left them no alternative.

The hopeful progress toward European unity would be undermined. The French and Italian Communist parties opposed the creation of the European Common Market as a conspiracy of monopoly capitalism. Until quite recently, they have consistently fought progress toward European unity. Lately they have come to accept the European Community as a fact of life; they now say they seek to make it more "democratic" and to transform it, by "a process of innovation . . . in the spheres both of institutions and of general orientations," as Berlinguer expressed it. They can be counted on to reorient the Common Market towards closer relations with the state economies of Eastern Europe and toward the more extreme of the Third World's demands for a "new international economic order." It can be assumed that they will not encourage European political unity to foster cooperation with the United States; rather they will urge it, if at all, to encourage Third Force tendencies. And over time either governments with Communist participation will pull the others towards them, or deep fissures will open up in the European Community between the traditional Atlanticists and the "New Left." Either outcome would be destructive of European unity and Atlantic solidarity.

Thus, whatever hypothesis we consider, Communist participation in governments of Western Europe will have a profound impact on the international structure as it has developed in the postwar period. We cannot be indifferent or delude ourselves that the advent of Communists to a significant share of power in Western Europe would be anything less than a watershed in Atlantic relationships.

The American Response

The attitude of the United States towards such developments must of necessity be complex. The crucial role must be that of European governments; the final decision must be that of the European voters. We cannot substitute for either.

In the end, the Communist parties in Western Europe find their opportunities less in their inherent strength than in the demoralization, division, or disorganization of their opponents; they succeed only when the democratic system seems unable to solve the social problems of the day—when the center does not hold and societies become polarized. Violence—such as that currently tormenting Italy—drives many to support Communism in desperation, convinced that drastic remedies are required to end a state of siege which has now spread to the press and other media.

The basic causes of Communist gains thus go deep and are not easy to remedy. In many European countries disillusionment with democratic government and democratic leaders is pervasive. In an era of peace, in a world of bureaucracy and mass production, there is no galvanizing crisis and little opportunity for heroic performance. A relativist age debunks authority and puts nothing in its place as an organizing principle of society. Massive impersonal bureaucracy disillusions the citizen with the responsiveness of his government, and simultaneously makes the task of elected officials more difficult. In too many democratic countries the young are offered too little inspiration; their elders too often have lost confidence in their own values. Too frequently democratic leaders are consumed by winning and holding office and are unable to demonstrate the force of conviction and philosophical self-assurance of their radical opponents.

The very success of Western societies in maintaining prosperity at a level undreamt of even forty years ago sometimes contributes to their malaise. Intellectuals condemn society for materialism when it is prosperous and for injustice when it fails to insure prosperity. The widespread economic difficulties of the last four years—recession and inflation unparalleled in a generation, to a large extent induced by the extraordinary increase in oil prices—fuel the frustration of all whose hopes for economic advancement are rebuffed. The interdependence of economies causes inflation and recession to surge across national boundaries, compounding the sense of individual impotence.

And yet, with all these difficulties, the democratic forces of the West have it in their power to determine whether the Communist parties have opportunities to succeed. They have the capacity to put their economies on the path of steady noninflationary expansion. They have the intellectual capital and the resources to usher in a new period of creativity. Anti-Communism, while important, is not enough; there must be a response to legitimate social and economic aspirations, and there must be reform of the inequities from which antidemocratic forces derive so much of their appeal. With able leadership—and Western cohesion—the democracies can overcome their challenges and usher in a period of dramatic fresh advance.

In this process it is vital that the United States encourage an attitude of resolve and conviction. The governments of Europe must know that they can count on our moral and political support in resisting the accession of Communism to governmental power.

First, we must frankly recognize the problem that we will face if the Communists come to power in Western Europe, and we must understand the practical decisions this will impose on us as a nation. We must avoid facile projections which seek to escape difficult choices by making the most favorable assumptions about what might happen. We must have a program for encouraging the forces of moderation and progress in this critical period and for rallying them should a Communist party nonetheless prevail.

Second, we must avoid giving the impression that we consider Communist success a foregone conclusion by ostentatious association or consultation with Communist leaders or by ambiguous declarations. Communist success is not a foregone conclusion; United States hesitation or ambiguity can, however, contribute to it. Communist parties are riddled with weaknesses and internal strains, and marked by a fundamental flaw: parties that do not speak for the humane values which have inspired the peoples of the West for centuries are unlikely to appeal to a majority in a Western nation except in a moment of unsettling crisis. In no Western European country has the Communist party ever fairly won more than about a third of the vote. Their most powerful weapons are fear, distrust, and discouragement; their principal asset is the myth of their inevitability. Therefore, we do our friends in Europe no favor if we encourage the notion that the advent of Communists and their allies into power will make little or no difference to our own attitudes and policies. I am speaking less of formal statements—which depend on tactical judgments difficult for any outsider to make—than of a clear and unambiguous U.S. attitude.

Some have argued that such a policy would be counterproductive, that it would encourage Communist protest votes. I believe the opposite to be true. On balance, I consider it important that Europe know of America's interest and concern. Many voters in allied countries value the friendship of the United States and appreciate the security supplied by the Atlantic Alliance. We should not ignore them, or demoralize them, or undercut them. The gradual gains scored by the Communist parties over the past years occurred—by definition—at the margin, among voters who had not voted Communist before, who did not vote by anti-American reflex, who for one reason or another were persuaded that the Communists have now become acceptable or indispensable.

There is no evidence that voters are influenced to vote *Communist* by American anti-Communist attitudes. On the contrary, the real danger may well be the other way; many usual opponents of the Communist parties may be lulled by voices, attitudes, and ambiguities in this country implying that our traditional opposition has changed. Paradoxically, we even weaken whatever moderate elements may exist in Communist movements by settling too eagerly for verbal reassurances.

If the United States has a responsibility to encourage political freedom in the world, we surely have a duty to leave no doubt about our convictions on an issue that is so central to the future of the Western Alliance and therefore to the future of democracy. Human rights is not an abstraction concerned only with judicial procedures and unrelated to basic questions of political and geopolitical structure. We cannot fail to reckon the setback to European freedom that will result if Communist minorities gain decisive influence in European politics; we must not close our eyes to the effect on freedom throughout the world if as a result the global balance tips against the West.

Third, the United States should conduct its policies toward its allies in a way that strengthens the moderate, progressive, and democratic governments of Western Europe. We must, on the one hand, avoid demands or lecturing which, whatever the intrinsic merit, magnify domestic fissures in European countries or the sense of impotence of European governments. At the same time, the United States can contribute to a sense of accomplishment by offering vigorous cooperation in joint efforts to solve common problems in the fields of diplomacy, arms control, energy, and economic growth. This was the purpose of the economic summits among Western leaders begun by President Ford at Rambouillet and Puerto Rico, and continued successfully in London by President Carter.

The unity and cooperative action of the democracies is crucial to all that America does in the world. Western unity defends not only our security but also our way of life and the most basic moral values of our civilization. On this we cannot be neutral. To foster these principles deserves the same dedication and commitment that inspired the most imaginative periods of American diplomacy.

The stagnant societies of the East to which I have referred serve as both a warning and a hope. They remind us that the West's latent intellectual and political vitality, even more than its material prosperity, is the envy of the world. The winds of change are ultimately blowing from the West. The men and women of *Eastern* Europe are certainly aware that the West, for all its doubt and sense of spiritual dilemma, is the vanguard of modernization, the vital source of learning and of much of modern culture, and the haven of the free human spirit. The developing countries yearning for progress also turn to the West, not the East, for assistance, support, and the measure of what man can achieve when he aspires. Our technology, our creativity, our unequaled economic vigor, not some bureaucratic doctrine of economic determinism, are the forces that will shape the future, provided we mobilize the energies of free peoples.

This is not the time for resignation or acquiescence. It is a time for confidence, determination, and hope. The power of free men and women and free nations acting in concert, confident of their strength and of their destiny, cannot be matched by any totalitarian system or totalitarian movement. The spirit of freedom can never be crushed. But freedom can be lost gradually. Such a danger exists today in Western Europe, and that threat could have consequences not only in Europe but also throughout the community of democracies and the world.

If we cherish freedom, we will face the peril, marshal joint efforts to overcome it, and begin a period of new fulfillment for our peoples. Western Europe, our closest partner and the cradle of much of our civilization, is too precious to us for us to do otherwise.

Cover and book design: Pat Taylor